THE STATE AND ECONOMIC

EDITORS: Mel Watkins, University of Torc

16 STEPHEN MCBRIDE

Not Working: State, Unemployment, and Neo-Conservatism in Canada

Unemployment is once again a pernicious and growing fact of life in Canada. Stephen McBride rejects economic interpretations of the return of high unemployment after decades in which Canada enjoyed almost full employment. He argues that the phenomenon can best be understood as the product of a political choice by policy makers – a choice which can plausibly be linked to the preferences and growing power of Canadian business in the post-1975 period.

This argument is based on an evaluation of the implications of the monetarist economic paradigm whose influence grew in the late 1970s, a comparative survey of the policy strategies followed in other countries and the employment outcomes associated with them, and a systematic examination of Canadian public policy in the macroeconomic, labour market, unemployment insurance, and industrial relations areas.

McBride's analysis reveals the state's increasing emphasis on addressing the accumulation demands of capital and a decreasing emphasis on the provision of concrete benefits (such as full employment and social services) to citizens. Much state activity can be understood as an attempt to legitimate by ideological means the change in the state's priorities and the shifting balance of benefits conferred by public policy. Thus the Canadian state has played an important role in managing the return to a high unemployment regime.

Stephen McBride is Associate Professor, Department of Political Studies, Lakehead University. He is co-editor, with Larry Haiven and John Shields, of *Regulating Labour: The State, Neo-Conservatism and Industrial Relations*.

Not Working:
State, Unemployment,
and Neo-Conservatism
in Canada

STEPHEN McBRIDE

UNIVERSITY OF TORONTO PRESS
Toronto Buffalo London

© University of Toronto Press 1992
Toronto Buffalo London
Printed in Canada

ISBN 0-8020-5998-8 (cloth)
ISBN 0-8020-6929-0 (paper)

Printed on acid-free paper

Canadian Cataloguing in Publication Data

McBride, Stephen Kenneth
Not working

(The State and economic life)
Includes index
ISBN 0-8020-5998-8 (bound) ISBN 0-8020-6929-0 (pbk.)

1. Unemployment – Government policy – Canada.
2. Labor policy – Canada. 3. Conservatism – Canada.
I. Title. II. Series.

HD5728.M33 1992   331.13'7971   C91-095141-1

Cover photo: Bruce Langer / *Chronicle Journal*

Contents

Preface / vii

1 Implications of Mass Unemployment / 3
2 Only in Canada? / 29
3 Economic Paradigms and State Policy / 57
4 Macroeconomic Policy / 71
5 Labour-Market Policy / 118
6 The Role of Unemployment Insurance / 159
7 The State and Industrial Relations / 189
8 Conclusion / 211

Notes / 223
References / 229
Index / 249

Preface

One of my abiding memories of time spent as an undergraduate student in the mid-1960s is of the confidence with which we were assured that mass unemployment was a thing of the past. Modern economic theory was said to have given governments the tools, and memories of the misery of the Depression the motivation, to banish this evil forever. This seemed to me both a good thing, if true, and an overstatement of the actual situation even at that time. Getting a decent job and keeping it seemed a little more difficult than the accepted model allowed.

Such vague misgivings were to be confirmed in the not-too-distant future. Before many years had passed the notion that the state could or should guarantee full employment was to be decisively rejected. When that happened, getting a job and keeping it were to become much harder for millions of people. This book is about the transition from an era of relatively full employment to the present one, in which unemployment rates in the range of 7 to 10 per cent are widely judged acceptable, even desirable. Since few, if any, of the unemployed share these sentiments, an obvious question to ask is why such rates of unemployment are considered satisfactory, and for whom.

The bulk of the book is about unemployment in Canada and the role played by the Canadian state. But since high unemployment is not a universal phenomenon within the capitalist world, a comparative dimension is also provided. This perspective seems to indicate that levels of unemployment are much more subject to political choice than the conventional wisdom in Canada would concede. As well as any empirical and theoretical value they may have, the book's findings may have some practical use for those, including the author, who consider that the state's first economic priority should be provision of full employment.

In completing a major project such as a book, one becomes increasingly conscious of the people and experiences that in a general way have influenced one's thinking. In my case, I owe debts to my parents, grandparents, parents-in-law, friends, colleagues, and fellow activists in a variety of organizations in England, Hamilton, Toronto, and Thunder Bay.

More specific acknowledgments are owed to those who provided direct assistance to me in completing this project. A major portion of the research was conducted with the assistance of a grant (No. 410-87-0308) from the Social Sciences and Humanities Research Council of Canada. The grant enabled me to, among other things, employ the valuable services of Brian McMillan as research assistant. The Department of Political Studies at Lakehead University is fortunate to enjoy the capable secretarial services of Eleanor Maunula and Karen Woychyshyn. Karen Woychyshyn took charge of this manuscript from its inception and coped with numerous drafts and alterations with good humour and efficiency. A number of provincial and federal government officials agreed to be interviewed and generously made available both their time and various documents and statistics which would have otherwise been hard to obtain. Harold Keeton, Gary Munro, David Nock, David Peerla, Michael Phillips, Paul Pugh, and Jeremy Rayner read and commented on drafts of various chapters. Bob Russell generously read the whole manuscript and reread portions of it; his comments and constructive criticisms at various stages were extremely valuable.

Responding to the anonymous readers of the University of Toronto Press and the Social Science Federation of Canada was always interesting and sometimes enjoyable. No doubt remaining disagreements can be discussed in more public forums. Virgil Duff was always a helpful editor, and I am especially grateful to the series co-editor, Leo Panitch, for his consistent support for this project, and to John Parry, for his editorial suggestions. The final product is better for advice received, though, of course, remaining errors are my own responsibility. The first draft of the manuscript was completed while I was on sabbatical leave in England at the University of York. My thanks go to Lakehead University for granting me a sabbatical and to the Department of Politics and Institute for Research in Social Sciences at York University for providing a perfect environment in which to write.

This book has been published with the help of a grant from the Social

Science Federation of Canada, using funds provided by the Social Sciences and Humanities Research Council of Canada, and their assistance is gratefully acknowledged.

Finally, this book would not have been written without the help and support of my wife, Jan, and our children, Emily, Morna, and Shona. As a small token of my appreciation, I dedicate the book to them.

Not Working

1 Implications of Mass Unemployment

This book begins with a simple descriptive observation: mass unemployment, once thought to have been banished, has returned as an apparently intractable feature of the economic and political landscape. This rather significant change has been accompanied by a major upheaval in economic theory. Keynesianism, the theoretical approach or paradigm that is said to have guided political decision makers in the period 1945–75, has been jettisoned in favour of new doctrines for which the loose term 'monetarism' will suffice at this stage. Monetarist economic theory provided the major policy platforms for neo-conservative parties that, in Canada as in a number of other countries, dominated political discourse in the 1980s. For many observers the adoption of monetarism and the return of mass unemployment are far from coincidental developments: neo-conservative state policies guided by monetarism are widely felt to have been a major cause of increased unemployment.

The issue of unemployment, its implications for the Canadian state and political system, and the degree to which the state itself is implicated in the return of high unemployment provide the empirical subject-matter of the book. The empirical investigation is conducted using a theoretical framework derived from two bodies of literature: the use of 'policy paradigms' to analyse changes in public policy and neo-Marxian writings on the theory of the capitalist state and the state's role in market economies. Some of the more pertinent of this literature is reviewed in chapters 1 and 3. The starting assumption is that the state's relationship to the problem of unemployment may tell us a great deal about the state in contemporary capitalist society. In particular, the perception that state policies may be responsible for at least part of the increased unemployment poses quite pointedly the issue of on whose behalf the state may be said to act.

The purpose of this chapter is to provide some basic information about the return of the unemployment problem in Canada and to link this change both to the economic theories or paradigms that have influenced Canadian policy makers and to discussions of actual policies that have been pursued by political decision makers. The discussion of policy paradigms, their links to specific policy areas, and their impact on the state's performance is continued in the third chapter. The intervening chapter places Canada's unemployment performance and political response in comparative perspective.

The Return of Mass Unemployment

One of the basic facts in any discussion of unemployment is the official rate of unemployment. Ignoring minor fluctuations, we can see from Table 1.1 that the rate jumped sharply at the end of the 1960s, grew fairly steadily through the 1970s, and jumped sharply again in 1981–2. Since then it has declined somewhat, though it still remains very high by the standards of the 1960s. In the late 1960s, the rate had averaged 4 per cent, compared to 6 per cent in the 1970s and over 9 per cent in the 1980s. Put differently, the unemployment rate in 1986 was 282 per cent of that twenty years earlier. Clearly these figures indicate a situation dramatically different from that which obtained in the lengthy period of prosperity that followed the Second World War.

It can also be doubted whether the official statistics gauge fully the depth of the problem. It is regularly argued that the real rate is considerably higher. In an early analysis of the return of mass unemployment, Gonick (1978: 118–23) identified several categories of people without jobs who were not considered unemployed for purposes of the official statistics. These included 'discouraged workers' (i.e. those who had stopped looking for work because they believe that there is none to be had, women not in the labour force because jobs and adequate day care facilities are not available, participants in government-sponsored training programs, students who would prefer to work if jobs were available, and former workers who were forced into early retirement. In 1977 Gonick considered that the 'real' rate, counting in the above categories, might run as high as 20 per cent. Even simply including discouraged workers would, in his opinion, raise the rate to around 12 per cent. Other studies, using different assumptions and calculations, produced

TABLE 1.1
Unemployment rate, Canada, both sexes, 15 years and over

Year	Unemployment rate (%)	Year	Unemployment rate (%)
1966	3.4	1979	7.4
1967	3.8	1980	7.5
1968	4.5	1981	7.5
1969	4.4	1982	11.0
1970	5.7	1983	11.9
1971	6.2	1984	11.3
1972	6.2	1985	10.5
1973	5.5	1986	9.6
1974	5.3	1987	8.9
1975	6.9	1988	7.8
1976	7.1	1989	7.5
1977	8.1	1990	8.1
1978	8.3		

SOURCE: Canada, Statistics Canada, *Historical Labour Force Statistics 1990* (Ottawa 1991)

somewhat lower estimates. Deaton (1983), for example, calculated that including discouraged and involuntary part-time workers would have raised the rate in 1982 from 11 per cent to 12.7 per cent.

Statistics Canada has recognized the problem of adequately representing labour market conditions through appropriately defining unemployment. Surveys have compared unemployment according to nine different definitions. Some of the rates turn out to be higher and others lower than the 'official' rate. One rate that to some extent captures the category of discouraged workers is definition 'R7.' In R7 'the definition of unemployment is expanded to include persons not in the labour force who have sought work in the past six months, but are not currently looking for "labour market related" reasons. The reasons included the belief that no work is available, waiting for recall to a former job, having found a new job, and, waiting for replies resulting from previous job search' (Statistics Canada 1983a, April: 90). Under the official definition, such persons are not counted as being unemployed. Table 1.2 provides a comparison of the official and R7 unemployment rates.

This book will use the official unemployment rate in its analysis. But the implication of what has been said above should be duly noted: there are reasonable grounds for believing that unemployment, serious as it is, is understated by the official statistics. Similarly, although unem-

TABLE 1.2
Unemployment: the official and R7 rates

	'76	'77	'78	'79	'80	'81	'82	'83	'84	'85	'86
Official	7.1	8.1	8.4	7.5	7.5	7.6	11.0	11.9	11.3	10.5	9.6
R7	7.9	9.0	9.4	8.4	8.5	8.7	12.5	13.3	12.5	11.6	10.6

SOURCE: Adapted from Statistics Canada, *The Labour Force* (February 1987, Cat. 71-001)

ployment is dealt with here primarily as a problem of the Canadian state – that is, as a national problem for which the statistics in Table 1.1 are the most significant reference point – the national picture hides considerable diversity in the impact of unemployment among particular groups and regions of the country.

Table 1.3 compares the national unemployment rate to that for selected age groups, and Table 1.4 shows provincial variations in unemployment rates relative to the national rate. A given national rate carries with it different meanings for particular age groups and regions. Whatever level of hardship a given national rate implies, therefore, will be unevenly distributed, with significantly greater hardship for some.

Further, as Sharpe et al. (1988: 19–28) point out, much of total employment is part-time (15.6 per cent in 1986) – and almost 30 per cent of part-time workers would prefer to work full-time. Similarly, average unemployment rates fail to record how many people were actually unemployed during the course of a year. In 1985, for example, the average rate of unemployment was 10.5 per cent. But 25.4 per cent of the labour force was out of work at some point during the year. The corollary of this, of course, is that only a minority of the unemployed were out of work for a whole year (20.4 per cent in 1986), and this is only a small fraction of the entire labour force (1.9 per cent in 1985). Nevertheless, the average duration of unemployment in the mid-1980s was over twenty weeks. So annual unemployment rates in the 10–11 per cent range translated, in the mid-1980s, into around a quarter of the labour force experiencing unemployment for an average period of over twenty weeks. Thus a substantial portion of the work-force, and family members, experienced the hardships of unemployment, and the prospect of it must have been a source of worry for many others.

While few would deny that there is some hardship associated with unemployment, it is sometimes said that to be unemployed in the context of the modern welfare state is far less challenging than in the past.

TABLE 1.3
Unemployment rate: both sexes, various age groups and national

	15–19	20–24	25+	15+ (National rate)
1970	13.9	7.5	4.2	5.7
1971	15.1	8.4	4.5	6.2
1972	14.0	8.7	4.6	6.2
1973	12.2	7.8	4.1	5.5
1974	11.6	7.6	3.9	5.3
1975	14.9	9.9	5.0	6.9
1976	15.7	10.5	5.1	7.1
1977	17.5	12.2	5.8	8.1
1978	17.8	12.1	6.1	8.3
1979	16.0	10.7	5.4	7.4
1980	16.2	11.0	5.4	7.5
1981	16.2	11.2	5.6	7.5
1982	21.9	16.8	8.4	11.0
1983	22.2	18.5	9.4	11.9
1984	19.9	16.8	9.3	11.3
1985	18.8	15.3	8.7	10.5
1986	16.8	14.3	8.0	9.6
1987	15.1	12.8	7.5	8.8
1988	13.2	11.2	6.7	7.8
1989	13.1	10.1	6.6	7.5
1990	14.2	11.8	7.0	8.1

SOURCE: Statistics Canada, *Historical Labour Force Statistics 1990* (Ottawa 1991)

Some aspects of this argument can be conceded immediately: for those eligible, unemployment benefits provide an essential cushion which makes their lot far better than that of those out of work in, say, the 1930s. But the costs of unemployment remain high for individuals and for society, and it is worth considering these costs.

Several Canadian studies have revealed a relationship between unemployment and various other social ills. The National Council of Welfare has linked the increasing proportion of Canadians living in poverty (14.7 per cent in 1981, 17.8 per cent in 1984) to increases in unemployment (Sharpe et al. 1988: 30). For individuals, the experience has been found to be 'traumatic ... characterized by dramatic shifts in economic power, personal support and self-esteem' (Borgen and Amundson 1984: 64). This situation gives rise to anxiety and stress and has been viewed as a threat to both physical and psychological health (Kirst 1983; Kramar 1984: 61). Testimony to an unofficial commission of inquiry in Newfoundland (People's Commission 1978) warned of a link among

TABLE 1.4
Provincial unemployment rates relative to the national rate, 1966–89

	Nfld.	PEI	NS	NB	Que.	Ont.
1966	5.8		4.7	5.3	4.1	2.6
1967	5.9		4.9	5.2	4.6	3.2
1968	7.1		5.1	5.7	5.6	3.6
1969	7.4		4.9	6.7	6.1	3.2
1970	7.3		5.3	6.3	7.0	4.4
1971	8.4		7.0	6.1	7.3	5.4
1972	9.2		7.0	7.0	7.5	5.0
1973	10.0		6.6	7.7	6.8	4.3
1974	13.0		6.8	7.5	6.6	4.4
1975	14.0	8.0	7.7	9.8	8.1	6.3
1976	13.3	9.6	9.5	11.0	8.7	6.2
1977	15.5	9.8	10.6	13.2	10.3	7.0
1978	16.2	9.8	10.5	12.5	10.9	7.2
1979	15.1	11.2	10.1	11.1	9.6	6.5
1980	13.3	10.6	9.7	11.0	9.8	6.8
1981	13.9	11.2	10.2	11.5	10.3	6.6
1982	16.8	12.9	13.2	14.0	13.8	9.8
1983	18.3	12.2	13.2	14.8	13.9	10.4
1984	20.5	12.8	13.1	14.9	12.8	9.1
1985	21.3	13.2	13.8	15.2	11.8	8.0
1986	20.0	13.4	13.4	14.4	11.0	7.0
1987	18.6	13.3	12.5	13.2	10.3	6.1
1988	16.4	13.0	10.2	12.0	9.4	5.0
1989	15.8	14.1	9.9	12.5	9.3	5.1

unemployment and alcoholism, drug use, vandalism, child abuse, and family breakdown. In Toronto the increased incidence of racism and discrimination, and associated destructive behaviour, has been linked to unemployment (Social Planning Council of Metro Toronto 1982). Similar studies in the United States (Brenner 1976) have related increases in the number of suicides, admissions to mental hospitals, crime, and certain types of physical disease to higher jobless rates.

Even a brief mention of these findings indicates substantial costs for the individuals who become unemployed, their families, and society. Many of the costs, such as personal unhappiness and gradual social deterioration, may be difficult to measure, although they are none the less real for all that. Others, such as the value of the lost potential production which results from having a substantial portion of the labour force 'unemployed,' are more easily measured. Even for the less quan-

TABLE 1.4
(continued)

	Man.	Sask.	Alta.	BC	CAN
1966	2.8	1.5	2.5	4.6	3.8
1967	3.0	1.7	2.7	5.1	3.8
1968	3.9	2.4	3.3	5.9	4.5
1969	3.2	3.2	3.4	5.0	4.4
1970	5.3	4.2	5.1	7.7	5.7
1971	5.7	3.5	5.7	7.2	6.2
1972	5.4	4.4	5.6	7.8	6.2
1973	4.6	3.5	5.3	6.7	5.5
1974	3.6	2.8	3.5	6.2	5.3
1975	4.5	2.9	4.1	8.5	6.9
1976	4.7	3.9	4.0	8.6	7.1
1977	5.9	4.5	4.5	8.5	8.1
1978	6.5	4.9	4.7	8.3	8.3
1979	5.3	4.2	3.9	7.6	7.4
1980	5.5	4.4	3.7	6.8	7.5
1981	5.9	4.7	3.8	6.7	7.5
1982	8.5	6.2	7.7	12.1	11.0
1983	9.4	7.4	10.8	13.8	11.9
1984	8.3	8.0	11.2	14.7	11.3
1985	8.1	8.1	10.1	14.2	10.5
1986	7.7	7.7	9.8	12.6	9.6
1987	7.4	7.3	9.6	12.0	8.9
1988	7.8	7.5	8.0	10.3	7.8
1989	7.5	7.4	7.2	9.1	7.5

SOURCE: Statistics Canada, *Historical Labour Force Statistics 1987* (Cat. 71-201);
Statistics Canada, *The Labour Force* (December 1989, Cat. 71-001)

tifiable effects of unemployment, it is sometimes possible to compute a direct economic cost. For example, if a known number of admissions to mental institutions or prisons result from a given increase in unemployment, these carry definite and calculable economic costs to society, in addition to the non-economic and incalculable costs of 'wasted' or 'ruined' lives.

Table 1.5 presents one of the most thorough attempts to estimate the social and economic costs of unemployment in Canada. A glance at the notes suggests that every effort was made to be reasonable in deriving these estimates. But even more conservative estimates, focusing directly on economic costs, yield figures of up to 9.3 per cent of GNP (Sharpe et al. 29). When expressed as a percentage of GNP or of the federal deficit,

TABLE 1.5
Estimated social cost accounting of unemployment in Canada, year-end 1982[1]

Item	Socio-Economic Cost of Unemployment[2] ($ Billion)
Lost Production[3]	41.0
Lost Earnings[4]	8.9
UI Benefit Payments	8.1
Social Cost of Unemployment – Related Stress Indicators[5]	7.4
Lost Tax Revenue to government[6]	7.4
Lost Education and Training, Depreciation of Human Capital[7]	2.7
Total Socio-Economic Cost of Unemployment:	$75.5 billion
Socio-Economic Cost of Unemployment as a % of GNP:	22.0%
Socio-Economic Cost of Unemployment as % of the Federal Deficit:	198%

Notes:
(1) Based on official second quarter 1982 data and annualized by straight-line extrapolation for year-end 1982.
(2) Based on the methodology developed by Dr. Harvey Brenner of Johns Hopkins University and used by the Joint Economic Committee of the US Congress to estimate the total social and economic cost of unemployment.
(3) Represents lost GNP per unemployed person multiplied by total unemployed.
(4) Difference between average weekly earnings and the average UI benefit paid.
(5) Methodology utilized by Leon Muszynski, Metro-Toronto Social Planning Council based on the work of Dr. Harvey Brenner. This calculation includes the direct economic costs associated with unemployment, including the increase in suicides, homicides, heart disease, mental institution and prison admissions and total mortality. It excludes the costs of child abuse, divorce, child poverty and alcoholism. Muszynski estimated the direct economic cost, using unemployment related stress indicators, at nearly $5,700 per unemployed person in 1970. This was adjusted by an inflation factor of 59% between 1970 and 1982, and multiplied by the marginal increase in unemployment over the same time period.
(6) Estimated individual, corporate and general sales tax revenue lost to all levels of government. This calculation of lost tax revenue is an underestimation since it excludes certain categories of consumption taxes, capital gains, natural resource revenues and property taxes. This has been calculated excluding a 2% frictional unemployment rate.
(7) Represents the estimated loss per capita cost of elementary, secondary and post-secondary education related to those unemployed in the 15-to-24-year-old age cohort. This figure is an understatement since it excludes the previous social investment in education for those who are unemployed and over age 24.

SOURCE: Deaton (1983: 15)

the costs are staggering, and it is clear that unemployment represents a major haemorrhage from our economic, social, and human potential. Data on public opinion suggest that this perception is, in a general way, shared by the Canadian public. Table 1.6 measures public responses to questions that posit a trade-off between fighting inflation and fighting unemployment. Though Johnston (1986: 119) concludes that 'Canadians are concerned about inflation at least as much as they are about unemployment,' he also concedes (128) that in the short run they are more sensitive to unemployment: 'Growth in unemployment can produce more dramatic shifts towards (aversion to) unemployment than growth in inflation produces in inflation aversion. The other side of the coin, however, is that concerns about unemployment can evaporate more quickly than can concerns about inflation.'

In the recent period of high unemployment, public aversion to unemployment has regularly outscored aversion to other economic problems such as inflation. Notwithstanding Johnston's caveat (124) that Canadians have an 'underlying permanent bias against inflation,' it seems fair to conclude that in the last decade, this focus generally has been outweighed by concerns about unemployment.

Given the high levels of unemployment, its economic and social costs, and the priority attached to the issue by the public, one might reasonably expect unemployment and solutions to it to dominate the political agenda. In fact, the issue has failed to realize its political potential. Government economic policy since 1975 has consistently placed greater emphasis on controlling inflation than on reducing unemployment. Examining why this has been the case, and how governments have justified their priorities, will tell us much about the nature of the state in late-twentieth-century Canada.

Implications for the State

This analysis of the political economy of unemployment in Canada synthesizes insights from two distinct approaches to the study of public policy and applies them to the state's response to unemployment. The two approaches are the policy paradigm literature, developed by some public policy analysts based in the political science discipline,[1] and neo-Marxian state theory.

The policy paradigm school emphasizes the impact of ideas on policy making and applies the concept of policy 'paradigms' to the evolution of policy. A policy paradigm can be defined as a series of principles that

TABLE 1.6
Inflation versus unemployment

Date		Study	Priority			(1)/(3)	(N)
			Inflation (1)	Both/No Opinion (2)	Unemploy- ment (3)		
Jan.	1971	CIPO 345	21.7%	33.7	44.6	0.49	(710)
Mar.	1975	CIPO 374	57.9%	7.2	34.9	1.66	(1,058)
Dec.	1976	CIPO 394	42.4%	9.4	48.2	0.88	(1,053)
	1979	QOL	36.1%	42.5	21.4	1.69	(1,436)
Feb.	1982	CIPO 458	42.5%	8.8	48.8	0.87	(1,048)
Spring	1982	Decima	33.2%	8.2	58.1	0.57	(1,495)
June	1982	CIPO 462.1	38.6%	4.8	56.6	0.68	(1,048)
Summer	1982	Decima	35.1%	4.5	58.3	0.60	(1,495)
Sept.	1982	CIPO 465.4	42.7%	5.7	51.6	0.83	(1,047)
Jan.	1983	CIPO 469.1	32.3	7.2	60.5	0.53	(1,055)

Sources: CIPO; Decima Quarterly Report
Items:
(1) CIPO 345 (January 1971): If the government of Canada had a choice between: (a) slowing down the rate of price increases, creating more unemployment [and] (b) reducing unemployment in Canada, but causing prices to rise as fast or even faster than at present, which of the two do you think the government ought to choose?
(2) Other CIPO studies: Which do you think the government should give greater attention to: trying to curb inflation or trying to reduce unemployment?
(3) Quality of Life: In your opinion, which is the more serious problem: inflation, or unemployment? (Not clear whether 'both equally serious' is a voluntary response only.)
(4) Decima: Many people say that government cannot fight inflation and unemployment at the same time. Which do you think should be the first priority of the federal government's economic policy: fighting inflation or creating jobs? ('Both' is a voluntary response.)

SOURCE: Johnston (1986: 127)

'express the current assumptions from which specific policy making can proceed, ... limit the appropriate set of policy instruments, and ... summarize the world view of the policy-making community' (Aucoin 1979: 15). An emphasis on paradigms puts ideology squarely back into the policy process.[2] Conflict between competing paradigms is an integral part of the policy process in times of crisis and change. Such conflict, of course, is hardly confined to disputes within the state's decision-making process. Rather, it characterizes the whole broad policy debate and the interactions between state and society. The replacement of one dominant paradigm by another can lead to major policy changes. In the economic sphere, replacement of the Keynesian paradigm by one that might loosely be called monetarism was an example of paradigm change fraught with policy consequences. The new paradigm also provided a different set of rationalizations with which to justify new policy priorities. It will be useful at this point to look, briefly and superficially, at the contents of these two paradigms. In chapter 3 they will be treated in more detail, and the implications of each for the contents of specific policy areas will be drawn out.

Both basic paradigms are concerned with the unemployment-inflation nexus of problems and were, therefore, drawn on for prescriptions in facing the economic problems of the 1970s and 1980s. Keynesianism, of course, has its origins in a different era – the mass unemployment of the 1930s. Keynes considered most of this unemployment to be caused by insufficient demand. He felt that there was no reason to believe that supply and demand would tend automatically toward equilibrium at a full-employment level. Therefore, if governments wanted full employment, it was up to them to manipulate aggregate demand appropriately, through either fiscal or monetary policy.

In the 1960s and 1970s, late-Keynesian, sometimes called 'post-Keynesian,' economic thinking began to modify the original Keynesian prescriptions quite considerably. First, the post-Keynesians began to consider the inflationary effects of operating the economy at levels of aggregate demand sufficient to produce relatively full employment. Incomes policy was conceived as one solution to such inflationary pressures and would, it was hoped, continue to make full employment possible while containing its inflationary side-effects. But it involved major adjustments to the Keynesian formula, which in the course of sustaining high levels of demand had encouraged trade unionism and free collective bargaining. Incomes policy involved state intervention into the centre-piece of the relationship between labour and capital – collective bargaining – and its delegitimizing effects rippled through industrial relations. Second, in the 1960s, the perception grew that unemployment not attributable to deficiency of aggregate demand was more widespread than had been anticipated. Management of aggregate demand was not only an inadequate response but would lead to unacceptable inflation. Other forms of state intervention, direct and acting on the supply side, were advocated to deal with structural unemployment.[3] Among these approaches was the concept of an active labour-market policy.

The rival paradigm – monetarism – became the preferred option for Canadian business during the 1970s and provided the theoretical basis for the neo-conservative initiatives in public policy that followed. Some reasons behind business's long-standing disquiet about the implications of Keynesianism are presented in chapter 3. On this basis, one might argue that monetarism, or something like it, has always been business's preferred option. But economic developments in the 1970s, and the perception of a growing challenge from labour, made it urgent for business to break out of the confines of the Keynesian paradigm. The monetarist alternative had the potential to solve a number of dilemmas faced by Canadian business (see chapter 3).

At a more technical level, monetarism became popular with state decision makers because of Keynesian theory's apparent inability to explain or deal with stagflation – the coexistence of high levels of unemployment and inflation. Monetarist theory states unequivocally that inflation is the greater of the two ills. An account of the causes of inflation and a series of policy prescriptions to end it occupy a significant portion of monetarist writings. Underlying this orientation is an analysis that suggests a natural rate of unemployment that is consistent with a constant rate of inflation, perhaps even zero inflation. A non-accelerating inflation rate of unemployment (NAIRU) carries an important implication for policy makers: that there is no need to accept some inflation in order to lessen unemployment. Monetarist theory suggests that no sustainable decrease in unemployment will result from such a strategy. Consequently, the policy priority should be to stop inflation and to allow unemployment to settle eventually at its natural rate. Some monetarists concede that the policies entailed in 'wrestling inflation to the ground' involve some short-term unemployment in excess of its natural rate. But, they argue, provided markets are allowed to operate freely, unemployment will ultimately fall to its natural rate. Keynesian policies of demand management, in the monetarist view, maintain unemployment below its natural rate only temporarily and cause a continually increasing rate of inflation.

Monetarism therefore focused on control of inflation, and Canadian economic policy since the mid-1970s is widely conceded to have reflected this approach (Riddell 1986: 18). State activity of the Keynesian type came to be seen as the basic cause of inflation: increased spending and deficits were said to be financed, in the end, by increases in the money supply. Monetarists sought to control the supply of money, reduce government spending, especially deficits and borrowing requirements, and ultimately reduce inflationary expectations. The last mentioned could occur only if a second significant element in the monetarist package were achieved: removal of impediments to the free operation of markets. Such obstacles included trade unions, spending on social services and welfare generally, and the existence of unemployment benefits and minimum wage legislation. Privatization of crown-operated facilities also would fit into the package, since it would remove the contribution to monopoly represented by state-owned operations. In addition, the sale of crown assets could reduce the deficit. What for monetarists were obstacles to the operation of market forces were, for Keynesians, key elements in the post-war settlement between capital and labour. They were the very substance of the Keynesian legitimation policies conceived in the Depression. Adoption of the monetarist paradigm implied vigorous reassertion of the primacy of market forces. Restoration of the priority of markets paradoxically might involve considerable state activity, at least initially, in a variety of policy areas.

In terms of the evolving effect of such paradigms, the following description of trends is fairly typical. From the end of the Second World War until around 1975, the dominant paradigm was Keynesian (including its late or post-Keynesian component). After that date, monetarism became more influential, although traces of the impact of the Keynesian school certainly could be detected.

The Keynesian paradigm that held sway between 1945 and 1975 included the state's commitment to 'high and stable levels of employment' (Canada, Department of Reconstruction, 1945; Wolfe 1977). Similar ideas informed policy making in other Western states. Even if this commitment was less honoured in Canada than in some other countries (Apple 1980: 16–18; Heidenheimer, Heclo, and Adams 1983: 123), the stated purpose of economic policy was high employment. In most countries, the collapse of this paradigm coincided with a much higher priority being placed on controlling inflation than on maintaining full employment (Hunter 1980: 45). Canada was no exception. While no single economic school of thought has achieved the dominance enjoyed by Keynesianism in economic discourse prior to 1975, new ideas, often described under the general label 'monetarism,' do add up to a re-emergence of pre-Keynesian economic thinking (Thurow 1984). In this sense one can speak of a new dominant paradigm, which is tolerant of and to some extent predicated on higher levels of unemployment than previously would have been acceptable. Empirical studies, both comparative (Zoeteweij 1983; Bruno and Sachs 1985; Therborn 1986; McBride 1988) and Canadian (Donner and Peters 1979; McCallum 1981; Kaliski 1984; Wolfe 1984), seem to confirm that the new policies have been associated with high and persistent unemployment. Clearly, conflict about changing the balance of advantage between classes and groups was partially expressed as conflict between competing paradigms.

The turning-point generally is considered to be 1975. In that year, the Bank of Canada announced its conversion to a policy of decreasing the rate of growth in the money supply. The Liberal government declared that the principal aim of both monetary and fiscal policy would be control of inflation. In line with that strategy, the growth of government expenditures was to be held to a level less that that of GNP (Wolfe 1984, 1985). Since 1975 also saw imposition of wage controls, a classic post-Keynesian measure, the sharpness of the break in paradigms can be exaggerated. It has been argued (Campbell 1987; Gonick 1987: 91–102) that the pre-1975 dominance of the Keynesian paradigm is an exaggeration – that it was not consistently applied to policy. The degree to which monetarism was applied after 1975 is also a matter of debate.

Yet the notion of a shift in paradigms continues to have some appeal. For most of the post-war period, policy debates about the proper course of macroeconomic and other policies tended to be conducted in Keynesian terms. From the mid-1970s, such debates showed the growing influence of monetarist doctrines. As long as the post-war boom lasted, much of the credit for economic growth and the attainment of reasonably full employment was given, rightly or wrongly, to implementation of Keynesian policies. As soon as the boom showed signs of faltering, the same policies began to be blamed for the economic difficulties. These paradigms therefore provided the language of economic policy discussions and established the framework within which policy problems and solutions were analysed and understood.

In the neo-Marxian framework, the state's actions (i.e. public policy) reflect the result of conflict between the interests of antagonistic economic classes. The precise nature of policy will be determined by the relative strengths of the classes, but the state will, in any event, seek to perform a number of basic functions. Specification of the functions performed by the capitalist state is one of three requirements that Panitch (1977b: 5–6) considered a fully developed theory of the state should meet:

It must clearly delimit the complex of institutions that go to make up the state. It must demonstrate concretely, rather than just define abstractly, the linkages between the state and the system of class inequality in the society, particularly its ties to the dominant social class. And it must specify as far as possible the functions of the state under the capitalist mode of production. It must undertake these tasks, moreover, not in an ahistorical way but in relation to the way the state's organization, its functions, and its linkages with society vary with the changes in the capitalist mode of production itself, and also vary with the specific conditions of a given social formation.

In this study, we shall be concerned mostly with the third of these requirements – specification of state functions – but such concerns do fit into the overall theoretical picture. Specification of state functions does not, of course, constitute an explanation of the state's actions, though the pattern identified may be suggestive of some explanations rather than others.

The distinction that James O'Connor (1973: 5–10) made between accumulation and legitimation provides a useful starting-point. O'Connor argued that a capitalist state must attempt to fulfil simultaneously these often contradictory roles. On the one hand, it must strive to facilitate vigorous profit making and capital accumulation. On the other hand, it must try to achieve harmonious social relations such that the state and the capitalist system itself retain legitimacy in the eyes of the population. The state's attempts to fulfil these mandates can be observed in its expenditure budget, and the inevitable tendency, for O'Connor, is for state expenditures to increase more rapidly than the revenues available to finance them. The tensions surrounding such a tendency will, of course, be accentuated in a general economic crisis. While the accumulation requirements of monopoly capital depend on state assistance in the socialization of costs and the maintenance of legitimacy, the same sector is strongly resistant to 'the appropriation of ... surplus for new social capital or social expense outlays' (O'Connor 1973: 9).

Hueglin (1987: 244–5) aptly comments that in these circumstances it is easy 'to see how this emerging pattern of double spending (for accumulation *and* legitimation) would result in a fiscal crisis of the state. Instead of supplying the public purse with tax funds for the state's welfare activities, business itself has become a recipient of public spending. The fiscal budget deficit resulting from such double spending may well be regarded as the ultimate manifestation of the structural contradictions in which the capitalist state finds itself enmeshed.'

Although O'Connor's account of fiscal crisis was quite influential in its day and continues to be cited by contemporary analysts of the period, it has encountered considerable criticism (see, for example, Elster 1982; Heald 1983; Albo and Jenson 1989); I intend to use the legitimation/ accumulation dichotomy as the basis of a framework for analysing state outputs, and so it will be useful to comment on some of the more serious criticisms. I shall explain how I shall use these concepts and, in the process, distance them from some of the theoretical problems attributed to O'Connor by his critics.

First, it has been said that O'Connor reduced 'legitimacy' to an insignificant residue and thus depicted labour as a dupe of capital. In similar vein, he has been accused of asserting that legitimation and accumulation were always and inherently contradictory – a situation soluble only in the long term through socialism. Second, he has been criticized for implicit functionalism, a mode of analysis and explanation that 'impute(s) needs to societies as if they were living bodies: it assumes a teleology without demonstrating the existence of goal-oriented planning mechanisms; and it involves circular reasoning, since any policy adopted is, by definition, functional, unless the system collapses' (Albo and Jenson 1989: 209n). Applied to the capitalist state, functionalism suggests that the state must and always will perform certain functions. It therefore explains the state's actions in terms of the functional requirements of capital without reference to human agency. Third, the difficulty of actually applying O'Connor's concepts to empirical material has received adverse comment. I shall deal with each of these potential problems in turn.

In this book, performance of the accumulation and legitimation functions is viewed as contradictory, but the contradictions involved are not inherently or permanently unmanageable, though the possibility always exists that they might become so. There are in fact lengthy periods in which the tension between the two either dissolves or becomes relatively easy to manage. The balance between stability and change has been the focus of analysis taking the regulation approach to political economy. This approach

asks how social relations take on stabilized forms – that is, how regulation occurs. Never assuming that reproduction of any social relation *must* occur, the task is to identify the institutionalized practices which stall contradictions and thereby contribute to reproduction ... The periods of stability in relations are never automatically or easily reproduced, however. Because social relations are contradictory, any moment of regulation always contains destabilizing pressures ... Therefore, longish periods of stability are punctuated by periods (perhaps almost as long) of crisis and instability. Moreover, a solution to any crisis is not predictable in advance; it is a product of politics, a solution constructed out of social conflict and conflict resolution. (Jenson 1989: 72–3)

Jenson's points are of relevance to a study of the state and unemployment. One implication of this perspective, in the context of criticisms levelled at O'Connor, is that when the subordinate classes struggled for and achieved real benefits, such as the full-employment and welfare-state reforms of the post-war era, they were not duped by capital, even though the concessions also contributed very nicely to capital accumulation. Legitimation, in that context, was based on real benefits and can be viewed as part of the 'institutionalized practices which stall contradictions.' In the circumstances of the 1970s, of course, it became much more difficult to achieve stability, and the contradiction between accumulation and legitimation became more difficult to reconcile. Much of this book is about the state's efforts to manage this more difficult situation.

On functionalism, I simply record my agreement with Gough (1979: 51) that 'whilst we must reject any functionalist explanation of the ... state, it is still useful to delineate the functions of the state, so long as they are used to indicate tendencies at work within the capitalist state.' The study of state policies can help us interpret the state's role without prejudging why the state performed as it did. The focus of this book, then, is on *how* the state managed the crisis that began in the 1970s.

Finally, although it may be difficult to apply these concepts empirically, especially because a single policy instrument may create conditions that are suitable for both accumulation and legitimation at the same time, this is a problem faced by all schemes for classifying state outputs. It is conventional, for example, to speak of economic, social, foreign, and various other policies. But the overlaps among these areas are so substantial that they are useful only at the most general level. A recent discussion of public expenditure analysis identified five ways of classifying expenditure (Likierman 1988: chapter 1). All were useful for specific and different purposes. But only the most formal methods (for example, classifying by department responsible for the expenditure) were watertight. In applying the concepts of accumulation and legitimation, we must construct criteria for gauging changes in the emphasis on particular types of activity. The criteria will be found in each of the chapters on substantive policy, and some general issues pertinent to their construction are addressed in chapter 3. Provided that satisfactory criteria are established and that any temptation to fit the evidence into the categories mechanically is resisted, the legitimation/accumulation schema focuses attention on how the state, through its policies, confers advantages and costs on social classes.

It does seem, however, that early analyses were unduly restrictive in adopting a simple dichotomy for assessing state activity. Panitch (1977b: 8), for example, adds the function of coercion, 'the use by the state of its monopoly over the legitimate use of force to maintain or impose social order,' and Panitch and Swartz (1985) document the increasing use of coercion in industrial relations. An analysis of the same policy area (McBride 1987b) has noted attempts to merge or combine the legitimation and accumulation functions or, more precisely, to devise legitimation measures that also promote accumulation. O'Connor's original formulation tends to define legitimation simplistically as government expenditures on social policy. This puts the concept on far too narrow a base. As a minimum, its material basis can be extended to include procedural rights, which, for example, enabled workers to express their demands (Bob Russell 1987). But legitimacy is also created by symbolic, persuasive, and ideological actions by the state. Carnoy (1984: 229) has argued that 'O'Connor's focus on the economic aspects of struggle in the State apparatus only implicitly touches on the ideological basis of State power. State legitimation for O'Connor ... is a question of material benefits accruing to the voting masses.'
It is particularly important to extend the range of the concept, since, as Chorney and Hansen (1980) have pointed out, fiscal pressures on legitimation activities since the onset of the economic crisis have failed to produce anything approaching a legitimacy crisis. Manifestations of such a crisis, of course, might have been suppressed by increased use of coercive methods. But symbolic and ideological activities by the state have probably substituted for more concrete legitimation activities. In this context, Hoover and Plant (1989: 41) have argued that 'Only by changing peoples' attitude to both the welfare state and the market can the potential legitimation deficit be overcome.'
Against a background of economic crisis, it is useful to draw a distinction between legitimation secured through provision of concrete benefits and that derived from ideological and symbolic state activities.

Henceforth I shall use the terms *concrete* and *ideological* to distinguish the two types of legitimation. The latter will cover the state's use of theory, documentation and information, argument, mystification, public relations manipulation, diversionary appeals (e.g. 'scapegoating'), co-opting of critics, and token or placebo policies[4] designed to create the impression of responding to problems but in reality doing little to resolve them.

The conjunction of Marxian and Weberian influences in the term *ideological legitimation* may be confusing. In fact, the theoretical terrain surrounding the process of 'changing peoples' attitude to both the welfare state and the market' is quite congested, and it may be worthwhile briefly to review some of the literature. The process should help to clarify the way in which 'ideological legitimation' is to be used.

Notwithstanding obvious differences between Weberians and Marxists, there are some points of connection, especially for those Marxists influenced by Gramsci (see Bocock 1986: chapter 4). Both Weber and Gramsci sought to understand the means, other than repression or coercion, by which a dominant group maintained its advantaged position in society. Weber's solution was that political authority, exercised on the basis of legitimacy, could sustain societies based on the dominance of a particular group. Legitimacy could be derived from traditional mores and values, from the authority of a charismatic leader, or from the operation of legal-rational rules and procedures. The last case is normal in advanced capitalist countries. Decisions and rules would be viewed as legitimate, and would therefore be obeyed and accepted, because of the nature of the procedures used in making them. For legitimacy to be conferred, it was important that the procedures be seen as binding both rulers and ruled and as carrying no necessary implications in terms of outcomes.

For Gramsci a social group could sustain supremacy by exercising intellectual and moral leadership based on hegemonic consent. A vast literature on hegemony has developed, and we shall concentrate on a few points of particular relevance. First, a central aspect of hegemonic rule is persuasion and organizing the consent of subordinate groups and classes. Consent is organized through political and ideological leadership, and hence the content of the ruling ideas and the means of establishing their dominance are of major interest. Second, however, hegemony does not operate solely at the level of ideas. It also assumes a material basis for acceptance of the dominant group's position. This implies that the ruling group takes into account the interests of other classes and has found ways of combining them with its own. This situation enables the ruling group to present its actions and policies plausibly as being in the interests of the people at large. Third, once successfully established, hegemony is virtually unnoticed in everyday political, cultural, and economic life.

Recent analysts (e.g. Jessop et al. 1988) have examined situations where hegemony has appeared either to disintegrate from within or to be contested from without. In these circumstances a struggle to establish a new hegemony ensues, and rival groups or classes can be said to engage in hegemonic projects. Jessop et al (1988: 162) define such a project as a 'programme of political, intellectual and moral leadership which advances the long-term interests of leading sectors in the accumulation strategy while granting economic concessions to the masses of the social base.' In this formulation, therefore, as with hegemony itself, the subordinate classes are subject to ideological leadership and also find certain of their economic interests accommodated.

Another approach is Edelman's (1964, 1971, 1975) concept of symbolic politics: consent in unequal, class-divided societies rests on a sociopsychological foundation. Governing élites manipulate the perceptions and beliefs of the population through management of symbols and political impressions. A highly sophisticated public relations strategy compensates or substitutes for real deprivation, and symbolic politics can sustain mass loyalties even in adverse circumstances.

The concept of ideological legitimation shares the social order/consent problematic with which these other concepts are concerned. Similarly, it is based on the view that state officials actively seek to shape popular perceptions and beliefs. If they are successful, they create legitimacy for the state's, and their own, activities. The concept is, however, distinct from each of those outlined above, and in some ways it is more appropriate in analysing the post-1975 era. In contrast to Weber's concept of legitimacy, ideological legitimation includes an emphasis on the content of state activities. In addition, it is more suitable for analysing the short- or medium-term management of the post-1975 economic crisis. Weber's major concern was with the underlying long-term basis of consent. The concepts of hegemony and hegemonic project deal with ideological issues but also emphasize the accommodation or compromise of material interests vis-à-vis subordinate classes. Ideological legitimation deals with circumstances where previous material concessions are being reduced. Edelman's concept of symbolic politics would appear well-suited to dealing with this type of situation but suffers from two defects: the presumed socio-psychological basis of mass acquiescence and its simplistic view of élite manipulation of the masses. Many of the activities described as symbolic politics also fit into the broader concept of ideological legitimation, which does not imply that ideas are simply a smokescreen used by the élite to delude the masses. The paradigms to be discussed shortly, and which play a key role in the organization of ideological legitimation, do not merely provide a set of manipulative prescriptions. They also provide a program for expressing the real interests of sectors of society in a way that permits their self-interest to be associated with a view of the general interest. By this means, a paradigm, such as monetarism, as a constituent of a broader, neo-conservative ideology, may supply the absolute conviction and self-belief necessary if the dominant class is to wage what Miliband (1987) has termed 'class struggle from above.' Thus we can concur with Whitaker (1977: 29–30),[5] who, though retaining the dichotomy between accumulation and legitimation, highlights the importance of ideology and consciousness in analysing the two concepts. Following Whitaker's advice, I shall pay considerable attention not only to what the Canadian state has done about unemployment but also to how it has presented these actions – its arguments, justifications, and so on.

This brief review of the state literature has identified a number of basic activities that states may perform. We can assume that the precise mixture of activities varies over time and in response to both political and structural influences. Nevertheless, for fairly lengthy periods a particular combination may be well established. During the long period of postwar prosperity, most capitalist countries developed a range of welfare-state policies and institutions and were committed, to varying degrees, to the goal of full employment. Their legitimation activities included a substantial component of material and legal-procedural benefits which have just been labelled concrete legitimation activities.

The economic crisis of the 1970s led to increasing criticism of activities associated with what I have termed concrete legitimation. This led in many countries to a series of assaults on particular programs and eventually to cutbacks in the state's performance in these areas. In some policy areas there was increased resort to coercive measures. Yet, as noted above, the widely anticipated legitimacy crisis failed to materialize. The argument to be developed in this book is that the 'legitimacy deficit' was filled by a considerable increase in the state's ideological legitimation activities. An integral part of this process was the decline of the Keynesian policy paradigm and its partial replacement by the monetarist alternative.

In retrospect it is certain that analysts of the fiscal crisis overstated the degree to which the state was locked into the dilemma of fulfilling both the accumulation and legitimation functions. In particular, the degree to which legitimation depended on material concessions of the Keynesian form was exaggerated. In practice, the state seems to have been able to avert a potential crisis of legitimacy by substituting other activities for some of those formerly identified with concrete legitimation. In addition, of course, while the flow of material benefits has been reduced and its form amended, the process has not ceased.

The state's capacity to manage such a process was not obvious at the time.[6] Nor did the substitutions occur in a neat and tidy or automatic fashion. In fact, the response was an untidy conflict between competing interests and their organizations, ideas, and proposals and was characterized by considerable uncertainty on the part of politicians and other state officials. The pattern of changes that emerged in state policy, however, usefully can be understood as a process of shifting emphasis on various paradigms followed by specifiable material outcomes. Behind this development, of course, lies the complex political struggle among social classes, organizations, and groups.

To note this situation is not to adopt a crude reductionist approach which would consider ideas as merely ideological rationalizations for underlying class interests. It would be equally hazardous, however, to ignore the relationship between class-based interests and the ideas they espouse. The approach adopted here seeks to establish the nature of the relationship through an examination of state policy. Linking ideology to interests or, in this context, paradigms to state activities may provide a significant refinement and improvement of the insights which each alone has to offer. As I have argued in a related context, however powerful particular classes may be, they do require policy strategies capable of expressing and realizing their interests. If they are to stand any chance of being implemented, policies must be rendered convincing at a variety of intellectual levels, to a fairly wide cross-section of the population. Faced with an economic crisis, a class, group, or political party may need the ideological-intellectual resources adequate to this task if it is to retain continued long-term support. Failure to develop such resources may undermine its credibility and erode its strength. Ideology, therefore, may help to determine the long-run balance of class power itself (McBride 1988: 304).

At a more specific level, how do the basic paradigms correspond to the state's various material initiatives? Both paradigms promote the accumulation needs of capital, but Keynesianism, in addition, pays greater attention to legitimation (Chernomas 1983), conceding real and concrete benefits to subordinate classes, as through provision of full employment and welfare programs and encouragement of trade unionism and collective bargaining. Given the theory's perception that lack of demand is a recurring problem in a free-enterprise society, these legitimation policies obviously have an economic or accumulation aspect as well. All these policies help keep demand higher than it would otherwise be.

The mutually reinforcing elements of accumulation and legitimation which Keynesianism seemed to guarantee was at the heart of the post-war settlement between capital and labour. In its post-Keynesian variant, this paradigm pays far more attention to direct state intervention to assist the private sector in its accumulation requirements. Post-Keynesians perceived that simple manipulation of aggregate demand by fiscal and monetary policy could no longer create the conditions for profitable capital accumulation. In addition, they backed away from what they saw as the inflationary implications of free collective bargaining under conditions of relatively full employment. State intrusion into the regulation of wages could result in a loss of legitimacy – a price that post-Keynesians were willing to pay.

In terms of concrete analysis, such policies represented a substitution of coercion for legitimation. To the extent that unions could be induced to agree to wage controls through entanglement in consultative mechanisms, perhaps combined with other trade-offs, the delegitimizing effects of controls could be minimized. The creation of tripartite or corporatist mechanisms to facilitate such trade-offs figured prominently in post-Keynesian plans to manage the economy. Where such mechanisms failed to develop, or broke down, compulsion generally followed.

The monetarist paradigm, of course, saw Keynesian legitimation activities and the levels of spending associated with them as a cause of the economic crisis of the 1970s. By removing obstacles to free operation of markets, and cutting 'wasteful' state expenditures, its proponents hoped to revive the discipline of the market, free up funds for investment, and restore the dynamism of the economy. In the monetarist paradigm, therefore, the priority of accumulation was unchallenged by Keynesian-style legitimation concerns. Thus one would expect the shift in economic paradigms to be accompanied by policy changes that would de-emphasize concrete legitimation activities.

For a number of reasons, it is unlikely that the impact of a macro-level paradigm shift on other specific policy areas will precisely coincide with the broader change. Nevertheless, over the period 1970–88 the change in paradigms and in emphasis on particular state initiatives should be discernible in all of the policy areas to be examined. To the extent that concrete legitimation activities have been sacrificed in order better to promote capital accumulation, without this having provoked a crisis of legitimacy, one might expect to find compensatory activity in other areas, such as increased reliance on coercion or on ideological legitimation. Such activity might also include a search for alternative means of concrete legitimation. One would expect the latter means to be relatively inexpensive, in view of the proclaimed fiscal crisis, and ideologically consistent in form with the individualism and private-enterprise ethos of the new paradigm. This book emphasizes the state's increased use of broadly ideological techniques to sustain legitimacy but also pays attention to other means of compensating for cutbacks in concrete benefits.

In practice, such compensatory efforts are unlikely to effect a smooth substitution for past patterns of legitimation. Much recent analysis of the economic crisis has focused on 'the contradictory effects of state intervention' (Bob Russell 1986: 309). Such contradictions emerged from the difficulties of the situation facing state officials in the mid-1970s, their own uncertainties in the face of complexity, and the clash of interests among different classes, groups, and organizations in society.

In this book, four areas of state policy are judged particularly relevant to unemployment: fiscal and monetary macroeconomic policies (chapter 4), labour-market policies (chapter 5), provision for the unemployed through unemployment insurance (chapter 6), and interventions into the conduct of labour–capital conflict via industrial relations policy (chapter 7). In-depth analysis of these policy areas will follow in subsequent chapters. Within these areas we shall look at the changing influence of policy paradigms, the extent to which state policy indicates the fulfilment of particular priorities and the changing balance between them, and the extent to which the state's actions were consistent with each other.

State action is, of course, influenced by many factors, including national economic conditions, the international economic environment, and the domestic and international balance of class, ideological, and political forces. While the focus of this study is on the nature of the economic theory or paradigm that informs state decision makers and that leads to changes of emphasis on the performance of particular state activities, the perceived relevance of paradigms is seen as being conditioned by the operation of other factors.

The Influence of Class

Although I would concede a significant explanatory role for structural factors in the national and international economic environment, it will be argued subsequently (see chapter 2) that these are secondary to political factors in understanding the state's response to economic crisis and its performance with respect to unemployment.

Chapter 2 presents a comparative perspective on Canada's unemployment record. Based on the comparative evidence, a case is made that variations in national unemployment rates are determined largely by the policy packages chosen and implemented by national states. The choice of policy package is itself strongly influenced by the nature of the dominant ideology and the economic policy paradigm embedded within it. These factors in turn seem closely linked to the balance of class forces. In most cases where business was dominant and labour was weak, the Keynesian full-employment commitment was abandoned with the onset of economic crisis in the mid-1970s. The monetarist paradigm provided the theoretical basis for a policy shift which clearly reflected the expressed interests and political dominance of business. The analysis of the Canadian case that occupies much of the rest of the book indicates that Canada fits this comparative profile rather well.

This book is concerned primarily with what the state did and how it managed the potentially delegitimizing effects of its strategy. Explaining the state's actions is not a major focus. However, the issue is addressed from time to time in chapter 2, in the substantive chapters, and again in the concluding chapter. The results seem to indicate growth in business dominance pertaining to construction of state policy. There is certainly evidence that suggests the mechanisms by which this is achieved in Canada. For example, Williams (1989) reports that business people have more extensive access to the state than labour leaders and that these contacts are more important, since business-state contacts tend to be associated with adoption of pro-business policy stances by state élites (233). Similarly, Langille (1987) has documented the formation and growing policy influence of the Business Council on National Issues. Interesting as these findings are, they must remain tangential to our primary focus. But given the vogue of state-centred explanations of state activity, it is worth noting that any state-centredness in the current manuscript is confined to the empirical subject-matter: what the state did. It does not extend to explanation. As chapter 2 makes clear, my reading of the comparative evidence is that state choices and policies are conditioned by a number of political factors behind which can usually be found class interests.

Summary

After a prolonged period of relatively full employment, there was a return in the 1970s and 1980s, in Canada as in many other Western countries, to high unemployment levels. This development carries with it considerable economic and social costs and has been the occasion of much public concern. Yet far from state policy being dedicated to solving the problem, there is considerable evidence that public policy is one of the causes.

As a preliminary step in exploring this situation, this chapter has identified some of the relevant policy areas and has suggested that the content of state policy in these areas will be shaped, in the first instance at least, by the economic theory or paradigm that most influences decision makers. The relation among economic theories, public policy, and economic performance provides the focus of this analysis of Canada's unemployment problem. But these factors are seen as ultimately being conditioned by the balance of class, ideological, and political forces.

2 Only in Canada?

National Variations in Unemployment Rates: Alternative Explanations

In chapter 1, I sketched the broad outlines of Canada's unemployment record. Subsequent chapters will present a detailed examination of the Canadian state's policy response. A major theme in this analysis will be that state policy has been not merely a response to unemployment but an active and causal agent that is responsible, to a significant extent, for the existence of the problem.

This argument rests partly on an interpretation of the policy consequences that flow from the logic of the monetarist economic paradigm once adopted and implemented by state officials. It is also partly derived from the comparative empirical observation that particular policy strategies have been associated with high unemployment levels in countries that followed them. Canada fits such a profile and has shared the high unemployment consequences. In contrast, countries that have pursued alternative policy strategies have often experienced quite low unemployment. This chapter is concerned with the development and substantiation of this contrast.

Clearly not all of the increased unemployment, in Canada or elsewhere, can be attributed to the impact of policy. In all Western industrialized countries, there have been pressures on the unemployment rate, and almost all these nations have experienced increases in unemployment since the 1960s. Such pressures have their origin in a faltering international economy. In the early 1970s four developments in particular harmed the economic health of the capitalist world: inflation originating in the financing of the Vietnam War, the collapse of the

Bretton Woods system of fixed exchange rates, the first oil crisis in 1973, and the buildup of productive forces in a number of formerly underdeveloped countries because of the internationalization of capital. All the capitalist countries experienced difficulties in coping with the impact of these changes in the world economy. One aspect of these changes was a general tendency to increased unemployment.

Table 2.1 shows the basic trend for most OECD countries. Although average rates of unemployment have increased across the board, some countries have maintained rather low levels, while others have lapsed into very high levels. Table 2.2 and Figure 2.1 provide additional illustration of this point. The number of countries with low unemployment, defined arbitrarily but not unrealistically as being less than 3 per cent, fell dramatically after the mid-1970s. A significant number began to experience unemployment above or close to 10 per cent. Although the categories in Table 2.3 are somewhat arbitrary, they do indicate the increasing differentiation between nations in the pre- and post-crisis periods and highlight those where performance deteriorated most. It will be argued that most of the variation can be explained by the policies pursued. Since this is not an uncontroversial argument, the next sections of the chapter will review some of the major explanations that have been advanced for observed variance in unemployment rates. The literature contains two broad types of explanation. The first hypothesizes that socioeconomic variables determine most of the observed difference in unemployment. The second focuses on political factors. The policy paradigm explanation is obviously an example of the second type.

The following section of the chapter reviews comparative evidence that leads to the rejection of economic explanations. Subsequently a variety of political hypotheses are discussed and reasons advanced for preferring the policy paradigm alternative. In the last part of the chapter, Canada is located within this comparative context.

Economic Hypotheses

This section of the chapter relies heavily on cross-national work conducted by Manfred Schmidt (1982a, 1982b, 1984, 1987) and Goran Therborn (1986). Their studies explore, among other things, the relation between unemployment rates and such economic variables as growth in wages, decline in profits, growth in the labour force, degree of integration into world markets, rate of economic growth, structural char-

TABLE 2.1
Average unemployment rates

	1965–9	1970–4	1975–9	1980–4	1985–8
Major seven OECD					
United States	3.7	5.3	6.9	8.2	6.4
Japan	1.2	1.3	2.0	2.4	2.7
West Germany	0.9	0.9	3.5	5.7	6.5
France	1.8	2.6	4.9	8.0	10.3
United Kingdom	1.7	3.1	5.4	10.3	10.5
Italy	5.5	5.7	6.8	9.0	10.3
Canada	3.9	5.7	7.3	9.8	9.1
Average	2.8	3.5	5.2	7.6	8.0
Others					
Australia	1.7	2.2	5.5	7.5	7.9
Austria	1.9	1.3	1.9	3.2	3.5
Belgium	2.2	2.5	7.0	11.3	10.8
Finland	2.5	2.1	5.0	5.1	5.0
Netherlands	1.1	1.9	5.3	9.9	9.8
Norway	0.9	1.4	1.9	2.5	2.5
Spain	2.6	2.6	5.8	15.6	20.3
Sweden	1.8	2.2	1.9	2.9	2.3
Switzerland	n/a	n/a	0.4	0.6	0.7
Average	1.8	2.0	3.9	6.5	7.0
Average, all of above	2.3	2.7	4.5	7.0	7.4

SOURCES: OECD *Economic Outlook* (December 1990); OECD *Labour Force Statistics 1965–85*

TABLE 2.2
Distribution of national unemployment rates over time

Unemployment rate (%)	1965–9	1970–4	1975–9	1980–4	1985–8
0–2.9	12	11	5	4	4
3–5.9	3*	4*	7	3	2
6–8.9	0	0	4*	3	3
9+	0	0	0	6*	7*

* Includes Canada

TABLE 2.3
Countries of low, medium, and high unemployment, 1970–4, 1975–9, 1980–4, 1985–8

	1970–4	1975–9	1980–4	1985–8
Low (0–2.9%)	Australia Austria Belgium Finland France Japan Netherlands Norway Spain Sweden Switzerland West Germany	Austria Japan Norway Sweden Switzerland	Japan Norway Sweden Switzerland	Japan Norway Sweden Switzerland
Medium (3–5.9%)	Canada Italy United Kingdom United States	Australia Finland France Netherlands Spain United Kingdom West Germany	Austria Finland West Germany	Austria Finland
High (6–8.9%)		Belgium Canada Italy United States	Australia France United States	Australia United States West Germany
Mass (9% +)			Belgium Canada Italy Netherlands Spain United Kingdom	Belgium Canada France Italy Netherlands Spain United Kingdom

NOTE: Countries underlined have moved categories since the previous period.

acteristics of employment (e.g. size of manufacturing or service sector), and pre-crisis unemployment rates.

Schmidt (1987: 172) summarizes the posited relationships:

International differences in rates of unemployment, it can be argued, are attributable to differences in the nature and the number of economic-structural obstacles to full-employment. Thus, for example, efforts to maintain full-employment are facilitated by low growth rates in labour supply, high growth of the gross domestic product (GDP) and low productivity growth, and a low degree of trade dependency, to mention just a few factors. In contrast to this, governments that are confronted with high labour supply growth rates, weak GDP growth and high productivity growth, heavy external dependence of the economy, wage rigidity, and the presence of industries with heavy adjustment problems will find it far more difficult to control unemployment effectively.

But Schmidt's studies (e.g. 1982b: 245–50) of the hypothesized relationships between unemployment levels and particular economic variables reveal, for the most part, little support for them. These findings are confirmed by Therborn (1986: chapter 1), who detects little, or in some cases no, relationship between unemployment and such factors as economic growth, labour-force growth, patterns of technological change, inflation, export performance, size of service sector, profit levels, labour costs, and levels of social expenditure or unemployment compensation.

Schmidt's own findings confirmed a relation between unemployment and only two economic variables. The first was degree of integration with the world market. The hypothesis that little political and economic integration would be more beneficial than extensive integration for a full-employment strategy was weakly confirmed. Once more, Therborn (51–3) provides some support for this conclusion. He notes that the five countries with the lowest unemployment were non-members of the European Community (EC) and speculates that critical aspects of their economic policy strategies would have been impossible had they been members.

The other, and more strongly confirmed economic hypothesis, is what Schmidt terms the 'constant structure hypothesis': 'It is frequently suggested that much policy-making can be understood in terms of incrementalism. A parallel pattern may be discerned in respect to economic systems. The structure, dynamics, and outcomes of an economy at time t [are] strongly dependent on the structure, dynamics and outcomes at time $t - 1$. One might thus argue that the differential rates of unemployment in the 1970's would be strongly associated with differential rates of unemployment in the preceding period' (1982a: 131).

Schmidt reports a medium-strength relation for this hypothesis. In itself, however, this merely begs the question: did economic or political factors account for good performance in the earlier period? In addition, a number of countries saw drastic deterioration in performance in the 1970s. In these cases, therefore, past performance did not predict later performance. Schmidt's analysis of the effect of individual economic factors (1982a: 138–9) reveals little support for the notion that unusually adverse economic factors account for deteriorating performance.

In a more recent work, Schmidt (1987) has attempted to assess the cumulative effects of economic-structural variables by constructing an index of economic-structural obstacles to full employment. The index included such factors as the existence of crisis industries, dependence on exports, growth rate, gap between productivity and growth, level of employment in manufacturing, labour-force growth rate, pre-crisis unemployment rate, and degree of wage differentiation within manufacturing. Each country was assigned a score depending on the number of factors blocking full employment. The major conclusion was 'the weakness of the statistical association between rates of unemployment and the index of structural obstacles to full-employment policy. Relative to the nature and number of economic-structural problems, the full-employment nations, except Japan, were by no means in a better position than the nations that were plagued by mass unemployment' (1987: 172–4).

Other studies can be cited to support this finding. Sweden, for example, has maintained very low unemployment since the onset of economic crisis. Yet it has been argued that the Swedish economy is highly sensitive to international economic fluctuations and suffers from an unfavourable industrial structure (Meidner 1984: 251–2). Much the same argument can be made about Austria.

Schmidt is careful to point out that his findings do not imply that economic factors are unimportant. But while in some countries economic factors, such as a recession, strongly affect the unemployment rate, in other countries they do not. And the difference cannot be explained by the economic variables themselves: 'The labour market responded immediately and directly only in certain countries, and in others a number of intervening variables interrupted the normal relationship between recession and labour market crisis ... It can be plausibly argued that intervening political mechanisms account for these different patterns of responsiveness' (1982a: 140).

The thrust of this argument, then, is that economic factors can either facilitate or hinder full employment. But they do not determine a particular labour-market outcome. Rather, political factors largely shape a country's level of unemployment. Proponents of this view, however, differ on what the key political factor might be. The next section of the chapter reviews the debate in the literature on this point.

Political Hypotheses

Three major political explanations for variations in unemployment rates are examined here: that party matters, that institutions matter, and that ideology matters. The last is the least well-defined but perhaps the most promising explanation.

Party and institutional explanations will be reviewed and criticized in turn. The critique will lay the basis for a fuller discussion of the ideology hypothesis. Criticism of the first two theories is not intended to suggest their wholesale rejection. Given the overlap among the three, this would be fool-hardy. Rather, the intention is to suggest that the ideological approach is better able to account for variations. But ideological dominance is obviously linked to the political parties that are, to a degree, its carriers. And policies derived from the dominant ideology may depend for their successful implementation partially on the pattern of group-state relations which has become known as corporatism and, possibly, on other institutional arrangements. Similarly, all these interconnections may themselves depend on a further underlying variable: the balance of class forces within countries.

Party

One of the clearest statements of this explanation is found in Hibbs's (1977) examination of the relation between party in office and macroeconomic performance. Hibbs considered that social democratic governments gave higher priority to maintaining full employment than governments of other political persuasions. If necessary, they were willing to tolerate higher inflation in order to 'purchase' high employment. Hibbs concluded that such priorities accorded well with the social base of such parties, as did the converse policy package with the social base of right-wing parties. Hibbs's general argument found support from other analysts. For example, Tufte (1978: 104) considered that 'the single most important determinant of variations in macroeconomic performance from one industrialized democracy to another is the location on the left–right spectrum of the governing political party. Party platforms and political ideology set priorities and help decide policies. The consequence is that the governing party is very much responsible for major macroeconomic outcomes – unemployment rates, inflation rates, ...'

Initial criticisms of the explanatory potential of party government tended to concentrate on the sample of countries used to generate these results (see Payne 1979). With a different set of examples than Hibbs's, much lower correlations were found between social democratic incumbency and specific macroeconomic results. Schmidt notes that where social democratic parties have dominated government for long periods, the relation found by Hibbs appears to hold. But in these cases, he argues, this may be the result of 'the coincidence of the dominant tendency in government and the extra-parliamentary balance of power' (Schmidt 1982a: 141).

It might also be argued that whatever pre-eminence party had in the era of the post-war consensus has been eroded by the breakdown in that consensus. The rise of neo-conservative thinking has not been confined to right-wing parties. In a comparison of the policies of the Conservative Thatcher government in Britain with those of New Zealand's Labour government, Boston (1987: 129) makes the general point that 'the past decade has witnessed a good deal of ideological flux within social democratic parties and many have moved to accept, often unashamedly, some of the policy prescriptions of neo-conservative scholars.' Yet, as Boston emphasizes, not all social democratic parties have moved in this direction. Whatever may have been true in the past, therefore, the policy implications of social democratic governments should now be viewed as highly differentiated. Given this situation, it is unlikely that party continues to 'matter' in the way posited by Hibbs.

This perception is reinforced if we take into account two types of evidence. The first involves the exceptional cases of Japan and Switzerland. Both have enjoyed exceptionally low levels of unemployment. Governments have long been dominated by solidly right-wing parties. Whatever explains their success, therefore, it cannot be the party complexion of their governments. The second type of evidence pertains to systems that have experienced alternation between left- and right-wing parties. In such countries cases can be found, as documented by Boston among others, of neo-conservative policies being adopted by social democratic governments – for example, New Zealand since 1984 and Britain after 1975. In both cases the policy shift was associated with high unemployment. But cases can also be found where, despite replacement of social democrats by right-wing alternatives, full employment has remained the major priority – for example, Sweden between 1976 and 1982.

In Sweden, all the major elements of Social Democratic labour market measures, a key instrument for maintaining full employment, were continued by the non-socialist governments (Webber 1983: 34). Indeed, expenditures increased markedly after 1976 (Henning 1984: 196–7), hardly the direction one might have anticipated on the basis of the party hypothesis. There is some evidence that adoption of expanded labour market measures – which included major interventions into the economy, deficit financing, and nationalizations – ran counter to the economic policy doctrines of the non-socialist parties (Webber 1983: 31). It seems reasonable, then, to infer that their reactions were determined by political constraints. One such constraint could be the existence of strong corporatist institutions. Another could be the ideological context in which non-socialist parties were forced to operate. Contrasting the situation, in this regard, with the case of West Germany, Webber (1983: 35) makes a telling observation: 'Social democracy governs in Sweden even when the Social Democratic Party is not in office, while social democracy does not govern in West Germany ... even when the SDP *is* in office.'

Given the variety of evidence briefly reviewed above, it is difficult to sustain an unqualified version of the dominant role of party. Party may matter, but to what degree is heavily contingent on other political factors.

Institutions

The application of institutional analysis to the explanation of policy outcomes has recently undergone a revival within political science. Three main types of 'neo-institutionalist' explanation of the employment/unemployment aspects of national economic performance have emerged, focusing variously on the structure of state-group interaction (corporatism), the nature of welfare-state 'regimes,' and the degree of autonomy enjoyed by central banks. Each will be reviewed in turn.

Over the last fifteen years a voluminous literature has developed on the phenomenon of corporatism – a structured pattern of bargaining between the state and key interest groups, especially those representative of labour and capital. The concept itself, and its empirical implications, have been the subject of considerable controversy in political science literature (see Panitch 1980; Ross Martin 1983; McBride 1985). It is widely claimed that corporatist structures give the state greater ability to manage the economy, including maintaining full employment while keeping inflationary pressures under control.

Tarantelli (1987) provides a clear exposition of this argument. In his view, corporatist or neo-corporatist arrangements are characterized by centralized collective bargaining, highly regulated industrial conflict, and co-option by the state of unions and employer's associations such that these groups are 'willing to accept, and strong enough to implement, a "fine-tuning" of economic policy' (95). The absence of these conditions means that inflation can be controlled only through a 'monetary crunch' which involves heavy unemployment and much lost output. The presence of such arrangements makes it possible to lower inflationary expectations by a formal or informal incomes policy, and this obviates the need for unemployment in order to bring inflation under control. Tarantelli's analysis is based on a study of sixteen industrialized countries, and his overall conclusion is that with a high degree of neo-corporatism, 'any given target rate of inflation can ... be achieved with lower costs in terms of unemployment' (101).

Other comparative studies provide sufficient support for this view to justify taking seriously the school of thought that claims a dominant place for corporatism. Goldthorpe (1984b: 337) notes that unions operating in corporatist arrangements have been relatively successful in sustaining governments' commitment to both full employment and adequate welfare state provisions. Quite a variety of policy techniques have been used to maintain employment levels, but the key element seemed to be partnership between unions and government. Similarly, both Cameron (1984) and Schmidt (1982a) report strong associations between corporatism and full employment. For Cameron, the association is between full employment and 'the structural preconditions for (corporatist) behaviour' (168). Thus he writes of the 'organizational power of labour' rather than of 'corporatism,' which, to him, implies a type of behaviour characterized by 'elite coalescence, cooptation, and participation in such wage restraining acts as incomes policies' (168). This mode of behaviour may or may not be associated with the structural preconditions. In effect, however, as Cameron notes, his concept of the organizational power of labour and others' concepts of corporatism have 'a near identity ... in measurement and empirical reference' (168). Schmidt's main finding is that 'corporatism is the best single predictor for differential rates of unemployment ... Strong corporatism is a sufficient but unnecessary condition for low rates of unemployment' (Schmidt 1982a).

In Schmidt's view (1982a: 252–5) corporatist institutions affect the rate of unemployment through a number of mechanisms: they may contribute to the salience of unemployment as a political issue, or they may contribute to capital accumulation, typically by way of incomes policies. But corporatist structures only partly explain low unemployment. Schmidt considers that earlier levels of unemployment act as a background determinant. More important, the extra-parliamentary distribution of power between 'the left and the bourgeois milieu' politically affects unemployment. We shall return to this factor presently when discussing the explanation that focuses on ideology.

The studies cited above show that the presence and strength of corporatist structures have considerable appeal as an explanation of differential unemployment rates. Yet there are some problems with the hypothesis. First, and notwithstanding the quantities of ink expended in describing and analysing corporatism, its defining characteristics remain disputed. This leads to some difficulty in empirically distinguishing corporatist from other systems of state-group interaction (Jordan 1984). How accurate are the rank-orders of degrees of corporatism that appear in the literature? Does Sweden have developed corporatism or something else: 'corporate pluralism', for example? Is it possible to have corporatism without labour involvement? There are several answers to questions such as these. Countries may be ranked as strongly corporatist in one study but as only weakly corporatist in another. The ranking will affect dramatically the association between corporatism and other variables, such as unemployment rate (see Therborn 1986: 98–100).

Second, a problem arises in considering the mechanisms through which corporatist structures supposedly help achieve full employment. One key mechanism, commonly mentioned in the literature, is corporatism's contribution to inflation control through wage restraint. With inflation thus under control, the state can take the steps necessary to maintain full employment. But in some cases, notably Sweden, there is considerable disagreement about whether the posited corporatist structures actually operated successful incomes policies.

Some studies (e.g. Marks 1986) have argued that wage restraint did operate in Sweden, albeit informally, and that this flowed from the existence of corporatist structures. Others, such as Andrew Martin (1985: 443–4), disagree. In his view, after the mid-1960s the centralized wage-bargaining system did not perform 'the function of an incomes policy,' despite attempts to make it do so. This analysis is consistent with Therborn's observation that although Sweden is generally ranked as strongly corporatist the ideology of social partnership is much weaker there than in a number of other European countries (Therborn 1986: 100; also Webber 1983: 30).

Third, there is the problem of the 'exceptional cases' of Japan and Switzerland. Both countries have very low unemployment; labour organizations and left-wing parties are weak, industrial relations are decentralized, and, rather than articulating an ideology of social partnership and collaboration, employers, particularly in Japan, tend to adopt a coercively paternalistic perspective. None of these conditions can be associated with the structural prerequisites of corporatism, and, in reality, corporatist institutions play little role in these countries. This factor led Schmidt (1984: 11–12) to posit two roads to full employment. One, typical of those Western European nations that have maintained full employment, rested on the power of labour and did use corporatist institutions. The other, typified by Japan and Switzerland, was based on the power of capital, which engaged in paternalistic relations with other social actors.

Therborn has used the same image of 'two roads to full employment' to advance a common factor between the two approaches:

The existence or non-existence of an institutionalized commitment to full-employment is the basic explanation for the differential impact of the current crisis. An institutionalization of the commitment to full-employment involves: a) an explicit commitment to maintaining/achieving full-employment; b) the existence and use of countercyclical mechanisms and policies; c) the existence and use of specific mechanisms to adjust supply and demand in the labour market to the goal of full-employment; d) a conscious decision not to use high employment as a means to secure other policy objectives. (1986: 23)

The commitment to full employment was institutionalized for two quite different reasons. In Sweden and Norway it resulted from the assertion of working-class interests by powerful labour movements. In Japan and Switzerland it emanated from a conservative concern with 'order and stability as being of equal importance to capital accumulation' (24). In the case of Swiss exceptionalism, Katzenstein (1984: 129–32) records that mass inter-war unemployment left an 'indelible mark on the country's collective memory' and that job security is viewed as essential to society's stability. In practice, Switzerland has been able to maintain full employment largely by the device of sending home foreign workers. Without this option, the country would have experienced an unemployment rate of around 10 per cent. In Japan the maintenance of full employment, often attributed to 'paternalism,' has been part of an essentially coercive strategy of social control directed against a work-force which, at least in the immediate post-war years, was far from quiescent either industrially or politically (Armstrong, Glyn, and Harrison 1984: 37–9, 72–80; Hirosuke 1986; Ichiyo 1986; Rokuro 1986; Sugimoto 1986). Both conservative examples of full employment imply the use of considerable coercion against labour – against foreign-born, temporary residents or domestic workers. Moreover, in both cases bourgeois concern with social stability can be linked, perhaps tenuously, for Switzerland, with previous assertions of working-class power.

Whatever its origins, however, state policy is based on an ideological commitment to full employment and on a determination to use various policy instruments to achieve this result. In the case of the two different 'roads,' the ideologies are different. In similar vein, in criticizing 'structural-determinist' explanations of unemployment differentials, Scharpf (1984: 70) has emphasized the importance of 'strategic choice': 'Different countries may differ in their performance profiles because they have *chosen* to pursue different priorities by different means.' Once again the element of ideology and policy choice emerges from this formulation.

The proposition that employment outcomes are determined by the nature of 'welfare state regimes' has been advanced by Esping-Anderson (1990), who argues that once they have become crystallized, such regimes function as 'independent causal variables' which 'systematically influence social and economic behaviour.' In particular, 'nations' capacity to maintain full-employment over the post-war period has been decisively influenced by the welfare state' (141–2).

Esping-Andersen identifies three welfare state regimes, each characterized by a cluster of social policy variables (26–9). The first is the 'liberal welfare state,' of which the United States and Canada are examples, and in which social benefits are typically modest and recipients often stigmatized. Such a regime reinforces the primacy of the market. 'Conservative welfare states,' exemplified by a number of continental European countries, are less concerned with reinforcing market forces than with preserving class and status differentials. State-provided benefits have little redistributive effect and, because of religious influences, are committed to preservation of traditional family roles and relationships. The 'social democratic welfare state' is infused with the ethos of universalism and promotes high levels of equally available benefits. Only it is 'genuinely committed to a full-employment guarantee, and entirely dependent on its attainment ... Neither of the two alternative regime-types espouse full-employment as an integral part of their welfare state commitment. In the conservative tradition, of course, women are discouraged from working; in the liberal ideal, concerns of gender matter less than the sanctity of the market' (28).

At a descriptive level, Esping-Andersen's categorization seems unobjectionable. Indeed, as he acknowledges (165), his placement of countries corresponds to that used by other writers in related models or typologies devised for somewhat different purposes. However, his account of the causal factors behind the development of particular regimes and, especially, the causal power of the regimes themselves, once crystallized, is open to criticism.

In the past Esping-Andersen has been identified with 'power resource theory,' in which levels of working-class mobilization account for variations in welfare state development and incorporation of goals such as full employment into the state's priorities.[1] His most recent contribution significantly modifies this approach and emphasizes the historical development of class coalitions in which the position of the rural classes assumes particular importance (18). In the post-war period (earlier in some countries, such as Britain), the disposition of the rising white-collar strata, rather than of the farmers, became the 'linchpin' for coalition formation: 'The political leanings of the new middle classes have ... been decisive for welfare state consolidation' (31). The analysis concludes: 'Middle-class welfare states, be they social democratic (as in Scandinavia) or corporatist (as in Germany) forge middle-class loyalties. In contrast, the liberal, residualist welfare states found in the United States, Canada and, increasingly, Britain, depend on the loyalties of a numerically weak, and often politically residual, social stratum. In this sense, the class coalitions in which the three welfare-state regime types were founded, explain not only their past evolution but also their future prospects' (33).

Despite its apparent plausibility, there are some problems with this analysis. First, the argument seems heavily determinist: once coalitions are formed and welfare-state regimes crystallized, they seem destined to persist and develop according to some kind of automatic pilot. The argument is inherently static and leaves little scope for alteration by current or future political developments. Second, the category of 'new middle class' is notoriously difficult to define and its presumed homogeneity cannot be assumed. Third, Esping-Andersen exaggerates the ability and desire of the new middle class in liberal welfare-state regimes to meet its welfare needs outside the state (i.e. privately). Given the nature of social provision in such regimes, middle-class recourse to private social benefits can be viewed as the product of necessity rather than of preference. Rather than being a proactive and decisive element, the class finds itself in a reactive posture.

These problems are replicated when the discussion turns to crystallized welfare-state regimes as independent causal variables that determine labour-market outcomes (and much else). Esping-Andersen notes the correspondence of labour-market and welfare-state profiles, as others have done, but fails to establish that the lines of causality run from welfare state to labour market. Moreover, he has not thoroughly investigated the possibility that some other variable explains the correspondence. This leaves the analysis open to the charge of being institutionally reductionist.

Another neo-institutionalist approach emphasizes the impact on labour-market outcomes of the degree of autonomy enjoyed by central banks. In a study of Sweden, Norway, Denmark, and Finland, Uusitalo (1984) observes that adoption of monetarist economic policies is correlated to the autonomy of central banks. In Finland and Denmark, where the central banks are well protected from political influence, monetarist doctrines have found more favour than in Norway and Sweden, where the central banks are much less autonomous. In the latter countries, Keynesian state interventionism has been the dominant mode of economic management, and, because of their control over the central banks, governments have been able to pursue integrated economic policies. This is an important point, and the potential exists for an autonomous central bank to use its authority over monetary policy to obstruct the full-employment policies of, say, a social democratic government. Similarly, there is little doubt that Uusitalo is correct to point to central bankers' affinity for monetarist economic doctrines. However, he leaves unexamined the relation of central banks to the structure and significance of finance capital in his four countries. Depending on what that relation is, a society-centred analysis, emphasizing the power of finance capital and its preferences in terms of economic paradigms, might have more to offer than the neo-institutionalist view that he favours. Central-bank autonomy would still be an important institutional variable, but its significance would be embedded in the context of class relations and the balance of class forces.

This criticism derives some support from another study which highlights central banks' autonomy as a key factor in explaining high unemployment in certain countries. In arguing that social democratic governments are constrained by autonomous central banks, Kurzer (1988) is always careful to emphasize the connection among this institutional factor, its ideological preferences, and the dominance (or otherwise) of financial interests within capital. Her careful investigation reveals that 'countries with independent central banks and an important financial sector are likely to pursue deflation and have high unemployment in the 1980s ... Belgium and the Netherlands belong in this category. Austria and Sweden are examples of countries in which the central bank is forced to cooperate with government and the financial sector occupies a subordinate economic position' (28).

Although Kurzer herself elevates the institutional variable to equal or higher status than the underlying structural variable of the dominance of financial capital, a careful reading of her article provides no particular basis for this assumption. It seems, rather, to be a normative statement, since the evidence, meticulously presented, does not seem to point in one direction or the other.

In short, the case for institutional determination of ideological and policy choices is not proven. But the significance of policy paradigms in either averting or contributing to unemployment is a central feature of these analyses. Criticisms of the institutional school, therefore, point away from structures as key determinants of economic performance, and toward ideology and policy choices, which will be analysed more carefully in the next subsection. However, even if the 'dominant ideology' hypothesis ultimately is judged superior, structures may either facilitate certain policy strategies or inhibit their implementation. The argument to be presented suggests that ideology matters most but cannot serve as the only explanation.

Ideology

Once economic-structural and political-structural variables are rejected as the principal explanation for differential unemployment rates, the most promising remaining explanation is that policies largely determine economic outcomes, including rate of unemployment. As will become apparent, however, there was no single 'magic formula' policy associated with low unemployment. Instead, countries that retained something approaching full employment used a number of policy instruments to achieve this result.

The argument, therefore, rests on the notion that the successful countries forged some mixture of policies which, in the conditions they were facing, produced full employment. As the mixture varied from country to country, different combinations of policies performed functionally equivalent roles. No particular mixture leads automatically to full employment, but incorporation of a commitment to that goal within the dominant ideology leads to a search for policies that, in the circumstances of the country, will produce the desired end. What the low-unemployment countries share is an ideology that ranks maintenance of full employment as the first priority. From this choice flow a number of secondary decisions about appropriate means.

As with the party and corporatist explanations, there is a body of literature that tends toward the conclusion that ideology matters most. Though less identifiable as a coherent school of thought than the others, its main conclusions are worth reviewing. A number of studies see mass unemployment as part of a neo-conservative strategy to tame the power of trade unions and enable economic adjustment to occur on terms favourable to capital (Blackman 1987: 318–19; McBride 1986). Policies are seen as either being designed to create unemployment or as withholding actions in order to allow unemployment to rise 'naturally.' Whiteley (1985) concludes that the monetarist approach to inflation consists of causing a recession in order to weaken trade unions' bargaining power.

In a significant study of British economic failure since the Second World War, Stephen Blank (1977) argued that Britain's ability to pursue domestic goals, such as full employment, was severely limited by external commitments. But contrary to the conventional wisdom which saw such external constraints – defence of sterling, balance of payment difficulties, and so on – as structural, Blank argued convincingly that they were really 'the result of a series of political choices made by post-war governments to restore and preserve Britain's role as world power' (675). In reality, then, although full employment was widely perceived to be a central part of the country's post-war consensus, it enjoyed less priority than other economic goals.

In a comparative study of unemployment in Britain and Sweden, McBride (1988: 307–10) pointed out the need to modify the image of post-war Britain as being governed by a Keynesian consensus which included an unequivocal commitment to full employment. In reality, full employment was only one of a series of proclaimed economic policy goals, and its relative priority, should conflicts occur, was not spelled out. Nor were the likely inflationary consequences of free collective bargaining in a context of full employment fully anticipated. To the extent that inflationary pressures were foreseen, the solution was supposed to lie in wage moderation by the unions. But the potential conflict was not addressed. While the Labour party may have been emotionally committed to full employment, its failure to devise a theoretically coherent strategy for achieving it was to plague the party throughout the post-war years and ultimately, because of Labour's regular adoption of wage controls, to undermine its base of support within the working class.

The Conservatives' attachment to full employment can be viewed as much more instrumental. Apart from the desire to escape their 1930s image of being the party of mass unemployment, the Tories found Keynesianism temporarily attractive because it promised to make economic management a matter of technique rather than politics and thus offered government some immunity from interest-group pressures. In a later era, it has been said that the attraction of monetarism was precisely the same, although the goal of escaping from interest-group pressures was to be achieved by different means (Bulpitt 1986). Such an instrumental attachment to Keynesianism hardly provided a firm foundation for the commitment to full employment.

In Sweden, in contrast, full employment seems to have been explicitly acknowledged as being the first priority of government, and the means to achieve it were much more carefully worked out. This approach was clearly based on a strong trade union movement and on Social Democratic dominance of government. But the bourgeois parties, whatever their private reservations, considered themselves locked into the full-employment commitment, which thus became a central feature of the hegemonic ideology.

It is precisely in the differences in degree to which full employment was entrenched in the post-war consensus of Sweden and Britain that McBride traced the different levels of unemployment in the 1970s and 1980s. Further consideration of the countries that maintained high employment tends to substantiate this approach. The primacy of full employment in Sweden has often been remarked on (e.g. Meidner 1984: 247). Similarly, Austrian economic policy during the 1970s has been characterized as being based on 'full-employment at all costs' (Pichelmann and Wagner 1984: 211). In analysing the experience of Austria, Norway, and Sweden, Bellemare and Poulin Simon (1988: 74–5) attribute great significance to the top priority given to full employment. The commitment must extend far beyond the rhetorical level and must impel governments, unions, employers' associations, and other groups to incorporate the ethos into their programs, attitudes, and behaviour. In

Japan and Switzerland, where the commitment is based on conservative reformism rather than social democracy, motivations may owe more to paternalism and preventive avoidance of crisis (Schmidt 1987: 180). Yet even there full employment seems to have achieved 'fact-of-life' or 'common-sense' status, and policy packages have been devised accordingly.

Many of the available policies that can ease unemployment have been summarized by Gerlach and Sengenberger (1984), from whose work Table 2.4 is reproduced. The Canadian experience in some of these policy areas will be explored in later chapters.

Attempts have been made to construct policy configurations typical of high, and low-unemployment countries. Lindberg (1985) distinguished three such patterns of inflation-control strategies, each with rather different consequences for unemployment. The first, exemplified by countries such as Britain, Canada, and the United States, consisted of allowing the market to correct inflationary pressures by permitting recession, and therefore unemployment, to dampen them. This was sometimes assisted by cuts in public spending and measures to weaken trade unions. Beyond this, policy tended to be restricted to macro-level instruments. Essentially this was a market-driven strategy. The second approach Lindberg characterized as hierarchical. A strong state élite such as Japan's relied on monetary policy and a variety of micro-level interventions (channelling of investments, export subsidies) to weather the crisis. Pressures on consumption and wages, rather than unemployment, were the chief cost of the approach. The third type Lindberg called solidarity. Bargaining occurred among the state, business, and labour about trade-offs between unemployment and inflation and the levels of profits and wages. The outcome for unemployment differed, as illustrated by the experiences of the Netherlands and West Germany. The result, in Lindberg's view, was determined by the balance of class power between business and labour. Where labour predominated and full employment was maintained, monetary and fiscal policies were supplemented by active labour-market pressures such as training, relocation, avoidance of public-sector lay-offs, and, on occasion, restraint of wages.

Therborn (1986) provides a more detailed picture of policy configurations, especially as these relate to unemployment levels. His analysis (26–8) provides the following profile of full-employment policy pack-

TABLE 2.4
A typology of active public policies toward full employment

Policies operating on the demand side		Policies operating on the supply side	
Aggregate demand management	Creation, maintenance, and reconversion of jobs	Active labour-market policy proper	Reduction of labour input
Instruments	*Instruments*	*Instruments*	*Instruments*
Monetary policy	Direct job creation in the public sector	Promoting geographical worker mobility	Reducing daily, weekly, and annual hours of work
Fiscal policy	Wage-cost subsidies (temporary or permanent)	Placement and counselling services	Reducing life-time employment through early retirement or lowering legal retirement age
Incomes policy	Subsidies to output, inventories, or goods purchase	Promoting education and training	
	Regional development	Rehabilitation	Increasing part-time work
		Integrating and reintegrating disadvantaged and hard-to-employ groups	Immigration and foreign worker policy

ages. In all cases the full-employment countries followed expansionary Keynesian-type policies, especially during the 1970s and the early threats to employment levels. Since some of the high-unemployment countries reacted in similar fashion, however, this factor is obviously insufficient to explain the differences. In the successful countries two other factors were also present. First, in addition to early expansionary fiscal policies, complementary monetary policies were also consistently followed. In particular, efforts were made to achieve and retain low real interest rates. Second, such expansionary macro policies were accompanied by 'nationally specific direct interventions in the market economy' such that 'the state in the low unemployment countries has significant control of one or more strategic economic variables on the market itself, a control which has been amply used to ensure full-employment. This has meant control of labour supply in Switzerland and Austria; of labour demand and of qualitative labour supply in Sweden; investment in Japan, Austria and Norway; and price and cost structures in Norway and Austria' (28).

The variety of interventions could indicate that countries were choosing an instrument appropriate for dealing with their most serious structural problems. Or it may simply reflect the ideological and class origins of the particular route being followed. In either event, adoption of such a complementary and consistent policy package has prevented the high levels of unemployment characteristic of most of the capitalist world since the mid-1970s.

Two points from Therborn's formula for full employment deserve to be emphasized. First different aspects of policy must complement each other. This can be illustrated by a comparison of labour-market measures in Britain, a country of very high unemployment, and in Sweden. The United Kingdom does have an extensive package of special measures to address unemployment: direct job-creation projects, work-experience and training schemes, and subsidies to retain labour and create employment (see Jackson and Hanby 1982). Expenditures on these programs have increased both in real terms and in comparison to overall trends in total expenditure, notwithstanding an initial attempt by the Thatcher government to cut these expenditures (Moon 1983: 325). The scale of expenditures on similar programs in Sweden may be greater, but also Swedish labour-market measures complement the overall macroeconomic stance: both types of policy are directed toward full employment. In Britain since 1975, and more emphatically since 1979, there has been a dislocation between the two types of policy. Since 1975 British governments, both Labour and Conservative, have made a basic strategic choice, albeit with different degrees of enthusiasm, that the route to economic recovery lies through public-sector restraint, reliance on market forces, and giving top priority to the fight against inflation. This choice 'undermined the possibility of a concerted national effort to reduce unemployment in the long-term' (Moon and Richardson 1985: 87). In Therborn's view, such policies have been 'the shortest and fastest route to mass unemployment' (30). Notwithstanding increased expenditures on labour-market policies, therefore, the measures become little more than 'a form of political insurance' or 'placebo' policies (Moon and Richardson 1985: 86–7, 182). In terms of the discussion in chapter 1, they represent ideological legitimation measures. In Sweden the same policies can better be viewed as concrete legitimation activities and in some of their aspects, such as training and relocation, as accumulation-oriented measures.

Second, while some type of direct intervention seems to be necessary in order to supplement macro policies, the extensive variation in form suggests that expansionary macro policies, if not sufficient, are at least necessary to produce full employment (Tobin 1987: 18–19).

The conclusions to be drawn from the literature that stresses ideology can be stated as follows. The policies pursued by various countries in the face of similar economic difficulties, and with comparable structural characteristics, do seem to have mattered. Some countries with few discernible structural advantages seem to have retained full employment without experiencing disastrous performance in other areas such as inflation. Other countries have lapsed into mass unemployment. The difference in performance seems attributable to policy.

But the choice of policy does not seem attributable solely either to party incumbency or to the presence of corporatist institutions – or, given bourgeois dominance in Japan and Switzerland, in a straightforward way to the balance of class forces. Policy differences do, however, seem attributable to the nature of the dominant ideology and, more specifically, to its inclusion of a commitment to full employment. In particular, policy strategies for full employment seem to have been chosen where either social democracy or paternalistic conservatism dominated. In countries with liberal market ideologies, the full-employment commitment, where it established itself at all after the war, seems to have been weakly entrenched and was easily sacrificed with the return of hard times. The next section of the chapter will attempt to locate Canada within the comparative context outlined above.

Canada in Comparative Context

Policy Configuration

Canada's own policy configuration in the face of economic crisis will receive detailed attention in subsequent chapters. Here it will be sufficient to anticipate some of the main findings. At the level of macroeconomic policy, Canada since 1975 has pursued relatively restrictive fiscal and monetary policies. Inflation has been identified as the principal economic problem, and its control has been seen as the chief economic policy priority. The Bank of Canada has been the main actor in monetary policy. Its concentration on inflation control has, however, received the enthusiastic endorsement of successive ministers of finance. The following statement by Michael Wilson can serve as an example: 'Monetary policy must continue to stand firm against inflationary pressures. Fiscal policy must ease the burden on monetary policy and contribute directly to increased confidence and to lower interest rates' (Wilson 1984: 5–6). 'Easing the burden' has tended to mean efforts to reduce the deficit. Notwithstanding evidence that shortfalls in revenue, partly caused by the recession itself, have increased the deficit, the government has attributed poor economic performance to the size of the deficit and has relied for its reduction on expenditure restraint more than would seem warranted.

An apparent attempt to establish an 'active' labour-market policy in the late 1960s and early 1970s faltered and ultimately faded away. Fairly large sums of money continue to be spent on such programs, but, as a percentage of both federal expenditures and GDP, they have gradually declined since the early 1970s. Since unemployment remains much higher than in the early 1970s, resources have decreased even more relative to the size of the problem they are supposed to ease. Indeed, given the macroeconomic stance adopted, any other outcome would have been contradictory.

Expenditures on unemployment insurance (UI) are several times those on 'active' labour-market measures. Essentially, therefore, the government compensates individuals for their unemployment rather than preventing the experience – consistent with a market-driven strategy and the toleration of fairly substantial unemployment. Changes in the UI system in the 1970s and 1980s have tended toward greater restriction. While by no means ungenerous, UI benefits certainly have been affected by the macroeconomic paradigm and, in particular, the desire to restrain expenditures.

In industrial relations, the trend, too, has been in the direction of greater restriction and, indeed, coercion: restraint of wages both by incomes policies and by ad hoc back-to-work legislation for particular groups of workers. Such measures are, or course, entirely consistent with inflation control, though the degree of interventionism inherent in them makes them undesirable for monetarists. Among their other effects, the reduction in effective demand represented by forgone wages probably causes some unemployment.

Reviewing other policy areas, we do not find that the Canadian state has seized control of any of the 'strategic economic variables in the market itself' – a strategy pursued, as Therborn noted, in countries with low unemployment. Such measures would have been in conflict with the basic macro-economic stance of governments after 1975. The failure to use such measures is, therefore, quite in tune with the overall strategy.

Canada's policy profile is therefore consistent with that predicted for a high-unemployment country by the comparative literature.

Explanations

In his comparative survey of economic-structural factors inhibiting full employment, Schmidt (1987) identified four major obstacles faced by Canada: high dependence on exports, rapid growth in the labour force, high pre-crisis unemployment, and the existence of a number of industries in crisis. Schmidt's data show (173), however, that Canada's structural position was no more difficult than that of most of the countries considered, including several that kept unemployment very low in the period (1974–82) covered by his study. Canada's unemployment rate was thus considerably higher than warranted by structural difficulties and therefore, requires a political explanation.

The three political explanations outlined earlier in the chapter rested respectively on party incumbency or extra-parliamentary strength, institutional characteristics, and content of the dominant ideology. At first glance, however, Canada's high unemployment levels seem heavily 'overexplained.' The social democratic party (the New Democrats, or NDP) in Canada has never held office federally and has, for almost all of its existence, been the third party. Corporatist institutions are relatively undeveloped in Canada, and trade unions, by European standards, are relatively weak in terms of density of organization and, above all, integration into the policy-making system. Finally, while Canada's political culture may contain a 'Tory touch' and a 'socialist tinge,' its mainstream is solidly liberal, albeit with a greater tolerance for a strong state than its southern neighbour.

In Canada, left parties are weak. Their pressure on the state to implement full-employment strategies has been muted. There is some evidence that industrial militancy and strong performance by the CCF-NDP in opinion polls spurred introduction of post-war welfare and industrial relations reforms, including announcement of a commitment to maintain high levels of employment. But certainly neither the parliamentary strength of the NDP nor its level of support in the country as a whole could deter the other parties from reneging on the commitment. In some countries, as the comparative evidence makes clear, incumbent social democratic governments similarly reneged on the same promise. And even in countries without strong left parties, bourgeois governments sometimes maintained the commitment. The weakness of the Canadian left, then, facilitated, rather than determined abandonment of the pledge.

The percentage of the labour force organized into trade unions (often called 'trade-union density') in Canada is low compared to the Scandinavian countries and Austria. It is, however, comparable to West Germany and some other European countries. Both trade union structure and the state-regulated collective bargaining system are, however, very decentralized, which fact has impeded establishment of corporatist structures, as have the absence of a strong centralized business association, Canada's economic dependence on the United States, the balkanization of economic decision-making resulting from Canada's federal system, and the low legitimacy ascribed to unions (DiGiacomo 1977: 148, 155–6; Panitch 1979: 78–85).

Despite these obstacles, however, in the mid-1970s corporatism was 'on offer.' As part of its reaction to the imposition of wage controls, between 1976 and 1978 the Canadian Labour Congress (CLC) advocated creation of corporatist decision-making structures (McBride 1983). Even after that date, there was high-level support for corporatism or tripartism, which foundered only partly on internal labour opposition to the proposals. Among other reasons for the failure of the CLC's corporatist initiative was the refusal of state and business élites to countenance the scope of shared decision-making that animated the CLC leadership, particularly its president, Joe Morris.

The CLC proposed[2] that Parliament create a tripartite board or agency that would have jurisdiction over a specified policy area and would help develop regulations and future amendments to the founding legislation. The Council for Social and Economic Planning would be involved in 'reviewing draft legislation; reviewing current practice; proposing improvements to law and practice; initiating new programmes, and projects' in a wide range of policy areas, including old age pensions, workers' compensation, health, maternity, unemployment and other welfare benefits, family allowances, minimum wages, and development of national industrial strategy. The CLC's proposals were quite explicit on the need for tripartite rather than multipartite bodies, arguing that other groups were represented through government's expression of the public interest or, in the case of unorganized workers and consumers, through the CLC itself. The CLC noted that 'such delegation of powers does no violation to our Parliamentary form of government since the tripartite body would be responsible through a Minister to Parliament.'

Beneath the Council for Social and Economic Planning, a secondary level of boards and agencies would carry out administrative and planning functions over the council's sphere of jurisdiction. Such boards and agencies would be responsible to the council and hence indirectly to Parliament. The CLC went into detail on only one of the secondary-level boards, a proposed Labour Market Board. This board would have authority over the following areas of public policy: labour-market forecasting, manpower training and retraining; worker mobility grants; immigration regulations; and UI. The board would in addition 'have the power and authority to channel investment funds, both public and private, or to hold back on proposed projects so that cyclical and regional unemployment be evened out.'

The CLC proposed a rather comprehensive set of corporatist decision-making structures. This ambitious plan failed to come to fruition for a variety of reasons (Finn 1978). Government and business refused to restructure the labour-capital-state relation so drastically, partly because of a perception that labour was weak and internally divided and that the CLC leadership would be unable to deliver its side of any bargain.

The comprehensive nature of the CLC's proposals, itself explicable in terms of the CLC's misinterpretation of signals received from the government, seems to have stimulated governmental caution. The CLC seems to have gone further in a fully corporatist direction than anything foreseen by Ottawa. The government's response, therefore, tended to focus on the desirability of consultation and partnership in order to avoid the excesses of adversarial collective bargaining (Malles 1976; Munro 1977). Such a response undermined the ability of the CLC leadership to win labour's support for its initiative.

The absence of corporatist structures in Canada cannot simply be taken as a 'given' of the political landscape. Canada's labour movement was not strong enough in the late 1970s to force creation of corporatist structures. Some in organized labour feared that such structures would co-opt labour into institutionalized class collaboration (see United Electrical Workers 1979). But internal opposition cannot entirely explain the CLC's failure. Government and business were simply unwilling to accept creation of decision-making corporatist structures, thereby undercutting the efforts of the CLC leadership to convince its followers that corporatism was a viable option. Without an expression of interest from the 'other side,' the CLC's position was untenable. Thus Canada does not have corporatism in part because business and the state chose not to have it. Labour's weakness was no doubt a contributing factor, but ideological preferences probably also weighed heavily. And the wan-

ing of the post-Keynesian paradigm and the rising influence of monetarism signalled that corporatist collaboration and interventionism were
decreasingly attractive for both the state and the business élites. Both
the balance of class power and the dominant ideology explain the absence of corporatism in Canada.[3]

From the mid-1970s, it was also clear that the dominant ideology in
Canada, and the more specific policy paradigms comprising it, were less
and less concerned with maintaining full employment. In this respect
the Canadian example fits quite well into the earlier comparative discussion. It would appear that the full-employment commitment was
never lodged too firmly within the dominant post-war ideology.

Robert Campbell's thorough study (1987) of the Keynesian experience
in Canada certainly points to this conclusion. Although the nation's
post-war economic successes were often attributed to the success of
Keynesian policies, Campbell concludes (chapter 8) that even the modest version of Keynesianism adopted by economic decision makers was
never fully applied. Budgets, for example, tended to be passive rather
than countercyclical. Policy goals were not limited to those favoured
by the Keynesians, and the priority of various goals was contested rather
than the subject of consensus. Full employment certainly does not seem
to have been the primary goal of government: 'The economy experienced a few brief periods of 'full' employment, but there were far more
jumps than declines in the level of unemployment. In thirteen years in
the post-war period, government economic policy was unsuccessful in
preventing a substantial rise in the level of unemployment. In six other
years, government policy did not encourage a fall in the level of unemployment. In the remaining years, a low level of unemployment was
the result of healthy economic conditions' (191).

If this was the extent of the commitment in the relatively amenable
post-war conditions, it is unsurprising that in the more difficult 1970s
the commitment quickly disappeared. The monetarist paradigm suggested that government action to lower unemployment beneath its 'natural' level was pointless – a convenient hypothesis.

Although Canada's inability to achieve and maintain full employment
is 'overexplained', failure to establish a commitment to full employment
in the post-war economic consensus in itself explains the policy configuration adopted by Canadian governments in the face of economic
crisis.

Summary

Despite a shared international experience of economic crisis since the mid-1970s, nations have varied considerably in unemployment rates. This chapter has reviewed literature directed to explaining this situation and rejected economic explanations in favour of political ones. The political explanation stressing incorporation of a full-employment commitment within the dominant ideology was judged most promising. I identified a number of policy profiles representative of the way Western states responded to the crisis. It is apparent that Canadian policy fitted the market-based configuration which was associated, here and elsewhere, with high unemployment. Why did the Canadian state follow a strategy of high unemployment? Each of the three political explanations seemed relevant: a weak left-party milieu, lack of corporatist institutions, and absence of a commitment to full employment from the dominant ideology. It was concluded that though all three were relevant, absence of a full-employment commitment was sufficient in itself. Underlying all the political explanations for adoption of a high-unemployment strategy was a balance of class forces in which business was predominant. Whatever may have been the case in Japan or Switzerland, Canadian business's ideology did not perceive full employment as being in its interest. This was indicated in the 1970s by its growing enthusiasm for monetarism. While lack of commitment to full employment became most apparent after the onset of economic difficulties in the mid-1970s, it could also be discerned during the long post-war boom: unemployment had been relatively high in comparative terms during that era. The policies pursued by the Canadian state seem to have reflected business's agenda rather well.

3 Economic Paradigms and State Policy

In preceding chapters the following argument began to take shape. The
return of high levels of unemployment in Canada, rather than stimulating the state to massive efforts to eliminate the problem, was accompanied by increased tolerance of it. Acceptance of unemployment was
associated with replacement of the dominant economic theory, Keynesianism, by a new one, monetarism. The latter was used both to justify
and to shape government policy. It provided a theoretical basis for
defining unemployment as a less serious problem than inflation. Since
measures taken to control the latter had the effect of increasing the
former, it was reasonable to attribute some of the increased joblessness
to state policy and to the new paradigm that guided it.

Such shifts in policy and ideas produced a change of emphasis in the
state's priorities. The onset of economic crisis caused far greater attention to be paid to the accumulation requirements of capital. Satisfying
accumulation and legitimation came to be viewed as a zero-sum game.
Keynesianism had addressed accumulation demands while simultaneously taking care of legitimation, not least by pledging and attempting
to deliver full employment. But among business and its political allies,
the perception grew in the 1970s that concrete legitimation expenditures
could no longer be afforded and that they contributed to the economic
crisis. The new paradigm rationalized measures designed to shift the
emphasis of state activity much more firmly to the accumulation side
of the ledger.

This is an appropriate point at which to present a more detailed
account of the various economic theories, approaches, or paradigms
that have been identified. Each approach or paradigm is a complex
system of ideas that contains different currents or emphases. The sketches

that follow may fail to represent adequately the complexity of the approach, and not all those identified with it would concur with the rendition presented here. But these systems of ideas entered policy and political debates in considerably simplified forms – sometimes ones that their founders might well have repudiated. The question of whether Keynes was himself what later came to be termed a Keynesian is both valid in itself and of broader applicability. In each sketch, my concern is to give a useful summary of the main ideas of the theoretical approach rather than, necessarily, those of its founder. Special attention will be paid to identifying what each paradigm has to say about the four policy areas examined in the present study: macroeconomic policy, labour-market policy, unemployment insurance, and industrial relations.

Keynesianism

Keynesianism is derived from the works of John Maynard Keynes and especially his 1936 publication, *The General Theory of Employment, Interest and Money*. Writing as he did in a period of mass unemployment which the neoclassical economic orthodoxy of his day was unable to explain, Keynes challenged several postulates of that system. The neo-classical paradigm held that capitalist economies had an automatic tendency, via adjustments in prices, wages, and interest rates, toward full employment. Unemployment was either frictional, as with persons temporarily out of work while looking for a job, or voluntary, as with workers who priced themselves out of jobs by insisting on excessive wages. Keynes accepted that these types of unemployment did exist but considered that most unemployment in the 1930s was neither frictional nor voluntary. Instead, he argued, most of it was involuntary and caused by insufficient aggregate demand in the economy – an eventuality regarded as impossible by the neoclassical paradigm because of its acceptance of Say's Law, which held that supply creates its own demand.

Aggregate demand is made up of consumption, investment, net exports, and government spending. In the event that these did not equal potential output, a deflationary gap could be said to exist and unemployment would result. In Keynes's opinion, there was no reason to suppose that supply and demand would tend toward equilibrium at a full-employment level, and demand deficiency was, therefore, quite likely under capitalism. If governments wanted full employment, they had to manipulate aggregate demand to the necessary level – by adjusting their own spending or by stimulating private-sector consumption or investment through tax cuts or changes in interest rates. Either fiscal or monetary policy could be used to achieve the desired result, although it was anticipated that fiscal policy would play the greater role.

These proposals clearly envisaged a much greater macroeconomic role for government than formerly. Though extensive state intervention had previously been anathema in capitalist economics, Keynes's ideas, both in general and in detail, were designed to save rather than subvert the capitalist system. Keynes's context was the delegitimizing effect of mass unemployment in the 1930s and the threats to capitalism from communism and to liberal democracy from fascism. In this context his ideas, as his perceptive contemporary Harold Macmillan was quick to observe, offered a 'middle way' between communism and fascism that reformed the system but preserved its essentials.

The Keynesian solution consisted of greatly expanded state intervention in the running of the economy without, however, undermining the prerogatives of private enterprise and, in particular, private ownership; the latter's negative significance was denied, and its merits, in terms of the promotion of freedom and initiative, asserted.

Keynes argued that increased government intervention was 'the only practicable means of avoiding the destruction of existing forms in their entirety and ... the condition of the successful functioning of individual initiative ... It is certain that the world will not much longer tolerate the unemployment ... (which is) ... inevitably associated with present-day capitalistic individualism. But it may be possible by a right analysis of the problem to cure the disease whilst preserving efficiency and freedom' (Keynes 1936: 380–1; also 1926: 50).

Pursuit of full employment would necessitate the 'socialization of investment,' but not involving extensive state ownership: 'It is not the ownership of the instruments of production which it is important for the State to assume. If the State is able to determine the aggregate amount of resources devoted to augmenting the instruments and the basic rate of reward to those who own them, it will have accomplished all that is necessary' (Keynes 1936: 378).

The argument that nationalization of the means of production was unnecessary to ensure adequate investment rested on three propositions. First, a transfer of power had taken place within large corporations. Owners of capital (shareholders) had become separated from management of enterprises. As a result, the goals of the corporation were concerned much less with profit and much more with the stability of the corporation and its reputation in the eyes of the public and its customers

(Keynes 1926: 42–3). In these circumstances formal nationalization was irrelevant. Second, as far as direction of investment under capitalism was concerned there was no cause for complaint – the right things were being produced in the right way. The only problem centred around the volume of investment (and hence employment). State intervention should be concerned with volume, not direction (Keynes 1936: 379–80). Third, there were many advantages to the exercise of private initiative and responsibility. Decentralization and the exercise of self-interest were said to promote efficiency; most important, by widening the field of personal choice, economic individualism protected individual freedom. For these reasons, 'The important thing for Government is not to do things which individuals are doing already, and to do them a little better or a little worse but to do those things which at present are not done at all' (Keynes 1926: 46–7).

The attraction of these ideas, once an adequate theoretical account was constructed of how they might be realized, was obvious. A commitment to full employment was a massive advance for labour. Similarly, the Keynesian paradigm adopted a relatively benign view of trade unions, saw positive benefits in the encouragement of collective bargaining, and supported welfare state measures, including unemployment benefits for those temporarily out of work. All of this was very positive from a labour perspective. In addition, permanently high aggregate demand offered seemingly endless opportunities for expansion by capital. Keynesian theory, in short, created the possibility for the state to meet its accumulation and legitimation objectives simultaneously and without significant conflict between them.

Given such an apparent coincidence of interest, the 'age of ideology' was widely proclaimed to have ended. Lipset (1955: 171), for example, proclaimed 'I doubt very much that in an era in which Keynesian economics are almost universally accepted, in which various institutional safeguards have been created to prevent unemployment, and in which the conservatives find depressions politically impossible will witness strong controversy between left and right.'

Such was the spirit of the age. Keynesian-style policies seemed capable of maintaining the necessary conditions for capital accumulation while legitimating the system at the same time. But drawbacks from capital's point of view were identified in Keynes's own era and loomed large in the debates in the 1970s (cf. Kalecki 1943; Gonick 1987b: 81–4). In particular, as *The Times* pointed out in January 1943: 'The first function of unemployment ... is that it maintains the authority of master over man ... The absence of the fear of unemployment might ... have a disruptive effect upon factory discipline ... with full-employment the worker would have no ... moral obligation to refrain from using his new found freedom from fear to snatch every advantage he can' (cited in Gonick 1987: 82–3).

The first part of the quotation anticipates an authority problem for capital; the second hints at the dangers of a profit squeeze for capital and of an inflation problem for society, once the bulwark of unemployment were removed. Kalecki thought that the authority problem was the more serious source of capital's ambivalence about and ultimate opposition to full employment. The problem has two dimensions. Capital's authority over its work-force was threatened by full employment. But so also was its authority vis-à-vis the state. As Sawyer's (1985: 137) discussion of Kalecki's ideas puts it:

Under laissez-faire capitalism the level of employment strongly depends on the 'state of confidence'. If the confidence falters, then so does investment, and thereby output and employment. Confidence is a fragile flower which needs great care, i.e. policies which industrial leaders approve of. Thus the use of public expenditure to maintain the level of demand is seen to remove considerable power from capitalists, whose threats not to invest if confidence is harmed become less potent ... The social function of the doctrine of 'sound finance' is to make the level of employment dependent on the state of confidence.

The Canadian version of Keynesianism (cf. Campbell 1987: chapter 2) was sensitive to these type of concerns. The federal government's famous 1945 White Paper on Employment and Income stopped short of promising full employment, preferring the phrase 'high and stable levels of employment' (Canada, Department of Reconstruction, 1945). The focus was on the demand side of the economy, leaving the supply side to look after itself or, more accurately, leaving it to the private sector to take care of. This arrangement minimized the scope for state intervention possible within a Keynesian framework. The possibilities inherent in Keynes's discussion of the 'socialization of investment' were resisted, and the government's role was limited to management of aggregate demand through fiscal and monetary policy. Elsewhere, more interventionist versions of Keynesianism were adopted that addressed the supply side as well as demand. In Canada such interventions were post- or modified Keynesian, rather than part of the original package. Canadian Keynesianism remained focused on the demand side, and limited state intervention was a basic feature.

In terms of the components of aggregate demand, which the state was henceforth committed to managing, the 1945 White Paper emphasized the contribution of exports. Wolfe (1984: 55) notes that the White Paper represented 'a rather unique synthesis of the traditional staples-led approach to economic development with the Keynesian theory of demand management and fiscal stabilization.' Throughout the post-war period, there were supply-side interventions by the state in such areas as immigration, commerce, taxation, transport, and energy – in effect, applications of Canada's traditional state-based economic development policies rather than interventionist Keynesianism. They were directed toward capital accumulation (Gonick 1987: 91).

Post-Keynesianism

The version of Keynesianism originally adopted in Canada tended to focus on one type of unemployment – that caused by deficiencies in aggregate demand. Canadian unemployment rates in the 1950s and 1960s ranged from around 3 per cent to over 7 per cent. In most years levels were higher than the rate that the economists of the day considered to represent full employment. Arguments began to be made that not all of this unemployment was of the demand-deficient variety and that Keynesian-style aggregate demand measures were unlikely to be appropriate or sufficient. Modifications produced by these arguments are often referred to as post-Keynesianism.[1]

Further modifications were induced by concerns in the 1950s and 1960s about the allegedly inflationary effects of high employment. At or close to full-employment levels of aggregate demand, the argument ran, the balance of power in collective bargaining shifted toward trade unions (as anticipated earlier by The Times and analysts like Kalecki). If business, as was likely with high demand, granted wage demands that exceeded increases in productivity, then inflation would result.

A British economist, A.W. Phillips (1958), detected a long-run relation between unemployment and changes in wage rates. When unemployment was high, wages changed little (low inflation); when unemployment was low, higher rates of inflation were recorded. His analysis was interpreted to mean that decision makers could trade off levels of unemployment and inflation. In Canada this notion had been widely accepted by policy makers by the mid-1960s (Riddell 1986: 9). The effect of incorporating this notion into the dominant paradigm was considerable.

First, the concept and goal of full employment became less focused. Policy makers came to believe that they could choose from a range of unemployment rates and corresponding inflation rates. A desirable combination was a far more elastic concept than the original notion of full employment. In practice, the definition of full employment tended to creep upward. Second, Phillips's ideas, and the interpretations placed on them, provided a theoretical rationale for demoting full employment from the single most important goal of economic policy – a status it never achieved in reality – to one significant goal among others. Third, use of increased unemployment to tame inflation began to be legitimized: it could be argued that achieving a given rate of inflation justified a certain rate of unemployment. Also, blame for this 'necessary' joblessness could be transferred to trade unions, since, the theory suggested, their excessive wage demands triggered the inflation which, in turn, stimulated a government response (Gonick 1987: 98). Similarly, wage controls could be depicted as the price of continuing the commitment to full employment. Clearly, such arguments also anticipate some later ones: in monetarist parlance, unions could be blamed for the mass unemployment that resulted from application of generalized deflationary measures.

Post-Keynesianism represents a theoretical and interventionist policy response to two factors largely ignored in Canadian Keynesianism. First, its practitioners considered that the inflationary effects of high employment needed to be controlled and that incomes policies were an appropriate instrument to achieve this goal. Second, they increasingly came to believe that non-demand-deficient unemployment was more widespread than anticipated and that aggregate demand management was an inadequate response.

Non–demand-deficient unemployment is usually broken down into a number of categories (cf. Hughes and Perlman 1984: chapter 2): frictional or job-search, seasonal, structural, and regional varieties. Seasonal unemployment can result from such factors as climate changes or the entry into the summer-job market of students and school-leavers – particularly difficult for Canada's many communities dependent on one or two seasonally concentrated forms of work.

Structural unemployment results from imbalances in labour demand and supply caused by ongoing changes in industrial structure. Products and skills may become obsolete and demand for them evaporate. Population movements may stimulate relocation of industry. Some workers may be or become 'unemployable' – lacking the skills, attitudes, or motivation to obtain work under existing labour-market conditions. Such unemployment is generally classified as structural and, being of longer term than the frictional type, is considered a more serious problem. Persistent regional unemployment can be considered a special case of the structural type, coexisting sometimes with very high national levels of aggregate demand. It can hardly be considered demand-deficient unemployment. From a post-Keynesian perspective, it exists because of a supply-side problem: regional maldistribution of factories and capital. There are not enough firms and plants in a region, but workers may be unable or unwilling to move elsewhere.

Some economists see structural and frictional joblessness as making up an irreducible minimum which constituted the full-employment rate of unemployment – in the early 1960s, about 3 per cent. Later, when it was claimed that accelerated economic change caused by technological innovations had increased structural unemployment, estimates rose to 6 per cent and even higher.

Post-Keynesians remained committed to full employment at far lower levels than these. But increasing aggregate demand to cope with non–demand-deficient unemployment was pointless, and so they advocated other forms of state intervention, direct and acting on the supply side, to deal with structural unemployment. Labour-market policies, such as training and relocation, were designed to cope with the unemployment effects of economic restructuring. These will be analysed in chapter 5. Post-Keynesian labour-market policies were distinct from macroeconomic policies, but complementary. Macroeconomic policy was to ease the demand-deficient type of unemployment, while labour-market policies were to take care of the non–demand-deficient, non-frictional type. In this perspective then, labour-market policies assisted legitimation through helping create full employment. The training component would provide a suitably skilled work-force, thus performing an accumulation role. Training could also reduce inflationary pressures caused by 'bottlenecks' in the supply of certain skills. To the extent that inflation still remained, incomes policies were conceptualized as a solution, though they might involve conflict with trade unions and have delegitimizing effects. But this was a price that the post-Keynesians felt it necessary to pay under inflationary conditions.

Monetarism[2]

The monetarist paradigm gives top priority to controlling inflation. Its popularity coincided with the development of rapid inflation in the 1970s which, contrary to the conventional wisdom, occurred in combination with high unemployment. Monetarism suggests that state interference in the operation of economic markets causes this situation.

The monetarist policy prescription involves the state's withdrawal from much direct intervention in labour and other markets. The main aim is to control inflation, in part through reduction in state spending and intervention. With inflation under control, it is argued, unemployment will gravitate to its 'natural' level. Full employment is not an objective unless it is arbitrarily defined as being equal to the natural rate. Since the theory considers it possible for actual unemployment to be higher than the natural rate, some role may exist for labour-market policy – measures to assist the labour market to function efficiently and thus lower the jobless rate to its natural level.

Although monetarist theory conceives of a natural rate of unemployment, it does not envisage it as an immutable constant. Labour-market policies can reduce the natural rate. As one would expect from the ideological position incorporated in the theory, such policies are seen as desirable to the extent they complement and improve market forces. Robinson (1986: 383–98) provides a useful list of illustrations, as follows.

Improved labour-market information and functioning. For instance, a bigger and more efficient employment service might improve the efficiency of the labour market itself.

Training and retraining programs. These might hasten the adjustment of labour supply to demand. While strict monetarism might see this as a function for employers, others concede a role for government, especially where skills acquired are transferable between employers.

Mobility and relocation assistance. This would enable workers to move to places where jobs can be found.

Selective measures. These might increase either the supply of workers or the demand for them. Examples might include encouragement of early retirement, temporary employment subsidies, and, at least for some categories of the unemployed, job-creation schemes. The latter would enable target groups to acquire work experience and habits; a typical target group would be youth.

Like post-Keynesianism, monetarism emphasizes supply-side labour-market measures, but monetarist prescriptions are passive and minimalist, designed to promote the adjustment of labour supply to the demand for labour. The economy, however, is driven by market forces, and there exists no state commitment to full employment.

The monetarist view of the labour market also takes a more restrictive approach to trade unions, collective bargaining, and provision of unemployment benefits. These are seen as impediments to the proper functioning of the labour market and as driving unemployment above its natural level. Trade unions are an obstacle because they can use their monopoly power to bid up wages with disruptive and inflationary effects on prices. Given monetarist hostility to direct state control of markets, wage and price controls are not seen as an ideal answer. The creation of 'short term' unemployment to restore the discipline exerted by market forces is one solution (cf. Showler 1981). Legislative changes to reduce the 'excessive' powers attained by unions is another. Such changes, of course, shift the balance of power toward the employer. They represent an increase in state intervention, justifiable because directed toward restoring the unfettered operation of market forces. Since they deprive unions of some of their existing powers and status, they reduce the state's legitimation activities. If the argument outlined in chapter 1 is correct, one would expect the state to develop either alternative forms of concrete legitimation or some ideological legitimation to compensate for these actions. Failing this, or in addition, the state might increase its coercive activities.

Privatization of industry is seen as removing another obstacle to market forces: the contribution to monopoly represented by publicly owned industries (Barratt Brown 1984: 81). Similarly, privatization of government services creates additional profit-making opportunities for the private sector. On a one-time basis, proceeds from the sale of such operations can be applied to deficit reduction, tax cuts, or other monetarist measures. Monetarists also oppose unemployment benefits and legislation on minimum wages, which enable workers to refuse jobs at wage rates the market might determine. The effect, from their perspective, is to keep unemployment higher than it might be otherwise. In addition, unemployment benefits are regarded as contributing to greater labour-force participation than would otherwise occur: some individuals allegedly seek work in the expectation that they will soon become eligible for unemployment benefits. Monetarist strategy may also include tax reforms, aimed at redistributing incomes upward in order to reward initiative and create pools of capital for investment that will create future job opportunities.

A monetarist strategy restores capital accumulation through allowing market forces to operate free of state interference. As Chernomas (1983: 133) notes: 'In essence, monetarist policy and rhetoric is an effort to restore the rightful place of depression into the dynamics of the capitalist economy.' This, in turn, means the end of the full-employment commitment, strong pressure on wages and social services benefiting the working class, and strong pressures on working-class organizations, particularly trade unions. Adoption of such a strategy does not preclude periods of relative prosperity and fluctuations in the unemployment rate. It is not a recipe for permanent depression. But it accepts rather than seeking to regulate the cyclical nature of a capitalist economy. In doing so it also accepts unemployment rates that reflect the business cycle. One possible outcome is a legitimation crisis. Preventing development of such a crisis places a tremendous premium on the presentation of government policy (Fine and Harris 1987: 386) or ideological legitimation.

The four chapters that follow deal with substantive policy areas: the macroeconomic sphere, labour markets, unemployment insurance, and industrial relations. In each case we shall be concerned, first, with the extent to which the policy area can be understood in terms of the shift of policy paradigms anticipated in the theoretical chapters. Second, it is important to ascertain whether such a shift, to the extent it has occurred, produced the predicted change in state priorities. Given the difficulties discussed in chapter 1 of applying the concepts of legitimation and accumulation, it is necessary to establish criteria to help in judging the extent to which one or other receives emphasis. Such constructed types (see McKinney 1966) are provided in each chapter. To the extent that the empirical material is conducive to this type of analysis, these types will help us identify accumulation and legitimation concerns in each area. In addition, the analysis will seek to identify measures that plausibly can be linked to ideological legitimation or coercion.

Summary

This chapter has presented sketches of the economic paradigms that have contended for the attention of state policy makers in the recent past. Keynesian policies seemingly avoided conflict between accumulation and concrete legitimation. Indeed, provision of the latter was envisaged as guaranteeing the former. The primary policy goal, in theory at least, was full employment. In practice, other goals tended to intrude and often took priority. Actual enthusiasm for the Keynesian paradigm may have fallen well short of the degree to which it was publicly espoused. Keynesianism placed great emphasis on macroeconomic policy – management of aggregate demand by way of fiscal and monetary policies. Backing up macroeconomic policies was provision of the social wage in various ways, including unemployment benefits for those who might become temporarily jobless and recognition of trade unions and free collective bargaining. Little role was envisaged for labour-market policies. The main problems encountered in applying this paradigm were inflation in the 1970s and a perception that labour organizations had gained too much power.

The 'post-Keynesian' variant responded to inflation by advocating a degree of coercion. Post-Keynesians were sensitive to the destabilizing effects of inflation, promoted stable prices as an economic goal co-equal to full employment, and were prepared to impose incomes policies in order to achieve these goals. Doubting the efficacy of demand management policies in coping with structural unemployment, they advocated much more active labour-market policy. The more activist stance encountered two major problems in the 1970s. First, labour's approval of the Keynesian consensus declined as its bargaining rights were eroded by wage controls and other coercive measures. The state withdrew some of the concrete legitimation measures that labour had enjoyed since the war. Second, business was scarcely better pleased with post-Keynesian intervention. The unravelling of the social basis of Keynesianism paralleled its theoretical difficulties in the face of economic crisis.

With the advent of monetarism, we can detect unchallenged emphasis on accumulation through restoration of market forces. State activities shifted away from those measures that had performed a key legitimation role under the post-war Keynesian settlement between capital and labour. It has been predicted that such a change would be accompanied by increased resort to ideological legitimation and coercion and by a search for appropriate alternative means of concrete legitimation. Under monetarism, the state sought above all to control inflation. Increased economic competitiveness was also a goal, but the state relied on market forces rather than its own activity to achieve it. Macroeconomic policy was characterized by control on money supply and government spend-

TABLE 3.1 Paradigms, policies, and problems

Paradigm	Types of state activity	Primary policy goal(s)	Policy mixture	Problem(s) encountered
Keynesian	Accumulation through macro-level state economic management, plus (and in part through) concrete legitimation	Full employment	1 Macroeconomic policy: aggregate demand management via fiscal and monetary policies 2 Social wage and welfare state 3 Unemployment benefits 4 Recognition of trade unions and free collective bargaining 5 Supplementary role for labour-market policy	Authority (labour discipline) Inflation
Post-Keynesian	Accumulation through increased state micro-intervention plus (and in part through) concrete legitimation plus some coercion (e.g. incomes policies)	Full employment and stable prices	1 Macroeconomic policy (fiscal, monetary, and social wage) 2 Enhanced role for labour-market policy (especially on the supply side) 3 Incomes policy 4 Use of unemployment benefits in job preservation and creation	Authority (labour discipline) Legitimation Blocked restructuring of capital accumulation

Monetarism	Accumulation through freeing market forces
	Decreased concrete legitimation
	Increased coercion and ideological legitimation
		Stable prices (no inflation)
		Enhanced competitiveness through restructuring
			1 Macroeconomic policy (control of money supply; reduction of government spending and deficits; reductions in social wage expenditures)
			2 Labour-market policy (some role for improving operation of the labour market)
			3 Removal of obstacles to market forces
			  (i) Trade unions
			  (ii) Unemployment benefits and minimum wages
			  (iii) Privatization
				Legitimation
				Unemployment

ing and reductions in the deficit and in social wage expenditures. The paradigm recommended measures to lessen the power of trade unions, restrict unemployment benefits, and privatize government operations, in order to improve the operation of market forces. The theory posited a significant role for labour-market policy – one that would perfect rather than replace the market.

The major anticipated problems connected with the monetarist paradigm are unemployment and a loss of legitimacy derived from provision of concrete benefits. Table 3.1 summarizes predicted relations among paradigms, types of state activity, policies, and anticipated problems. We turn, in the next chapter, to an examination of trends in macroeconomic policy.

4   Macroeconomic Policy

This chapter begins by presenting a brief overview of macroeconomic policy in the 1970s and 1980s. In light of the theoretical debates reviewed in previous chapters, a number of issues require attention. How valid is the paradigm-shift interpretation of recent macroeconomic policy? To the extent that such a change occurred, did the state give greater priority to accumulation and decrease its concrete legitimation activities? Did ideological legitimation take on a higher profile? These questions are explored in later sections of the chapter, which, in a general sense, answers them in the affirmative. Assessing such issues will enable us to probe more deeply into the content of macroeconomic policy than is done in the initial overview. Subsequent chapters will assess the extent to which other policy areas exhibit similar shifts attributable, in the first instance at least, to policy paradigms and with similar implications in terms of the balance between the state's priorities.

The chief components of macroeconomic policy are fiscal policy and monetary policy, and comprehensive wage control policies of the type in effect in Canada between 1975 and 1978 can also be included. Fiscal policy can be defined as the government's use of its powers to tax and spend. By determining the balance between revenues and expenditures, governments affect the level of aggregate demand in the economy. Aggregate demand normally is expanded when the budget is in deficit and reduced by a budget surplus. However, existence of a deficit need not imply a deliberate effort by government to increase aggregate demand. During recessions, revenues fall, and, to the extent that income-maintenance and social security programs are in place, expenditures increase. Such expenditures act as 'automatic stabilizers' for the economy, since demand remains higher than it otherwise would have. The impact of such stabilizers can be affected by the government adjusting the coverage and generosity of such programs. Given established programs, however, a deficit caused by their operation is non-discretionary or cyclical in nature. Beyond these limits, a government may adopt a discretionary expansionary or restrictive fiscal stance. Monetary policy consists of the state's attempts to influence the supply of money and its rate of growth, along with such variables as exchange rates, interest rates, and availability of credit. Prices and incomes policies ostensibly restrain inflation. If successful, they tend to control incomes more effectively than prices and thus either freeze or reduce the share of wages in national income (Nuti 1972: 433–7).

Responsibility for the conduct of each of these areas rests ultimately with the government of Canada and, in particular, the minister of finance. Within the state apparatus, the minister's autonomy in formulating and implementing policy varies considerably according to policy area. The revenue budget, for example, is determined largely by the minister of finance and the prime minister, but expenditures are much more subject to bargaining between the minister and other cabinet members (Doern, Maslove, and Prince 1988: 47). For incomes policy, implementation of the legislation was delegated to an Anti-Inflation Board. The Bank of Canada is the major player in monetary policy. In cases of major policy disagreements, however, the minister is empowered to issue a written and public directive to the Bank (Rymes, 1986: 180). Although no such directive has ever been issued, the possibility of that being done gives ultimate political responsibility for monetary policy to the minister of finance.

Comparative evidence, reviewed in chapter 2, suggests that countries that avoided mass unemployment tended to pursue expansionary fiscal and monetary policies during the mid-1970s economic crisis. Restrictive policies were the strategy in many countries with high unemployment. In most cases, the strategic choice made by governments seemed closely connected to the balance of class power between capital and labour. Governments in countries with strong labour movements tended to retain full employment as the major priority of economic policy. They were prepared to operate expansionary fiscal and monetary policies, complemented by appropriate initiatives in subsidiary policy areas. In most countries where business was powerful, it tended to advocate restrictive policies aimed, above all, at controlling inflation, and such concerns were reflected in government policy. The policy stance adopted by Canadian governments in the face of economic crisis is therefore of prime interest.

Trends in Macroeconomic Policy

There seems little doubt that 1975 does represent a sort of 'great divide' in the stated aims of Canadian fiscal policy. After that date the fight first against inflation and later against the size of budget deficits came to dominate government pronouncements on fiscal matters. The change in emphasis was accompanied by introduction of compulsory wage controls and adoption of monetary gradualism by the Bank of Canada. From 1975 the government thought that resolution of unemployment depended on first eliminating inflation and/or deficits.

These dramatic developments in state policy came after a period of heightened wage conflict between labour and capital. Beginning in the mid-1960s, waves of industrial militancy signalled the willingness, first of private-sector workers and later of public-sector employees, to fight to improve their material position. Stiff resistance from business indicates that the terms of the post-war balance of power between the two were being contested and redrawn. The debates over paradigms and policy changes within the state should be understood in this context.

The new orientation was part of a comprehensive package tabled in the House of Commons on 14 October 1975 by Finance Minister Donald Macdonald:

1 Fiscal and monetary policies aimed at increasing total demand and production at a rate consistent with declining inflation.
2 Government expenditure policies aimed at limiting the growth of public expenditures and the rate of increase in public service employment.
3 Structural policies to deal with the special problems of energy, food and housing, to ensure a more efficient and competitive economy and to improve labour-management relations.
4 A prices and incomes policy which establishes guidelines for responsible social behaviour in determining prices and incomes of groups, together with machinery for administering those guidelines and ensuring compliance where necessary.

The fiscal and monetary stances outlined in this statement can be characterized as ones of gradual or incremental restraint. In the face of crisis, therefore, the initial posture was restrictive. To what extent was this stance actually implemented?

Fiscal Policy

Table 4.1 summarizes the federal government's revenue, expenditure, and deficit/surplus position from 1970 to 1986. The information is presented in current dollars and as a percentage of gross domestic product (GDP). The current dollar column shows how easy it is to understand the common argument that expenditures and deficits were far from restrained throughout the entire period. But the other column presents a rather more qualified picture.

As a percentage of GDP, for example, expenditures were restrained in the 1976–81 period. Hicks (1983) notes that constant dollar expenditures, excluding debt costs, declined by 6.3 per cent in the five years prior to 1982. In a context where 75 per cent of programs were either statutory or subject to indexing provisions, Hicks regards this as evidence of considerable fiscal restraint. The increase in 1982 and subsequent years is usually attributed to the impact of automatic stabilizers triggered by the deep recession in 1982. Even in the years when expenditures were restrained, however, the deficit was a sizeable proportion of GDP. The revenue column provides part of the explanation. In 1975 revenues amounted to 18.5 per cent of GDP (down from 19.7 per cent in the previous year). After 1975 this proportion was never equalled. From this situation emerges the 'revenue shortfall' explanation of the budget deficit, discussed more fully below.

The argument that federal expenditures have been quite restrained since 1975 finds some support from an examination of trends in major expenditure items. Table 4.2 summarizes such trends, as a percentage of GDP.

From these tables it is apparent that since 1975, except during the 1982–5 recession, program expenditures have declined. The increase in total budgetary expenditures can, therefore, be explained entirely by the increase in public debt charges, which more than doubled as a percentage of GDP between 1975–6 and 1988–9. Such charges are a function partly of increased deficits and an accumulating debt load but also of the prevailing rate of interest. Interest rates are in turn partly a function of the government's own monetary policy.

A more detailed breakdown of expenditure items will be presented later in the chapter. In terms of the categories in Table 4.2, only defence

TABLE 4.1
Federal government revenues, expenditures, and surpluses or deficits 1970–88
(National Accounts Basis)

| | Current ($ billions) | | Surplus/ | Percentage of GDP | | Surplus/ |
	Rev.	Exp.	deficit	Rev.	Exp.	deficit
1970	15.5	15.3	0.2	17.4	17.2	0.3
1971	17.3	17.4	−0.1	17.8	17.9	−0.1
1972	19.6	20.1	−0.5	18.0	18.5	−0.5
1973	22.8	22.4	0.4	17.9	17.6	0.3
1974	30.0	28.7	1.3	19.7	18.9	0.8
1975	31.8	35.6	−3.8	18.5	20.8	−2.2
1976	35.5	38.8	−3.3	17.9	19.6	−1.7
1977	36.7	44.0	−7.3	16.8	20.2	−3.4
1978	38.3	49.1	−10.9	15.8	20.3	−4.5
1979	43.4	52.8	−9.4	15.7	19.1	−3.4
1980	50.7	61.3	−10.7	16.3	19.8	−3.4
1981	65.0	72.3	−7.3	18.3	20.3	−2.1
1982	66.1	86.4	−20.3	17.7	23.1	−5.4
1983	69.6	94.6	−25.0	17.2	23.3	−6.2
1984	76.5	106.5	−30.0	17.2	24.0	−6.8
1985	83.2	114.7	−31.4	17.4	24.0	−6.6
1986	91.3	115.3	−24.0	18.1	22.8	−4.8
1987	99.1	122.0	−22.9	18.0	22.2	−4.2
1988	110.1	130.6	−20.5	18.3	21.7	−3.4

SOURCE: Wilson (1990: 151–2)

expenditures escaped the downward trend after 1975 (again except for 1982–5). Since transfers to other governments remained relatively constant, decreases have been concentrated in general expenditures and in transfers to persons.

The general thrust of the evidence is that government expenditures have been quite restricted in the post-1975 period. The same holds true of employment in the federal public service, which declined from 2.52 per cent of the labour force in 1975–6 to 2.03 per cent in 1985–6 (Zussman 1986: 262). Despite restraint measures, the federal deficit has risen quite considerably, as indicated in Table 4.1. The size of the deficit, in dollar terms or as a percentage of GDP, has been used to justify ongoing expenditure restraint.

The actual size of the deficit is reasonably easy to establish. But many analysts believe that the existence of a deficit does not necessarily indicate an expansionary fiscal stance. In the late Keynesian era, it became

TABLE 4.2
Federal budgetary expenditures as a percentage of GDP, 1970–1 to 1985–9

	Major transfers to persons	Major transfers to govts	National defence	Other	Program expend.	Public debt charges	Total exp.
1970–1	4.0	3.4	2.0	6.0	15.4	2.1	17.6
1971–2	4.4	3.8	1.9	6.3	16.4	2.2	18.6
1972–3	5.1	3.9	1.8	6.3	17.0	2.1	19.1
1973–4	5.1	3.7	1.7	6.6	17.1	2.0	19.1
1974–5	5.3	3.9	1.7	7.5	18.4	2.1	20.5
1975–6	5.7	4.1	1.7	7.9	19.4	2.3	21.7
1976–7	5.3	4.3	1.7	6.9	18.1	2.4	20.5
1977–8	5.4	4.0	1.7	7.0	18.1	2.5	20.6
1978–9	5.3	4.0	1.7	6.6	17.6	2.9	20.5
1979–80	4.6	3.9	1.6	6.2	16.3	3.1	19.3
1980–1	4.7	3.8	1.6	6.5	16.7	3.4	20.1
1981–2	4.8	3.9	1.7	6.5	16.8	4.2	21.0
1982–3	6.1	3.9	1.9	7.3	19.1	4.5	23.6
1983–4	5.8	4.3	1.9	7.3	19.4	4.5	23.8
1984–5	5.6	4.4	2.0	7.5	19.5	5.0	24.6
1985–6	5.5	4.2	1.9	6.3	17.9	5.3	23.3
1986–7	5.5	4.1	2.0	6.2	17.8	5.3	23.1
1987–8	5.2	3.9	2.0	6.4	17.5	5.3	22.8
1988–9	5.0	3.9	1.8	5.7	16.5	5.5	22.1

SOURCE: Wilson (1990: 144)

common to distinguish between the so-called structural deficit (the size the deficit would be if the economy were operating at full employment) and the cyclical deficit (the portion of the deficit attributable to the economy operating at less than full employment). The larger the structural component of the deficit, the greater the governmental stimulus.

Estimates of the structural deficit vary considerably, largely because of different assumptions about what constitutes 'full employment.' Recent government estimates have been based on an 'average rate of labour utilization' rather than on a full-use rate (Lalonde 1983a: 55).[1] In 1982, this was estimated to be equivalent to an unemployment rate of 6.3 per cent. (The actual rate in 1982 was 11 per cent.) Using this estimate, $9 to $12 billion of the $21 billion (national accounts) federal deficit could be classified as structural or cyclically adjusted (Lalonde 1983: 3). Lalonde also claimed that the structural portion could reasonably be subjected to inflation-adjustment:

a given nominal deficit will be less stimulative in an inflationary environment than in an inflation-free economy, ... Examination of the inflation-adjusted balance would help assess the impact of the fiscal position on aggregate demand ... The notion of inflation adjustment is quite distinct from (that of) cyclical adjustment ... Inflation adjustment is essentially a measurement-related issue that is associated with the well-known fact that conventional current dollar accounting methods can sometimes give misleading results in an inflationary environment. Cyclical adjustment, on the other hand, addresses the much more hypothetical question of what the budget balance would be, under a different 'more normal' set of economic conditions. As indicated earlier, it is useful to think of the actual deficit as comprising two components: a cyclical component and a structural component. It is also useful to identify the inflationary sub-component of the structural deficit in arriving at judgements as to appropriate levels of that deficit. (Lalonde 1983: 11; see also Annex F)

By these accounting conventions, some $7 billion could be regarded as an inflationary component of the structural deficit, reducing the apparent stimulus of a $21-billion deficit to between $2 and 5 billion.

If a full-employment rate of, say, 4 per cent were assumed, instead of the 6.3 per cent used above, then the structural deficit and corresponding fiscal stimulus would be smaller. Keynesian economists have estimated that on an adjusted basis the federal budget was in surplus in 1982 (studies cited in Chorney 1984: 28). Similarly, Bossons and Dungan (1983: 1) argued that the projected 1983 total government-sector deficit of $25 billion was 'entirely attributable to measurement errors and to the effects of the current economic depression. If the economy were at full-employment and the government surplus or deficit were correctly measured, the current taxation and expenditure programmes of all governments combined would yield a surplus of approximately $6 billion. As a result, the current fiscal position of Canadian governments is depressing rather than stimulating the Canadian economy.' Given these estimates, therefore, federal fiscal policy was restrictive, notwithstanding a $21-billion actual deficit.

The balance between the cyclical and structural components of deficits will also vary over time. Cyclical factors are widely conceded to have had greater significance after 1980 than they did before (e.g. Lalonde 1983: 1). Between 1975 and 1980, then, the structural component of the deficit was relatively more important than it became in the early 1980s.

Whether it represented a financial stimulus in the earlier period depends, of course, on the assumptions made in cyclical and inflationary adjustments.

Table 4.3 presents estimates of the cyclically and inflation-adjusted federal budget deficits, based on calculations from the 1983 *Federal Deficit in Perspective* (Lalonde 1983b). Under these assumptions, there was considerable fiscal stimulus in the 1975–9 period, especially in 1977–8, but much less thereafter. If a full-employment rate of output were assumed, the stimulus would be very mild in the earlier period and non-existent later. Later analysis by the Department of Finance, based on changes in the actual and cyclically adjusted budget deficits suggests that federal fiscal policy was restrictive from 1985 onward, with the exception of 1988–9, 'when increased public debt charges generated an expansionary change in the cyclically adjusted budget balance' (*Quarterly Economic Review*, June 1990, 41). Forecasts indicated that fiscal restraint would continue until 1994–5.

Any stimulus in the earlier period was delivered through forgone revenues rather than through stimulative spending (Wolfe 1985: 120–3). The impact on revenues of 'discretionary tax measures' is very significant. Excluding the effects of indexing personal income taxes, the amount of revenue forgone has been estimated at $8.89 billion in 1980–1 and $9.825 billion in 1982–3. Thus, as Wolfe points out, 'a substantial proportion of the structural component of the current federal deficit is the result of discretionary tax measures introduced by the federal government after 1970' (121).

Given the restraint on expenditures after 1975, it is clear that whatever fiscal stimulus was delivered by the federal government took the form of 'tax expenditures' rather than actual spending. Maslove (1981) has pointed out that the existing tax expenditure system produces certain allocations and equity outcomes. In particular, 'tax expenditure benefits flow disproportionately to higher income taxpayers. In 1978, for example, the highest 14% of tax filers received 52% of the total tax expenditures. As a percentage of total income, tax expenditures have remained fairly constant up to an income level of about $10000 to $15000 but from that point have increased quite dramatically as incomes rise' (241).[2] As we shall see, the transferring of resources toward the affluent is a feature of all three macroeconomic policy areas.

In summary, then, fiscal policy stance since 1975 does seem to have been restrictive. Expenditures have been strongly restrained, and the

TABLE 4.3
Cyclically and inflation-adjusted budget deficits 1974–82 (percentage of GDP)

	Actual budget deficit	Cyclically and inflation-adjusted deficit	
		Assuming 6.3% unemployment in 1982	Assuming 7.0% unemployment in 1982
1974	+0.8	+0.9	+0.6
1975	−2.3	−1.4	−1.8
1976	−1.8	−1.2	−1.6
1977	−3.5	−2.4	−2.7
1978	−4.6	−3.3	−3.7
1979	−3.5	−1.5	−1.9
1980	−3.5	−0.6	−1.1
1981	−2.4	+0.5	+0.1
1982	−6.0	−0.5	−1.2

SOURCE: Lalonde (1983: 57–65)
CALCULATION: Estimated cyclical budget deficit as % of GNP (Lalonde 1983: 61) minus inflation adjustment (calculated as the difference between the actual budget deficit as a % of GNP and the inflation-adjusted budget deficit as a % of GNP)

amount of stimulus provided through budget deficits is disputed but probably, on balance, quite small – at least from a full-employment perspective. Forgone revenues have provided any stimulus, redistributing income from less to more affluent individuals.

Monetary Policy

There is little room for debate on the stance adopted in monetary policy in the post-1975 period. After following a relatively expansionary monetary policy in the early 1970s, the Bank of Canada moved steadily toward restriction in 1974–5. Thereafter monetary policy presents a clear-cut case of restrictiveness.

In late 1975, the governor of the Bank of Canada, Gerald Bouey, announced the Bank's conversion to a policy of setting explicit targets for the growth rate in money supply. The growth rate of the selected indicator, M1, was initially set within the 10–15 per cent range. Later the target was steadily reduced. By 1981 the announced target stood in the 4–8 per cent range. The intention was gradually to reduce the rate of increase in money supply to the real growth rate of the economy. The Bank was largely successful in meeting its targets. Despite this, the

practice of setting specific targets was abandoned in 1982 because the
M1 statistic became increasingly unreliable at a time when banking practices and technology were undergoing rapid change. The Bank did, however, reiterate its commitment to monetary restraint:

The withdrawal by the Bank ... of its target range for M1 growth did not reflect any basic change in its approach to monetary policy. What it reflected
was that M1 had become an unsuitable aggregate to use in expressing targets
because its relationship to interest rates and total spending was no longer sufficiently reliable for that purpose. We have not yet succeeded in finding another aggregate that is suitable for target-setting. This affects the way of
describing our policy but not the policy itself. We continue to believe that
monetary policy must move towards a trend of monetary expansion that will
permit economic growth without inflation. (Bank of Canada 1982: 8)

Control of inflation has been the primary aim of monetary policy
since at least 1974. Inflation itself was attributed to 'highly expansionary
monetary and fiscal policies' followed in the major capitalist countries
in the early 1970s (Bank of Canada 1974: 8). The Bank's turn to monetary restriction was depicted as part of 'a coordinated national programme to wind down inflation' (Bank of Canada 1976: 5). The other
components were the government's commitment to restrain expenditure
growth and the wage and price controls that were to be implemented
by the Anti-Inflation Board. In the effort to halt inflation, monetary
restraint was viewed as essential, with the ultimate goal being a rate of
monetary expansion 'compatible with inflation-free growth of the economy' (Bank of Canada 1976: 10).

Monetary restraint affects inflation primarily through its impact on
interest rates, in effect creating high interest rates. In its 1978 Annual
Report, the Bank pointed out that, other things being equal, 'there is
an inescapable interrelationship between changes in the quantity of
money and changes in interest rate levels. The central bank cannot take
action to affect the one without the other. It is not possible, for example,
for the Bank of Canada to exert increased restraint on the growth of
the money supply without at the same time putting immediate upward
pressure on interest rates' (Bank of Canada 1978: 14). Ultimately, the
Bank argued, restraining expansion of money supply would reduce inflation, and interest rates would then become lower than they would
otherwise have been: 'But the first effect on interest rates is in the other
direction. These relationships are part of the nature of Canada's eco-

nomic system, so if the rate of monetary expansion is to be controlled, the interest rate consequences must be accepted' (Bank of Canada 1980: 6). Further upward pressure on Canadian interest rates resulted from the Bank's efforts to control the decline in the value of the Canadian dollar relative to the US dollar. Such a policy, the Bank argued, was consistent with its overall aim of reducing inflation.

From time to time the Bank has levelled veiled criticisms against government fiscal policy, alleging that it has been too expansionary, placing a correspondingly greater burden on monetary policy. In retrospect the Bank viewed fiscal policy in the 1970s as giving insufficient priority to containing and reducing inflation and attributed at least some of the increase in interest rates in the early 1980s to the flight of capital occasioned by introduction of the National Energy Policy (Bank of Canada 1986: 8–9).

Critics of Canadian monetary policy have pointed to the costs of the Bank's policy of monetary restraint and high interest rates. These include high unemployment, slow growth, bankruptcies, increased regional disparities including those in unemployment rates, and failure to bring inflation under control until a major recession occurred (Donner and Peters 1979; Reeves and Kerr 1986; Rymes 1986; Gonick 1987b: Part III). The Bank's policy has also contributed to the government's fiscal problems: 'The bank's decisions and their links with interest rates ... have had a major impact in the last several years on the growth of government spending, since debt-servicing costs have been the fastest growing item' (Doern 1985a: 72).

The Bank has from time acknowledged the costs and hardships – except for the last point – associated with its policy of monetary restraint. Always, however, it has justified the costs in terms of fighting inflation:

Inflation melts the glue that holds free societies together ... People sometimes talk about the cost of controlling inflation as being too high ... What Canadians should think more about is the cost of not dealing with inflation. To appreciate how heavy that cost would be one does not have to envisage the kind of economic and political collapse that has occurred in countries where inflation got totally out of control. All one has to do is envisage the consequences of temporizing with the problem, namely, recurring bursts of inflation checked painfully by bursts of financial restraint, a kind of stop-go stagflation. No one wants that. Yet that is the future we face if we do not address ourselves seriously to meeting the requirements for non-inflationary prosperity. (Bank of Canada 1981: 6, 10)

Since 1975, then, Canadian monetary policy has adopted a restrictive stance, with the aim of controlling inflation in fact outweighing any other goal.

Prices and Incomes Policies

In the early 1970s, the federal government attempted to engineer a voluntary program of prices and incomes restraint. Such efforts were unsuccessful, largely because of labour opposition (Berger 1973; Hawthorne 1973; Walsh 1975).

On 14 October 1975 the government introduced mandatory incomes controls under the rubric of its Anti-Inflation Programme. Though prices and profits were included in an attempt to 'sell' the program 'virtually all actors in the controls decision viewed the programme ... as a wage control' (Maslove and Swimmer 1980: xx). The legislation covered employees of large firms, public-sector and government employees, and professionals[3] and imposed guidelines for each of the three years of the program. In the first year the maximum allowable increase was in the 8–12 per cent range, depending on circumstances, and this figure was progressively reduced in each of the two subsequent years. All the provincial governments co-operated with Ottawa by extending the program or a matching provincial equivalent to their own public sector and to municipal employees. Indeed, the case has been cited as an example of intergovernmental co-operation (Maslove, Prince, and Doern 1986: 230).

The controls program was seen as a crucial element in a concerted attack on inflation. The fiscal and monetary policy areas, as outlined above, were the other elements in the anti-inflationary strategy. One distinctive feature of the program was its orientation toward gradual reduction in the rate of wage increases rather than, as in some countries, resorting to a freeze (OECD 1977: 29). The principle of gradualism was, therefore, built into all the three major policy areas crucial to the fight against inflation. We shall return to this aspect of Canada's anti-inflation policy later in the chapter.

In practice, to no one's surprise, the Anti-Inflation Programme was more effective in controlling incomes or compensation than prices (see Table 4.4). A Conference Board study cited by Gonick (1987b: 184–5) concluded: 'Controls resulted in a significant shift in income distribution in Canada away from persons and in favour of business compared to what would have occurred over the period (1975–8) in the absence of

TABLE 4.4
Price and compensation guidelines and outcomes under the anti-inflation policy
(percentage)

	Prices		Compensation	
	Guideline	Outcome	Guideline	Outcome
Year 1	8.0	6.2	9.7	9.3
Year 2	6.0	8.8	7.5	7.1
Year 3	4.0	8.7	5.7	5.4

SOURCE: OECD (1979: 36)

the programme.' As noted above, other elements of economic policy, such as increasing use of tax expenditures, had similar results.

Controls were allowed to lapse in 1978, but in June 1982 the federal government reintroduced them for its own employees (Swimmer 1984). Similar provincial programs effectively controlled public-sector workers for a two-year period beginning in 1982. In the federal case – and most provinces enacted similar limits – wage increases were limited to 6 per cent in the first year and 5 per cent in the second year. For public-sector workers, the program significantly affected industrial relations, an issue addressed in chapter 7. It contributed to fiscal restraint by enabling the government to reallocate the monies saved. It was touted as an example for the private sector to follow. The rate of inflation did, in fact, begin to decline, but probably because of the 1982 recession rather than widespread 'voluntary emulation' of '6 and 5.' To the extent that the recession itself was produced by the government's restrictive policies, especially monetary policy, the government might, of course, claim credit for declining prices.

Assessment

It is fair to characterize state economic policy in Canada since 1975 as restrictive. Rather than making full employment a major priority, government sought to control inflation and reduce state spending, and hence the size of the state. Such policies have at least tolerated and, more probably, led directly to the increased unemployment of these years. We now turn to the issues of changing paradigms, the balance between the state's accumulation and concrete legitimation activities, and the role of ideology.

From Keynesianism to Monetarism

It seems clear that Keynesianism has declined as the dominant paradigm within which economic policy is conceptualized. It has been replaced by monetarism – although those who accept the new paradigm do not all accept the monetarist creed in its more technical aspects. The Conservative government elected in 1984 is clearly comfortable with the implications of the new paradigm. But 1975 represents the turning-point that signalled the decline of the old and the development of the new. The transitions that became most noticeable in 1975, however, must be qualified at each state of the process.

Prior to 1975, Keynesianism was the dominant paradigm. But it was a somewhat diluted version of the possibilities inherent within the paradigm. In addition, many 'post-Keynesian' developments were already apparent. Moreover, as noted in chapter 3, other state initiatives could be traced to the traditional interventionism associated with role of staples in Canadian economic development. From 1975, monetarism became the major paradigm, but until 1984, at least, a strong admixture of post-Keynesianism can be detected both in government pronouncements and in policy. After 1984, monetarism became more clearly dominant, but in its looser form.

The view that Canada's Keynesian era was less Keynesian than is commonly supposed has been presented most comprehensively by Robert Campbell (1987). In Campbell's view, post-war federal budgets were largely passive. This was a far cry indeed from the activist counter-cyclical budgeting one might have expected from true Keynesians (191–4). Most stabilization occurred through the operation of Keynesian-style automatic stabilizers, but unaccompanied by complementary discretionary activity by the state. Campbell attributes the failure to act in a Keynesian way to unforeseen technical problems, inadequate statistical information and economic forecasting among them. But political factors also played a role: the ideology of the balanced budget may have faded somewhat compared to the 1930s, but it did not disappear, and new goals tended to be added to those at the heart of the Keynesian approach.

As goals multiplied, choices about competing policies became more difficult (207). Seasonal, regional, and sectoral problems in the Canadian economy led governments, from the mid-1950s onward, into a series of ad-hoc, supply-side, direct interventions into economic life: 'Many of these policies were tentative and half-hearted but, cumulatively, they extended the role of the state into far deeper waters than had been proposed by the Keynesian vision. An increasing number of economic items were displaced from the market and placed on to the political agenda. Economic policies were more and more directed to the supply side of the economy, to detailed, micro matters, and to the long-term, and in the process they became far more discriminatory and coercive than Keynesian policies' (210).

From the perspective adopted in this book, these policy developments are evidence of encroaching 'post-Keynesianism.' For Campbell they are non-Keynesian – beyond the scope of the Keynesianism adopted in Canada after the war. In any case, he argues, they were too ad hoc to constitute a new paradigm (213). To cope with this rather untidy policy-making picture, Doern, Maslove, and Prince: (1988: 2) prefer the term *state activism* to *Keynesianism*. Their term encompasses both Keynesian stabilization policy and the ad-hoc interventionism noted by Campbell.

While these points tarnish the image of a purely, or even predominantly Keynesian era, sufficient substance remains to justify retention of the designation. Social programs were devised and implemented and acted as automatic stabilizers of aggregate demand in times of economic downturn, as they were intended. And the process of adding social programs continued as late as 1971, when unemployment insurance was expanded significantly. Further, as Wolfe (1985: 111) argued, while 'there is considerable debate as to how effectively countercyclical stabilization policies were implemented,' 'for 30 years following the end of the war, the federal government remained committed in principle to the use of Keynesian fiscal policies to stabilize the economy.'

The onset of economic crisis in the mid-1970s and associated loss of confidence in the Keynesian paradigm triggered two alternative sets of prescriptions within government circles. Both emphasized private-sector solutions and sought to foster more effectively the accumulation requirements of private capital. Yet the two alternatives disagreed profoundly on the best means for accomplishing these ends. Despite, or perhaps because of the theoretical disagreement over means, in practice Canadian governments from 1975 to 1984 sought to hedge their bets and combined elements of both alternatives. The first, post-Keynesianism, advocated intensification of state activism at the micro-, structural level of the economy. Examples were active labour-market policy to provide the skilled workers necessary for a growing economy, industrial strategy to assist growth sectors and encourage adjustment of uncompetitive sectors, and wage and price controls to control inflation. Monetarism, positing a less interventionist state that would permit and assist the free operation of market forces, was the other alternative. Donald Macdonald's statement on 14 October 1975, cited above, contained elements of both approaches: fiscal and monetary restraint was to be accompanied by wage and price controls and by structural policies 'to ensure a more efficient and competitive economy and to improve labour-management relations.'

The Bank of Canada's conversion to monetary gradualism provides the clearest indicator of the monetarist paradigm at work within the state. From 1975 to 1982 the Bank set targets for the rate of increase in money supply. Even after that date the Bank made it clear that its basic approach remained the same, despite its abandonment of a specific target. During the whole period, the Bank in its annual reports and other public statements offered a monetarist analysis and prescriptions for the economic ills facing the country.

The growing intrusion of the monetarist analysis into the state is also reflected in the governments' major policy statements and budgets. References to fiscal restraint, as in 1970's throne speeches, were strengthened after 1974. Table 4.5 also indicates an increased prominence for monetarist arguments regarding fiscal restraint.

With the possible exception of the 1977 speech, the references show increasing severity toward fiscal excesses and insistence that government represented a burden on the economy. Yet in 1980 the resurrected Trudeau government emphasized post-Keynesian interventionism. While promising to continue expenditure restraint and to reduce the deficit in an orderly manner, the government added the proviso that this would not be 'to the exclusion of other objectives such as reducing unemployment and promoting industrial growth. Improving the efficiency of the federal government is as important an objective ... as reducing the deficit. My ministers believe that Canadians want more effective government, not necessarily less government' (*Hansard*, 14 April 1980, 6). Essentially the same position was enunciated in the 1983 Throne Speech. So these pronouncements suggest that the forward march of monetarism was halted in the early 1980s and did not resume its advance until the election of the Mulroney government in 1984.

Budget speeches represent a major occasion for governments to outline their analysis of the economic situation and to highlight their priorities. The influence of the monetarist paradigm can be detected quite clearly in many of the post-1975 budget speeches. In 1976 Donald Macdonald (1976: 23) used his first budget speech to record his 'full support'

TABLE 4.5
References to fiscal restraint in throne speeches during the 1970s

30 September 1974	'The policy of the Government on inflation has been to pursue appropriate fiscal and monetary policies ... The Government will exercise restraint in its own expenditures with particular emphasis on improving effectiveness and efficiency in its existing operations while controlling expansion of new activities which, although desirable, would contribute to inflationary pressures.'
12 October 1976	'To create the climate necessary for [reduction of inflation and creation of employment] the Government will continue to practice fiscal restraint ... Determined restraint in fiscal and monetary policy is essential to the long-term control of inflation. The Government remains committed to a reduction in the growth of the public sector ... All federal programmes will be reviewed to identify those government activities which could be transferred to the private sector.'
18 October 1977	'The current unemployment situation ... [requires] ... immediate stimulus to the economy ... Further stimulus must not be allowed to compromise our objective of continuing reductions in inflation. The Government will continue to exercise responsibility in controlling its expenditures.'
11 October 1978	'The objectives of imposing more severe restraint on government spending are ... to encourage a more vigorous expansion of the private sector by reducing government's share of the nation's wealth ... to create a leaner and more efficient government ... The government is committed to reducing the size of the federal public service ... (and) to continued wage restraint in the public sector.'
9 October 1979	'My ministers will reduce the burden of government on the economy by better controlling expenditures. A new expenditure management system has been introduced ... to set strict overall spending limits, to ensure that all ministers accept full responsibility for spending restraint, and to require that funds for new programmes come from savings in existing programmes ... Any government has initiated action to reduce the size of the federal public service and to offer for private purchase and ownership Crown Corporations ... You will also be asked to approve "sunset" legislation to provide a regular opportunity for Parliament to judge whether government programmes and agencies need continue in their present form, if at all.'

SOURCE: Throne Speeches, *Hansard*

for the Bank of Canada's monetary policy, which, as we have seen, was monetarist. Macdonald noted that fiscal policy had precisely the same goal as monetary policy and that, in the circumstances, this could best be pursued by strict control over government spending. The same assurances formed part of Jean Chrétien's first budget speech in October 1977 (*Hansard*, 20 October 1977: 99). Similarly, Chrétien (1978: 5) explained mid-1970s inflation partly in monetarist terms: too much growth in government spending and too fast an increase in money supply. The stated objective of many of the tax measures announced in the budget was 'to strengthen the private sector without government interference' (16), a goal more monetarist than post-Keynesian.

The Clark government's budget in 1979 emphasized deficit reduction ('the fundamental objective of our fiscal plan'), endorsed the Bank of Canada's monetary gradualism, criticized the 'huge and swelling budget deficit' inherited from the Liberals, and proclaimed a new era of budgetary realism (Crosbie 1979). Despite the change of government in 1980, fiscal restraint and support for the Bank of Canada's monetarist policy were also features of Allan MacEachen's three budgets (MacEachen 1980: 3; 1981: 1; 1982: 3).

If MacEachen's budget statements sound monetarist,[4] however, Marc Lalonde's budgets of 1983 and 1984 demonstrate the continued influence of post-Keynesianism. Lalonde (1983a: 20) noted that the deficit was caused by a shortfall in revenues which was the result of tax cuts, rather than by runaway expenditures; that total government spending (including other levels of government) was in surplus between 1975 and 1982; that the federal structural deficit had declined as a percentage of GDP between 1978 and 1981; and that it was necessary to take into account the effects of inflation in calculating the real growth in national indebtedness. He continued: 'If we are to address the issue of deficits over the medium term in a realistic way, we must put rhetoric aside and look at the facts. We cannot eliminate the deficit quickly. To do so would require us to slash government programmes or to accept massive tax increases. Either course of action would jeopardize our prospects for economic recovery. But we must manage the deficit now to ensure that it will come down as quickly as possible.' In an accompanying document (Lalonde 1983b: iv), the minister stated that he did not hold the view that the deficit had to be brought down immediately and denied that its size had caused any severe 'crowding out' of private investment. In 1984 he took the same position: 'I remain committed to bringing the federal deficit down in a way that does not damage our economic prospects' (Lalonde 1984: 5).

State policy in the 1975–84 period was far more willing to intervene in the operations of markets than would be condoned by monetarists. A major survey in this period revealed significant differences between state and business élites. On issues such as social welfare policy, labour relations, government intervention in the economy, foreign investment, and taxation, business executives took positions considerably to the right of members of the state élite (Ornstein 1986). This suggests that enthusiasm for monetarism gained strength first in the business community but encountered resistance within the state. Prime Minister Trudeau spoke to the Canadian Club in Ottawa on 19 January 1976. While affirming the Liberal party's commitment to the free enterprise system, Trudeau went on to say:

Until I heard the shrill comments made by some businessmen during the past few weeks, I had thought the great depression of the nineteen-thirties had destroyed forever the notion that a free market economy, if unassisted by governments, would produce by itself the ideal state of steady economic growth, stable prices and full-employment ... Every reasonable person now recognizes the duty of the Federal Government to manage the country's economy in the interests of all its people and all its regions. That duty carries with it the consequent responsibility to intervene when necessary to stimulate employment, to redistribute income, to control inflation and pollution, to protect the consumer, to promote conservation, productivity, and an adequate supply of the things we need. (In Rea and McLeod 1976: 449–50).

Such sentiments clearly implied a non-monetarist role for the state. The Anti-Inflation Board and, in the early 1980s, the National Energy Programme and the megaprojects indicate that such a view did not remain at the level only of sentiments or fade entirely.[5]

While monetarist ideas clearly dominated monetary policy and probably shaped fiscal policy in the period 1975–84, the paradigm always faced rivalry from advocates of post-Keynesian state activism. In retrospect, the period was a lengthy transition between an untidy late-Keynesian era prior to 1975 and greater enthusiasm for monetarism after 1984.

In the years since 1984, monetarist ideas have enjoyed a rather more secure position. Though the Bank of Canada abandoned formal targets for the increase in money supply in 1982, it remained committed as before to controlling inflation by way of restraining the rate of increase in money supply and, as a result, keeping interest rates high. References to the economy in throne speeches have stressed the need to attain fiscal health by expenditure restraint. In budget speeches the need to reduce the deficit became something of a fetish. The virtues of competition, the private sector, and deregulation have been proclaimed regularly.

The approach was outlined early in the government's mandate (Wilson 1984) and has remained relatively unchanged. The government, he announced, has set itself four challenges:

first, to put our own fiscal house in order so that we can limit, and ultimately reverse, the massive build-up in public debt and the damaging impact this has on confidence and growth; second, to redefine the role of government so that it provides a better framework for growth and job creation and less of an obstacle to change and innovation; third, to foster higher investment, greater innovation, increased international competitiveness and a positive climate for the birth and growth of new enterprise; and fourth, to bring about these changes in a way that is fair, open and consistent with the basic sense of compassion, tolerance and justice that is characteristic of Canadian society. (2)

The arguments for the urgency of deficit reduction stressed the deficit's upward pressure on interest rates, crowding out the private sector, and its adverse effect on investor confidence:

We must take action to limit the deficit. We must assure savers and investors, in Canada and abroad, that the impressive gains we have made on inflation will be consolidated and continued and that the federal government will not place undue demands on Canadian capital markets. Such assurances can be provided only by responsible monetary and fiscal policies. Monetary policy must continue to stand firm against inflationary pressures. Fiscal policy must ease the burden on monetary policy and contribute directly to increased confidence and to lower interest rates. (5)

In subsequent budget speeches, Wilson regularly returned to these themes.

But the government's announced recipe for deficit reduction has focused mostly on expenditure. Reduced expenditures were projected to provide 84 per cent of the projected reduction in the deficit between 1984–5 and 1992–3 (Wilson 1988: 43). The imbalance in addressing expenditure and revenue has led some observers to the conclusion that rhetoric about deficit reduction serves as a 'Trojan horse' for a rather different agenda: reduction of the role played by the state (e.g. Doern, Maslove, and Prince 1988: 28). This too, however, is entirely consistent with the monetarist paradigm.

While budget rhetoric certainly conforms to monetarist principles, however, the rate of implementation has been incremental. The annual deficit declined as a proportion of GDP from 7.5 per cent in 1984–5 to 3.7 per cent in 1989. It was projected to decline further, to 2.8 per cent of GDP in 1990 (Wilson 1990). Even at this level, the deficit would substantially exceed that of the pre-recession year of 1981. This may be a monetarist government but it is proceeding cautiously. The change of paradigm certainly can be identified, but, as in previous periods, dominance is qualified.

A Shift to Accumulation?

Both the post-Keynesian and monetarist paradigms which contested the post-1975 period placed a very high premium on promoting capital accumulation. In the post-Keynesian view, capital accumulation could best be assisted in the mid-1970s by a variety of interventionist measures. Wage controls, through determining the outcome of free collective bargaining, served to stabilize a major cost of production. Provision of suitably trained personnel through training programs was conceived as a similar support to capital. In addition, investment in infrastructure could indirectly lower the cost of production. Selective direct state interventions could be undertaken as part of an industrial strategy. Through such measures the state could directly assist capital.

From capital's point of view, however, there were disadvantages. The degree of state involvement and control was of particular concern, since post-Keynesians generally proposed to maintain other elements of the post-war settlement, such as full employment and a welfare state. These commitments enabled labour to retain much of its bargaining power. Unsurprising, therefore, most representatives of capital tended to gravitate to the paradigm that involved a major realignment of class power. It is hardly coincidental that, within a year of the enactment of compulsory wage and price controls, Canadian capital organized itself into a high-powered association, the Business Council on National Issues, capable of aggregating the interests of capital as a whole.

In the monetarist paradigm, accumulation would be promoted through an increased role for market forces. As a corollary, the state would reduce its role and especially its commitment to moderating the outcomes of market processes on behalf of subordinate classes in society. The state could abandon its commitment to full employment and reduce welfare benefits. More coercive policies might restrict trade union rights. Labour's bargaining power would be reduced, and state intervention in the outcome of collective bargaining unnecessary. At the heart of monetarist accumulation policies was the attack on inflation which, it has been argued, 'lowers the scarcity value of accumulated savings or wealth' (Chorney 1989: 72) and thereby undermines capital's economic and social power. Thus our constructed type for detecting increased emphasis on accumulation uses such benchmarks as the state's providing fewer concrete benefits to subordinate classes, its efforts to redistribute income upward, and its attacks on state or working-class institutions that impede or moderate the operation of market forces.

Earlier chapters posited that in the conditions of the mid-1970s, and afterward, increased attention to accumulation would involve some sacrifice of the state's concrete legitimation activities. In this chapter, on macroeconomic policy, three types of evidence are reviewed, each of which tends to reveal such a shift. First, we shall review the degree of satisfaction of relevant interest groups with the trend of state policy. To the extent that business groups are broadly satisfied and labour and social-service client groups dissatisfied, one might infer that accumulation has been fostered and concrete legitimation sacrificed. Second, the effects of monetary policy, wage and price controls, and taxation policy on distribution of income promote accumulation to the extent that they assist the wealthy. Third, the pattern of expenditures and, in particular, the relative priority accorded social programs may reveal reduced emphasis on activities associated with concrete legitimation.

Satisfying Interest Groups

In an important article, Langille (1987) has traced the development and growing impact on state policy of the Business Council on National Issues (BCNI). While the BCNI's influence is by no means unlimited, Langille demonstrates that in key areas such as energy policy, free trade with the United States, and tax reform the BCNI's position has ultimately prevailed. Similarly, Atkinson and Coleman (1987) demonstrate the close and ongoing co-operative relationship between the state bureaucracy and the private sector. No crisis in state-business relations has existed in this era, and labour and low-income groups are profoundly dissatisfied with both the general trend and many of the specifics of state policy (cf. Wolfe 1985: 138). Most important, business, especially the BCNI, was able to induce government to adopt its macroeconomic agenda, giving priority to lowering inflation. Business wanted to keep the costs of labour and other inputs low in order to maintain competitiveness on world markets, and, through predictability of investment returns and borrowing rates, to create investor confidence. The specific reasons advanced for the concern with inflation may, however, be less significant for business than the symbolism that such a stance implies. Langille comments (57):

The zealotry with which the BCNI pursued its anti-inflationary crusade – even after inflation rates dropped to under five per cent, suggests that the concept symbolizes for them a whole set of policy prescriptions, values and attitudes about the role of government. Opposing inflation means opposing inflated wages and income expectations, the growth of government expenditures, the regulation of the free market and so on. It involves re-educating the post-war generations in the values of restraint, self-reliance and balanced budgets.

In terms of the distinction drawn in chapter 3 between the problems of authority and of inflation that business feared would result from full employment, Langille's analysis suggests that the attack on inflation represented for business primarily a means of resolving its authority problem.

In recent years, deficit reduction has become an article of faith. Indeed, as Chorney (1989) convincingly demonstrates, business's position on the public debt and the deficit has been remarkably consistent over the past sixty years. The position is based on 'the notion that most government intervention is misguided. The attack against deficit financing is (thus) essentially an attack against the growth of government' (7). During periods of war or economic growth, this view has tended to be expressed mildly and intermittently. When growth faltered in 1975, however, there was an explosion of opposition in the business community to the size of the debt and the contributions of annual deficits in increasing it – even though total accumulated net debt was a lower percentage of GNP than at any time in the previous fifty years (48).

Although the deficit remains high, the prominence of deficit reduction under the Mulroney government is one indicator of responsiveness to capital's expressed accumulation needs. And so, consistent with a constant refrain of business, is the theme of reducing the deficit by cutting expenditures (cf. Doern 1988: 29–31; Maslove 1985: 19). Generally, business associations specify the need to reduce or rationalize social programs and spending so as to reduce overall expenditures. But, more important, the overriding concern seems to be to reduce the state's role and to restore or establish the relatively unhindered operation of market forces. In current circumstances, therefore, business prefers its accumulation needs to be met through the operation of market forces rather than through active state participation. Since the state sector is at least partially amenable to democratic pressures, whereas the market is not, such a strategy can be viewed as an attempt to remove or reduce democratic input into the shaping of the economy. Since the political system remains liberal democratic, however, the strategy requires elaborate ideological justification.

Two of the arguments commonly advanced to justify reducing the deficit through cutting expenditures, and hence reducing the role of the state, run as follows (cf. Doern 1988: 25–7). First, it is said that interest rates rise when governments borrow to finance deficits and to pay interest on accumulated debt. Rising interest rates adversely affect private investment and certain types of consumer spending – a phenomena known as 'crowding out.' Second, consumers' and particularly investors' confidence is harmed by large deficits, largely because of their presumed inflationary effects. At bottom, then, the claim is advanced that economic health, employment, and prosperity depend on reducing the state's role and restoring the market's. That this is a heavily ideological argument became apparent when the performance of other countries, with a large role for the state, was considered in chapter 2.

In the Canadian context, the priority given to reducing the deficit proclaimed by the state can serve as a rough indicator of the priority given to accumulation – at least insofar as business accurately expresses its own best interests in demanding reduced deficits. Table 4.6 is based on a content analysis of budget speeches between 1970 and 1987. It records subjective assessments of the rank-order of major themes for 1970–5 (the Keynesian twilight), 1975–84 (post-Keynesianism v. monetarism), and post-1984 (more influenced by the monetarist paradigm). If the themes of 'deficit' and 'need to stimulate private investment' can be taken as surrogates for accumulation, the increased prominence of accumulation over time appears to be well demonstrated.

The fact that the deficit has remained high might seem to undermine

TABLE 4.6
Major themes in budget speeches, selected periods

Period	Rank-order of themes
1970–7	1 Inflation 2 Unemployment 3 Need for economic stimulation 4 Social justice/need to stimulate prviate investment
1976–84*	1 Need to stimulate private investment 2 Inflation 3 Unemployment 4 Deficit
1984–7†	1 Deficit 2 Need to stimulate private investment 3 Unemployment

*Until defeat of the Liberal government
†From election of the Conservative government

this hypothesis. However, if the attack on budget deficits is seen as being primarily about reducing the role of the state, the situation can be explained in the following terms. There is no necessary connection between the size of the deficit and such problems as inflation and lack of investor confidence. Actually reducing the deficit is, therefore, less necessary than the rhetoric proclaims. But adopting the goal of deficit reduction, especially when reducing expenditure to do so, creates a presumption against further state activism and intervention. Thus, even if the deficit falls little in the short term, protection of the ideological primacy of the market indirectly serves accumulation. In the longer term, of course, sizeable actual reductions may well occur. To the extent that these are concentrated in the social-welfare area, the unhindered operation of market forces, and with them business's preferred accumulation mechanism, is reinforced.

Reverse Redistribution of Income

Macroeconomic policy can foster capital accumulation quite directly by halting efforts to redistribute income from the affluent to the poor or by actually redistributing income in the reverse direction. Reverse redistribution assists the formation of pools of capital for investment purposes. In the period under discussion, there is evidence that each of the three major elements of macroeconomic policy contributed to accumulation in this way. A study of Canada's 1975–8 wage and price controls was cited earlier in the chapter. Its conclusion was that the program resulted in a significant shift of income from individuals and toward business.

Monetary gradualism has performed much the same role in two ways. Real interest rates (the nominal rate of interest minus the inflation rate) had become negative in 1974–5. In this situation lenders of money, in general those with large amounts of it, were in effect subsidizing borrowers. After 1975, real interest rates recovered and, despite some faltering in 1977–8, became consistently positive from the early 1980s onward (see Table 4.7). Since positive real interest rates maintain and expand the value of money, a result that particularly benefits the affluent, post-1975 monetary policy performed a classic accumulation service.

The effect of high real interest rates on accumulation is, of course, ambiguous. The high cost of borrowing deters some investment and has a deflationary effect on the economy. If inventories increase because of reduced demand, firms may have to borrow to finance them. Further, high rates may push up exchange rates, thus hurting sectors dependent on exports or exposed to competition from imports. High interest rates, however, are likely to find favour with bankers, financiers, and rentiers. Their impact on transnational corporations with other sources of capital is likely to be quite limited.

This phenomenon has led some observers to characterize monetarism, and monetarist policies, as the preferred paradigm of these sectors of capital. They suggest that the paradigm's rise is the consequence of a shift of power from nationally based industry to the banks (Bhaduri and Steindl 1983) or multinational capital. This argument rests not simply on the direct benefits to bankers and financiers but from the perception that 'monetarism intends to displace Keynesian policies which threaten the social power of the banking system by relegating it to one of the instruments of government policy in maintaining full-employment ... Keynesian policies entail an enormous strengthening of the national government's hand in the conduct of banking policy. This cannot find favour with the banks, unless they feel confident that the economic policies of the national government would be run more or less exclusively in the interests of "high finance"' (1).

For transnationals, the weakening of national governments may be beneficial to their operations. In any case they are less affected by high

TABLE 4.7
Nominal and real interest* rates, 1971–90

	Prime business loans		Long-term government bond yield	
	Nominal	Real	Nominal	Real
1971	6.48	3.68	6.95	4.15
1972	6.00	1.20	7.23	2.43
1973	7.65	0.05	7.56	−0.04
1974	10.75	−0.15	8.90	−2.00
1975	9.42	−1.38	9.04	−1.76
1976	10.04	2.54	9.18	1.68
1977	8.50	0.50	8.70	0.70
1978	9.69	0.79	9.27	0.37
1979	12.90	3.70	10.27	1.01
1980	14.25	4.05	12.48	2.28
1981	19.29	6.79	15.22	2.72
1982	15.81	5.01	14.26	3.46
1983	11.17	5.37	11.79	5.99
1984	12.06	7.66	12.75	8.35
1985	10.58	6.58	11.04	7.04
1986	10.52	6.42	9.52	5.42
1987	9.52	5.12	9.95	5.55
1988	10.83	6.73	10.22	6.12
1989	13.33	8.33	9.92	4.92
1990	14.06	9.26	10.85	6.05

SOURCES: *Canadian Economic Observer* 11-010 (Bank of Canada); ibid., 11-210
historical supplement 1985–89; ibid., 11-010, May 1991
*Real interest rate = nominal rate minus CPI.

interest rates in particular countries. Such arguments are suggestive of
a social base within capital for policies that clearly harm some sectors
of capital. Even those sectors of capital hurt by high real interest rates
may benefit from the efficiency-inducing effects of reduced demand and
high interest rates. Such circumstances make pressures to shed labour
and reduce labour costs intense. Higher unemployment and the threat
of closures discipline labour, thus easing the 'authority problem' identified previously.

The notion that high interest rates may assist the accumulation of capital
is reinforced by Table 4.8, which shows the relative balance between
assets and debts for particular population groups. Clearly the impact of

TABLE 4.8
Debt as a percentage of total assets, families and unattached
individuals, spring 1984

Total assets ($)	Debt as % of total assets
Negative	189.3
0–999	75.7
1,000–4,999	50.4
5,000–14,999	47.9
15,000–29,999	44.4
30,000–49,999	32.2
50,000–74,999	19.3
75,000–99,999	13.4
100,000–149,999	9.3
150,000–199,999	7.9
200,000–299,999	5.3
300,000 and over	3.3
Total	12.5

SOURCE: Canada, Statistics Canada (1984: 67)

high real interest rates will vary significantly. For the well-off, they may
be a source of increasing wealth.

A similar effect flows from the federal government's payment of interest on the accumulated public debt. Table 4.9 shows the increasing
burden of debt charges. (For an interesting discussion of whether these
charges really represent a burden on society see Chorney [1989: 30–7].)
Most of Canada's public debt is owed to Canadian individuals or institutions that have lent their money to the government in various ways.
Thus payments on the debt identified in Table 4.8 constitute transfers
from the tax-paying public to the debt-owning public. The two categories
will overlap, but such transfers can function as a means of wealth accumulation. In Canada this seems to be the case. In 1986–7, for example,
over 85 per cent of the gross public debt was owed to holders of Treasury
bills, Canada Savings Bonds (CSBs), domestically owned marketable
bonds, and superannuation accounts. While a broad cross-section of the
population are 'owners' of public debt in one form or another, the bulk
is likely held by the more affluent. Probably the most widely owned
component of public debt is CSBs. Yet families with incomes of $60,000
or over are more than twice as likely to own CSBs as families earning
$15,000 to $24,999, and in 1984 families with wealth of over $100,000

TABLE 4.9
Gross public debt charges, 1970–1 to 1989–90

	As a percentage of		
	GDP	Budgetary revenues	Budgetary expenditures
1970–1	2.1	12.7	12.1
1971–2	2.2	12.8	11.7
1972–3	2.1	12.0	11.1
1973–4	2.0	11.5	10.5
1974–5	2.1	11.1	10.4
1975–6	2.3	12.6	10.6
1976–7	2.4	13.7	11.6
1977–8	2.5	16.0	12.3
1978–9	2.9	19.1	14.2
1979–80	3.1	20.3	15.9
1980–1	3.4	21.9	17.1
1981–2	4.2	25.2	20.2
1982–3	4.5	27.8	19.1
1983–4	4.5	28.2	18.7
1984–5	5.0	31.7	20.6
1985–6	5.3	33.1	22.9
1986–7	5.2	31.1	22.9
1987–8	5.3	29.7	23.1
1988–9	5.5	31.9	24.9
1989–90	6.0	34.1	27.2

SOURCES: Wilson (1988: 85); *Quarterly Economic Review*, Special Reports, March 1991 (Ottawa: Department of Finance)

owned 73.6 per cent of the value of CSBS (*The Distribution of Wealth in Canada*, 1984, Statistics Canada Catalogue 13-580, 67, 78). Public debt charges represent a payment from taxpayers to holders of public debt, who are disproportionately from the more affluent sector of society. Provided that real interest rates are positive, such payments may contribute to accumulation, an effect reinforced if the tax system contains regressive elements, whereby a relatively greater tax burden is imposed on the less affluent.

The effect of high interest rates on sources of income may be observed in Table 4.10, which shows that share of national income paid in interest has increased over the past twenty years. Canada's tax system contains major elements of regressivity and has become more regressive in recent years. Further tax reform measures introduced by the Conservative gov-

TABLE 4.10
Distribution of Canada's domestic income: selected years (% of total)

	1967	1970	1975	1980	1987
Labour incomes	71.2	72.6	71.2	69.4	67.7
Pre-tax profits	13.7	11.8	14.7	16.1	13.2
Interest/investments (rentiers)	4.4	5.4	7.1	10.8	10.1
Farm income	2.4	2.0	2.9	1.5	1.3
Unincorporated business	9.0	8.4	6.0	5.2	8.3
Inventory evaluation adjustment	-0.7	-0.2	-2.0	-3.0	-0.6

SOURCE: Reproduced from Donner (1988: 17)

ernment are likely to enhance the regressive nature of the tax system (McQuaig 1987; Muszynski 1988).

Tables 4.11 and 4.12 show the changing origins of federal budget revenues, first as a percentage of GDP and then as a percentage of total federal revenues. Table 4.11 demonstrates the relative decline in budget revenues as a percentage of GDP and indicates the shifting composition of revenues over the past decade – most notably, the decline in corporate taxes, with clear implications for accumulation, and the increased role of unemployment insurance (UI) contributions. Heightened reliance on contributions makes the tax system more regressive. The incidence of these contributions operates relatively independent of income, given an income ceiling and fixed-rate contributions. If the employers' portion of such contributions falls ultimately on labour (through being considered by employers as part of the wage-benefit package) or consumers (through being passed on in price increases), then the regressiveness and contribution to accumulation increase correspondingly. (The financing of the UI system is dealt with in chapter 6 below.)

McQuaig (1987) has documented the way in which successive adjustments to Canada's tax system since the early 1970s have favoured business and affluent individuals and families. Loopholes, tax breaks, and 'tax expenditures' have accomplished this result. Referred to by the Department of Finance (1985: 1) as 'selective tax measures,' tax expenditures generally take the form of tax exemptions, deductions, credits, reduced tax rates, or tax deferrals and serve policy goals ranging

TABLE 4.11
Changes in federal budget revenues as a percentage of GDP, 1975–6 to 1989–90

	1975–6	1989–90	1989–90 as % of 1975–6
Personal income tax	7.4	7.7	104
Corporate income tax	3.4	2.0	59
Sales and excise tax	3.9	3.8	97
UI contributions	1.2	1.9	158
Other tax revenues	1.2	0.7	58
Non-tax revenues	1.4	1.2	86
Total budgetary revenues	18.4	17.3	94

SOURCE: Wilson (1990: 141)

TABLE 4.12
Changes in federal budget revenues as a percentage of total revenue, 1975–6 to 1988–9

	1975–6	1988–9	1988–9 as % of 1975–6
Personal income tax	40.3	44.3	110
Corporate income tax	18.2	11.3	62
Sales and excise tax	21.1	22.2	105
UI contributions	6.5	10.8	166
Other tax revenues	6.3	4.3	68
Non-tax revenues	7.7	7.1	92

SOURCE: Wilson (1990: 142)

from encouragement of investment to assisting the disabled. The scope
and size of revenues forgone as a result are difficult to estimate (Department of Finance 1985: 4–7), but the sums involved considerably
exceed the annual budget deficit. In 1983, for example, when the annual
budget deficit stood at $21 billion, over $34 billion in personal tax plus
over $16 billion in commodity tax expenditures went uncollected be-
cause of 'selective measures.' Over $5 billion (1982 figure) was forgone
in corporate taxes – an unusually low figure because the depth of the
recession meant that many corporations were unable to use available
deductions (Department of Finance 1985: 6). (In 1979, for example,
this item had totalled almost $9 billion – an amount almost as large as
the federal deficit in that year.) For the period 1972–81, Blais and Vail-

lancourt (1986) estimated that corporate tax expenditures represented a reduction of about 35 per cent of the nominal tax rate. Use of tax expenditures had increased significantly over the period.

Not all tax expenditures are accumulation devices. Many personal tax measures, such as non-taxation of strike pay, exemptions for dependent children, child tax credit, and the basic personal exemption, are concrete legitimation initiatives.[6] But many others assist the affluent. One of the largest single items among personal income tax measures in 1983 was the tax advantage on savings in registered pension plans and registered retirement savings plans, estimated at $4.9 billion. Statistics Canada (1984) reveals that almost 75 per cent of the value of such plans was held by the top 15 per cent of wealth owners. The advantages accrued overwhelming to the wealthy, and it seems fair to regard it as an accumulation device. Maslove (1981: 233–41) has argued more generally that tax expenditures involve allocational and equity consequences and that the benefits flow disproportionately to those with higher incomes. Perhaps it is precisely because the distributional consequences are little understood that tax expenditure has been preferred over direct expenditures.

To the extent that these measures favour the affluent, their scope and prevalence seem symptomatic of the state's determination to stimulate accumulation. Since the revenues forgone exceed the size of the deficit, the government's obsession with reducing the deficit, primarily by expenditure restraint, appears increasingly ideological in origin and decreasingly based on even the pretence of scientific economic theory. Such a focus seems to rest more on reducing the scope of the state per se and increasing the autonomy of market forces than on balancing the budget. Since social expenditures bear the brunt of restraint, the exercise looks like a cutback in concrete legitimation activities elaborately camouflaged by rhetoric and hidden disbursements of tax expenditures.

Spending Priorities

Some sense of the Canadian state's priorities in expenditure restraint can be obtained by examining trends among and within the expenditure envelopes featured in federal management since 1979. The system was obviously not designed to provide data in a way consistent with the type of analysis being conducted here. Nonetheless we can draw some tentative conclusions about the relative balance between accumulation

and concrete legitimation activities. Table 4.13 provides basic information about federal spending patterns between 1978 and 1986.
Public debt payments show the most dramatic expansion. Apart from
this, only defence has increased its relative importance. Both social
development and economic development envelopes spent less, propor-
tionately, in the mid-1980s than in the late 1970s. Economic development, however, fell off after receiving increased priority during the Liberal
government's activist phase in the early 1980s.

The Liberal government's expenditure projections for 1980 emphasized economic over social development. Given the rigidities of spending within the various envelopes, this amounted to an intention
incrementally to shift new resources into the favoured envelope. While
economic development programs cannot automatically be presumed to
contribute to accumulation, nor social development programs to concrete legitimation, the announced emphasis was consistent with a shift
in priorities. The criteria developed by the cabinet's economic development committee were intended 'to support capital development and
to de-emphasize current consumption much of which was held to be
"disguised welfare or social policy"' (Doern 1981b: 30). 'Efficiency' was
often proclaimed as an important goal of public policy. Seemingly this
reflected the influence of post-Keynesian ideas about economic development and the state's role as a handmaiden to private capital. The
trend should not, however, be exaggerated.

Lithwick and Devlin (1984) have traced the economic development
motif in Liberal priorities, which reached its apogee with the tabling of
Economic Development for Canada in the 1980's in November 1981
(Government of Canada 1981). While conceding that the document
represented a significant forward step in the government's conceptual-
ization of economic development, Lithwick and Devlin characterize it
as 'insubstantial' and unaccompanied by a major shift in resources.
Certainly the BCNI was by no means unhappy with a document whose
generality was more to its liking than a conceivable full-fledged industrial strategy, devised by cabinet members such as Herb Gray, might
have been (Langille 1987: 58–9).

The government was at best ambivalent about its own role in relation
to the private sector. Occasional interventions into markets were accompanied by a generally hands-off attitude toward the bulk of the
private sector. Donald Johnston, minister of state for economic and
regional development, explained in a 1983 speech: 'My role is to provide
support for economic development, not to direct it' (cited in Lithwick

TABLE 4.13
Federal envelope expenditures as a percentage of total federal outlays, 1978–86

Fiscal year	Fiscal arrangements	External Affairs	Parliament/services to government	Defence	Economic and regional development	Social development	Public debt
1978	7.2	2.8	5.9	8.5	14.8	48.1	12.5
1979	6.3	2.8	5.7	8.6	13.4	49.7	14.8
1980	7.0	2.7	4.2	8.5	15.0	46.0	16.5
1981	6.6	2.4	5.0	8.6	15.2	43.9	18.2
1982	6.7	2.4	6.4	8.6	13.4	41.1	21.5
1983	7.1	2.5	3.5	8.8	15.0	41.9	21.2
1984	6.5	2.5	3.9	8.9	14.6	43.2	20.3
1985	6.0	2.7	4.1	8.0	13.6	42.2	22.5
1986	5.4	2.6	4.1	8.9	12.3	42.5	24.2

SOURCE: Doern, Maslove, and Prince (1988: 134)

and Devlin 1984: 155). The increased use of tax expenditures rather than direct expenditures was consistent with this general approach. Business tended not to view tax expenditures as interventionist (Doern, Maslove, and Prince 1988: 140).

The influence of 'efficiency' and post-Keynesian ideas generally can be traced in such diverse areas as transport and labour-market policy. But, as Doern (1983b: 20–3) makes clear, the new emphasis by no means enjoyed unchallenged primacy. Competing and contradictory ideas such as stability and regional equity on the one hand, and deference to markets on the other, continued to influence economic development policy. In short, the post-Keynesian interventionism of 1980–4, except possibly for the National Energy Program, may have been rather half-hearted. Nonetheless, expenditures within the envelope for regional and economic development did increase somewhat and were to decline only after the election of the monetarist-influenced Conservatives.

The Conservative government's economic development policy has favoured greater reliance on markets to achieve accumulation. Continued state intervention, however well intentioned, is seen as simply distorting market signals and hindering the ability of markets to provide incentives and co-ordination for economic growth. The decline in relative spending on economic development since 1984, therefore, indicates not a lesser desire to foster accumulation but rather an assessment that this objective will be better served by the free market. Since the unhindered operation of market forces produces its own set of winners and losers, this preference has been described as 'a way of altering the social contract in Canada without saying so' (Prince 1986: 17). It is on this point, rather than any disagreement about the need to support accumulation, that differences between the Conservatives and their Liberal predecessors centred. They both thought that the state's role was to assist private-sector accumulation and growth but disagreed, to an extent, about how active a role the state must assume to discharge its responsibilities. The Conservatives, however, have not consistently abstained from federal expenditures in such fields. As the 1988 election approached, the government promised major expenditures on a variety of projects such as the Hibernia oilfields off Newfoundland.

With respect to social policy, the two parties differed less. In the midst of the Liberal era, Prince and Rice (1981) argued that Canadian social policy was under attack as a general entity and undergoing a process of internal transition. The transition was designed to increase the selective and targeted components of social policy at the expense of the universal ones. The pressure on social policy stemmed from the perception that the state was too large and that social policy led to excessive expenditures, which resulted in the deficit and inflationary pressures. Wolfe (1985), among others, has demonstrated that the relation between such perceptions and reality is slight at best. Social programs were, and are, the biggest component of federal spending. But their existence and size antedated the deficit problem. Like other expenditures, they have been subject to restraint since the mid-1970s. Prince and Rice (1981: 108) attributed the attack on social policy to the general influence of neoconservative ideology and to the sheer size of the social welfare budget, which made it the logical target of restraint.

Faced with such an offensive, social policy ministers sought to justify their programs in terms of their contribution to national economic development – as, for example, in the argumentation surrounding the National Training Programme, analysed in chapter 5. Such manoeuvres testify to the priority that accumulation had acquired relative to concrete legitimation within decision-making circles. The degree to which social programs were maintained in the early 1980s has been attributed largely to their 'marketization' – their adaptation to serve economic ends (Maslove 1984b: 2). Spending on social policy did in fact rise more quickly in the 1980s than had been envisaged by the Liberal government, almost entirely because of automatic stabilizers activated by the severely depressed economy.

After an abortive attempt to partially deindex pensions, which demonstrated that considerable public support still existed for welfare state programs, the Conservative government moved more cautiously in social policy. Nevertheless state support for social programs was eroding – stretching them 'to the tearing point' (Rice 1987: 212). The increasing selectivity and targeting begun by the Liberals meanwhile continued apace.

Alongside expenditures on social policy, a 'hidden' welfare system has arisen based on providing benefits through the tax system. While these measures have benefited low-income individuals, they have also been generous to high-income earners. In addition, the process of increasing selectivity has intensified under the Conservative government. Rice points out (1987: 222) that in the first full year of Conservative budgetary control, universal programs grew by 6.8 per cent, compared to 39.9 per cent for selective programs. In the last year of the Liberal government, the growth rates were 8 per cent and 7 per cent respectively. The increased targeting of social benefits might conceivably be viewed as a new form of concrete legitimation activity. But where such measures were accompanied by cutting or eliminating benefits for other needy groups (see McQuaig 1987: 327–8 for examples) channelling assistance 'to those most in need' might better be viewed as ideological legitimation. Since high-income earners are the chief beneficiaries of selective programs in social policy, such as RRSPs, one can detect growing attention to accumulation in an area previously considered legitimation.

The State and Ideological Legitimation

The anticipation that the state would intensify its ideological efforts stems from the situation posited in this and earlier chapters. Faced with economic crisis, the Canadian state has followed restrictive monetary and fiscal policies, supplemented by occasional wage controls. These policies have been associated with increasing unemployment. Pursuit of this course by the state has been consistent with the positions taken by representatives of business and capital and has been opposed by labour and other groups. Tolerance of high unemployment has undermined an essential component of the 'post-war settlement' characteristic of Canada and most other countries. Public concern about unemployment has been exacerbated by pressures on social programs. Thus state policy, which has accented accumulation, has eroded its provision of two key concrete legitimation initiatives: full employment and the welfare state. In other words, the state's role in these two key activities has taken an increasingly zero-sum form.

Tremendous pressure has been placed on politicians to justify their policy responses to the economic crisis and to persuade the public either that their response has been the most appropriate or, perhaps, that it has been the only one possible. It is not suggested that the state has borne the sole or even the principal burden of justifying its economic strategy. Obviously elements in civil society supportive of the state's posture have sought to legitimize its priorities and methods. But the state itself has been impelled to engage in active ideological legitimation by the persistence of public support for components of the post-war settlement and of beliefs that governments can solve pressing economic problems. As late as 1980, Barber and McCallum cite pollster Allan Gregg's argument that 'although Canadians are perfectly well aware we have some serious problems they believe that all of these problems – even inflation – can be solved by government. On "solvability" tests, you get amazing results. More than 70% of Canadians believe that our problems can be solved, wholly or partly. People even believe that their leaders are being too pessimistic.' Shaking these beliefs was part of the objectives of ideological legitimation. The state's preferred response to economic crisis has been to limit its own role and to tolerate some problems (unemployment) in the name of allowing market forces to solve others (inflation, the deficit).

One element in the ideological legitimation process has been gradual implementation of policies resulting in a shift from concrete legitimation to accumulation. We saw earlier in the chapter that in all three macroeconomic policy areas changes of emphasis were consciously gradual.[7] The governor of the Bank of Canada noted that the gradualism of the co-ordinated attack on inflation avoided 'the severe economic disruption and concentrated social strain that would be involved in an all-out attack designed to produce quick results' (Bank of Canada 1976: 6). A gradual approach, stood a better chance of 'attracting the public understanding and support required for a successful outcome' (Bank of Canada 1977: 5). The following year the governor cautioned that anti-inflationary policies involved real costs and that success ultimately depended on 'Canadians showing willingness to accept that cost. How well a society will react to a situation of this kind depends of course on many things, but there are limits to the tolerance that it will show' (Bank of Canada, 1978: 7).

Underlying such comments is awareness of the delegitimizing effects of actions taken to counter inflation. A gradual approach had two benefits. First, the costs of the strategy were spread out, and this made it possible that people might become accustomed to the new reality. Second, gradualism provided time in which people might be persuaded of the wisdom of the macroeconomic approach adopted. The second process is what has been termed ideological legitimation.

While the Bank of Canada would not play the leading role among state agencies in such a process, the Bank (1980: 1) noted that it had been involved to an unusual extent in discussions of interest rate policy and in explaining its position. By 1985 the governor was able to record 'a much clearer public appreciation these days that pursuing inflationary policies in the hope that this will somehow ease other economic problems is worse than futile' (1985: 9). But he complained that there was much less public understanding of the Bank's continued emphasis on the dangers of inflation at a time when the inflation rate had dropped to 4 per cent. Continued efforts at public persuasion would, therefore, be necessary.

The state's persuasive activities have been noted in some recent literature. Doern and Phidd (1983: 317–21) draw attention to the use of 'exhortation and symbolic policies and policy.' By exhortation they mean 'a whole series of potential acts of persuasion and voluntary appeals to the electorate as a whole or to particular parts of it.' Symbolic politics is the demonstration of concern about a problem or group 'because to show no concern at all may be both uncaring and inhuman or, somewhat more basely, politically unwise.' Any actions that result are quite inadequate to resolving the problem or meeting the group's needs. Given pressures on politicians to be seen to be doing something about particular problems, Doern and Phidd judge symbolic politics to have reached epidemic proportions (318).

Stanbury and Fulton (1984: 284–93) have constructed a typology of 'suasion' techniques. Five types are discernible in Canada: *pure political leadership*: 'the use of exhortation by politicians to persuade citizens to alter their beliefs and ultimately their behaviour on the basis of emotional and or logical appeals without any inducements to do so' (284) (as in the government's attempts, analysed below, to convince people of the correctness and rectitude of state policy, through throne and budget speeches and efforts to document or 'textualize' the state's response); *consultative mechanisms* used to involve potential opponents in decision-making and/or implementation with a view to co-opting or neutralizing them; *suasion* with the threat of further action in the event of non-compliance; *mass suasion* through advertising or other forms of paid communications; and *monitoring agencies* and the use of unfavourable publicity against those regarded as behaving unacceptably.

Throne and Budget Speeches

Throne speeches, though often highly general in tone, are intended to present the government's priorities to Parliament and the Canadian people. Budget speeches present its assessment of the economic situation and typically contain fiscal and other measures designed to realize its economic goals. Budget speeches, and to a lesser extent throne speeches, have become major media events and so provide excellent opportunities for governments to communicate with the electorate and to legitimate state policy ideologically.

There seems to be general consensus that in recent years budgets have contained a broad range of goals – an 'astonishing array of measures' (Purvis and Smith 1986: 32–3) – and that there has been 'a rise in the more evident use of federal budgets as tactical occasions' (Maslove, Prince, and Doern 1986: 238). In short, they have become highly political occasions where governments seek to impose their agenda and to persuade the uncommitted that economic policy is on the right course.

An earlier section of this chapter traced the growing prominence of monetarism. The tenets of this paradigm supplied most of the arguments to justify the state's changing policy stance, especially its growing emphasis on accumulation and reliance on market forces. Some thirty-six throne and budget speeches, delivered between 1970 and 1988, were analysed, with attention paid to statements and measures connected to two major problems: inflation and the deficit, and unemployment. The results of this analysis are summarized below, in Table 4.14 and the discussion of it. Inflation and the deficit are treated as a single policy problem for the following reasons: first, each problem served as justification for a similar policy stance, albeit in different periods; second, in the monetarist paradigm the deficit was a primary cause of inflation, and so the two issues to some extent could and did substitute for each other; and third, as the inflation rate declined in the mid-1980s it no longer served to justify the overall policy stance, and hence the size of deficit entirely displaced inflation after 1984.

Table 4.14 identifies, for each of the problems, the percentage of speeches in which statements about the cause and negative effects of the problem were made and measures geared to solving the problem announced. Most speeches emphasized the negative impact of inflation and the deficit while passing over, mostly in silence, that of unemployment. This was one means by which ministers of finance sought to justify their choice of strategy. Virtually the only identified negative effect of unemployment was passing reference to its human and social costs. Failure to emphasize its economic impact is significant in itself. Governments were far more voluble about the negative effects of inflation, which, they said, harms confidence and inhibits investment; causes high interest rates; harms consumers, the elderly, and those on fixed incomes; reduces government's ability to respond to problems; causes unemployment and recession; reduces the competitiveness of industry; and creates social tensions.

The major solutions advanced for both inflation and the deficit were expenditure restraint and deficit reduction backed by a restrictive monetary policy. These tended to be coupled, in periods of high inflation, with measures to protect those hardest hit and with calls for greater consultation with business, labour, and government. The extent to which such consultations may have performed an ideological legitimation role is considered presently. On the supposition that measures to protect the weak were less than adequate, one might also categorize such measures, announced in over a third of the speeches, as ideological legitimation.

The most common solutions announced to deal with unemployment were efforts to stimulate the private sector to create jobs and active labour-market policy measures. The latter were announced in twenty of the thirty six speeches analysed. Whether such pronouncements merely symbolized government concern about unemployment, and hence were a form of ideological legitimation, or represented a real effort to deal with the problem will be considered more fully in chapter 5. The conclusion may, however, be anticipated here: active labour-market measures throughout most of the period were largely symbolic.

Earlier sections of this chapter have made it clear that the announced policies of fiscal and monetary restraint, justified in the speeches as necessary to deal with inflation and the deficit, were implemented. The speeches went to some lengths to identify those problems as the most important, partly through dwelling on their negative consequences while

TABLE 4.14
Percentage of throne and budget speeches (by period) offering statements about the causes, negative effects, and solutions to selected economic problems

	Inflation/deficit			Unemployment		
	Causes	Negative effects	Solutions	Causes	Negative effects	Solutions
1970–6	77	46	46	31	15	54
1976–84	67	60	67	53	20	80
1985–8*	50	88	88	38	13	75
Entire period	67	61	64	42	17	69

NOTE: In combining inflation and the deficit, I have avoided double counting.
*Includes speeches of Clark government (1979–80), to group PC speeches

all but ignoring those of unemployment. Such arguments constitute one part of the state's ideological effort; other parts are represented by symbolic and oft-announced measures to deal with the victims of the economic crisis. As already indicated, labour-market policies fit into this category. Other ideological legitimation activities are considered below.

The Macdonald Commission

The Report of the Royal Commission on the Economic Union and Development Prospects for Canada comprises three large volumes and is accompanied by seventy-two research reports. Although not the only report to provide a justification for state policy, it is by far the most comprehensive. A number of other reports that contributed to the 'documentation' of state policy are dealt with in chapters 5 and 6. This is not the place to attempt a comprehensive review of the Macdonald Report. Rather a number of the report's findings will be summarized, and its usefulness noted in legitimating past public policy as well as its anticipated future direction.

The report is heavily based on advice received primarily from the economics profession (Carmichael, Dobson, and Lipsey 1986; Simeon 1987). The profession's consensus, in terms of the distinctions used in this book, can be described as broadly monetarist. The commission's acceptance of this viewpoint led it to advocate greater reliance on market forces and reduced state intervention. This position rested in part on a perception that international competitive forces had already eroded the state's policy independence. Rather than attempting to retard operation of market forces, the commission recommended embracing them – hence the commission's support for free trade with the United States. The market-forces orientation also led to advocacy of recasting the welfare state in such a way that efficiency, adjustment, and adaptation became major features. The strategy of deficit reduction through fiscal restraint was endorsed, though the commission did consider, given reduced inflation, that monetary policy might be eased somewhat. Should inflation recur, a temporary incomes policy was recommended.

The report regretted that unemployment was so high but considered that the non-accelerating inflation rate of unemployment (NAIRU – see earlier chapters for a discussion) had risen to between 6.5 and 8 per cent. Of this, the commission believed some 1–2 per cent was attributable to the UI system. Unemployment might be lowered by restricting the generosity of the UI system. This argument could be used to legitimate the limitations on UI already introduced in the 1970s (see chapter 6) and also to encourage further restriction. The high NAIRU level – an estimate that even the commission warned should be treated with caution (II, 285) – could also be used to legitimate the high unemployment in Canada. The concept of NAIRU suggests that unemployment can be reduced beneath that level only by accelerating inflation. The fact that the rate is not subject to precise or, some would have it, even rough measurement means that it can be used to justify any prevailing rate of unemployment. In fairness to the commission, however, it attributed Canadian unemployment in excess of 6.5–8 per cent to demand deficiency. Nevertheless, the commission's use of NAIRU rather than full employment served to legitimate the trend of public policy over the preceding decade.

Consultation and Co-optation

Fournier (1986) has documented the state's growing use of consultative mechanisms. Increasingly, such devices have been used to bring together representatives of the state and those of business, labour, and other private-sector interests in an attempt to forge a consensus about specified problems or issues.

Task forces and similar mechanisms, such as royal commissions and other types of public inquiry, are a cost-effective means of improving the government's range of information and policy advice. Their reports, whether unanimous or by majority, can be used to document or textualize the problems faced by government and the validity of certain responses rather than others. Their 'documentation' aspect has already been referred to as a form of ideological legitimation. Such mechanisms also may contribute to ideological legitimation by the very process of consultation and the demonstration of concern implied by their creation. Blair's (1984: 95) study noted: 'Compared with the degree of influence the task force mechanism exerts on the policy-making process, its impact on the consultative environment is more far-reaching ... In facilitating the development of a better level of understanding among members of this diverse group (of interest group leaders), the task force mechanism makes an invaluable contribution to the consultative mechanism.' Such results confirm that this type of consultative process helps to legitimate the state's actions. There is evidence, however, that the best results are attained when the issues for discussion are quite specific (see Waldie 1986: 178ff.) and not innately conflictual.

Certainly there are examples of this approach that failed to deliver ideological legitimation. The role of labour representatives on the Forget Commission examining UI provides one example and is considered in chapter 6. Similarly, while the Macdonald Commission's report may have textualized the economic approach favoured by the government, it failed to achieve its mandate to be 'an instrument of consensus building.' Banting (1986a: 49) notes: 'The primary economic and ideological conflicts of the country had been built into the Commission from the outset, and the process of writing a report would inevitably become an effort to fashion a consensus acceptable to the major interests in the country.' Since labour's representative dissented from the majority report, no consensus emerged. The report (Banting 1986a: 61–3) noted the growth of consultative mechanisms, supported the trend toward consensus-building advisory bodies, but remained wary about and rejected the development of over-powerful quasi–decision-making bodies. These could be used to block market-driven adjustment processes and hence ran counter to the commission's free-market ethos.

Probably the most transparent and least successful attempt to use consultative processes to foster ideological legitimation was the National Economic Conference held in Ottawa in March 1985. The two-day meeting involved many interest-group representatives and was chaired by Prime Minister Mulroney and attended by all his top cabinet members. In his opening address, Mulroney reminded the 140 delegates that he had 'promised that the people represented would play a major part in determining the direction the Conservative government will take' (*Fi-*

nancial Post, 30 March 1985: 2). But Michael Wilson's key-note address focused on deficit reduction and how to achieve it. The *Financial Post* reported: 'Wilson, the only minister to formally address the conference, left the audience in no doubt that deficit reduction had resumed its place as the government's number one budget priority. What he wanted from conference delegates in the way of guidance on the reduction, he said, was "how, how much, and how fast"' (30 March 1985: 1). Deficit reduction dominated the talks, much to the pleasure of the Conservative government, which could now claim that the deficit-reduction measures introduced in the 1985 budget were the products of extensive consultation.

Such claims were clearly self-serving: nothing approaching consensus emerged at the conference. Many participants, especially but not exclusively those representing labour, perceived the conference as an exercise in manipulation (*Globe and Mail* 25 March 1985; *Financial Post*, 30 March 1985). Given such perceptions, it contributed little to ideological legitimation. Notwithstanding such failures, increased use of consultative bodies is testimony to the legitimating effects that can be conveyed by process and procedure, even where no measurable impact on policy results.

Suasion with Inducements

During the period 1982–4, the federal government implemented a policy of public-sector wage controls, known from the percentage increase permissible in each year as '6 and 5.' Swimmer (1984) mentioned three possible explanations for the policy. One of these, that it formed part of a coercive grand design to remove collective bargaining rights from federal employees, is addressed in Chapter 7. The other two in different ways fit the notion of ideological legitimation rather well. One takes at face value the government's claim that it was trying to set an example of restraint which, it hoped, would be emulated by the private sector. Although rejected by Swimmer as an adequate explanation of policy, the stated rationale might still produce public relations benefits. The other, favoured by Swimmer (246–60), is that the government was 'grandstanding.' It singled out public-sector employees as scapegoats for inflationary pressures. In a time of recession, when public servants were widely viewed as enjoying a privileged and protected position, such a stance pandered to a fairly common prejudice. The '6 and 5' program was imposed 'mainly to show businessmen that the government was serious about slowing inflation' (*Toronto Star* 6 December 1983, cited in Swimmer 1984: 257). In ideological terms, therefore, the program might be expected to garner both broad public support and the support of a key interest.

Advertising

Government advertising also may be a useful instrument of ideological legitimation. Notwithstanding methodological difficulties in calculating the volume of federal expenditures on advertising, spending has increased rapidly since the early 1970s. In 1970 the federal government was the twelfth-largest national advertiser. From 1975 it was normally the leading spender (Stanbury, Gorn, and Weinberg 1983: 165–6).

Not all or even most state advertising, of course, is aimed at persuasion and hence directly at performance of ideological legitimation. Much of it simply seeks to convey information or to promote broadly acceptable behaviour. An example would be promotion of increased concern about road safety. But even advertising of this nature tends to increase the government's visibility and may symbolically demonstrate concern about particular issues or groups. In a context of constraints on programs and expenditures, it may well be an important political and ideological factor. Trebilcock et al. (1982) have drawn attention to the possibilities of the state's use of information: either making perceived benefits greater than real ones or obscuring the erosion of real benefits.

It seems common in the limited literature on this subject to link expansion of advertising with the onset of economic and fiscal difficulties in the mid-1970s (e.g. Stanbury, Gorn, and Weinberg 1983: 154). The reality of the constraints inhibiting governments from using more traditional instruments such as direct expenditures seems generally accepted. From this perspective, then, the government substitutes an inexpensive policy instrument for one more expensive and thus no longer available. To the extent, moreover, that the constraints themselves were induced by forgoing revenues and, through deficit reduction, seeking to reduce the role of the state, then the use of advertising and other instruments would be even more clearly an ideological legitimation exercise.

Advertising is only one component in an array of instruments the state may use to attempt to 'define reality' (Stanbury, Gorn, and Weinberg 1983: 155). But it is one that is often neglected by observers, and, at least on the basis of expenditures, it appears to have been used increasingly since the economic crisis started.

Monitoring and Information Disclosure

Monitoring agencies and techniques of information disclosure were used periodically during the 1970s and 1980s. Inflationary price increases have been the most frequent targets of such agencies (Stanbury and Fulton 1984: 289). This technique seems largely symbolic: concern is demonstrated, but there is little evidence that monitoring has much effect.

Summary

The chapter opened by posing a number of questions about Canadian macroeconomic policy. Had there been a shift of paradigm from Keynesianism to monetarism? Had there been more emphasis on accumulation and less on concrete legitimation? Were there significant efforts to legitimate ideologically these developments? The evidence suggests that all these questions can be answered in the affirmative.

In the process, however, a number of qualifications and modifications were identified. The chapter's major findings were as follows. First, the principal goals of macroeconomic policy were to control inflation and reduce the deficit. Concern about unemployment surfaced periodically, but doing something about it never displaced other goals. In pursuit of its main goals, the state adopted a restrictive macroeconomic stance, which, it is widely acknowledged, caused some of the increased unemployment experienced throughout the period. Second, the basic economic strategy was both shaped by and justified in terms of the new dominant economic paradigm. Third, all three elements of macroeconomic policy – fiscal, monetary, and incomes – more and more promoted accumulation. Fourth, however, accumulation was delivered increasingly through reliance on market forces, with consequent reduction in the state's role. Fifth and finally, the change in policy was undertaken in a consciously gradual fashion. While the new priorities were introduced incrementally, considerable efforts were made to persuade the public of the rectitude of the new policies. In this connection we looked at a number of ideological legitimation techniques. We also saw that other policy areas, through serving as placebo or symbolic responses to the effects of the macroeconomic strategy, might serve to legitimate ideologically the basic approach. The role played by labour-market policies was advanced as an example and will be examined in detail in the next chapter.

5   Labour-Market Policy

The last three decades have witnessed the rise and fall of efforts to construct an active labour-market policy which would play a key role in overall economic management and adjustment. These efforts correspond to the changing fortunes of the economic paradigms with which we are concerned. The paradigm most identified with active labour-market policy is the post-Keynesian: attempts to implement its prescriptions in this sphere continued from the mid-1960s to the mid-1980s. Both the Keynesian paradigm which preceded it, and the monetarist one which came later, paid only limited attention to the policy area. In using the paradigms as a prism through which to interpret labour-market policy, I shall also be concerned to identify the implications of paradigm change for the state's priorities. The evidence in this sphere is suggestive rather than definitive. But arguably it adds a major dimension to understanding the place of labour-market policy in the state's implication in the unemployment issue.

Labour-market policy includes at least four major elements: actions to improve the way the labour market functions, such as provision of job-placement services, vocational counselling, and collection and dissemination of labour-market information to both prospective employers and employees; actions to influence the supply of labour, including mobility assistance, job training, and basic skills development; measures to influence the demand for labour, such as direct job-creation projects and wage or recruitment subsidies; and provision of unemployment benefits for those who become jobless. This chapter focuses on training and job-creation policies. Consideration of unemployment insurance is deferred until the next chapter, and provision of labour-market services will receive only passing reference. Before beginning a description and analysis of training and job creation, I shall connect the labour-market policy area to earlier discussions of macroeconomic paradigms and the state's role in a market economy.

The precise mixture and content of labour-market measures are linked to the dominant economic paradigm: Each paradigm assigns, explicitly or implicitly, a specific role to this policy area, and each shares a commitment to smooth operation of the labour market and provision of appropriate placement, counselling, and information services. In general, the latter area is not one in which policy differences derived from the basic paradigms play a big part. Beyond the basic services, however, the approaches do assign a somewhat different role to labour-market policy. These roles are derived from the implications of the macroeconomic policies favoured by each paradigm. In all cases, labour-market policy is viewed as subsidiary to macroeconomic policy and is designed to complement it.

From a Keynesian perspective, macroeconomic policy bears the overwhelming responsibility for ensuring full employment, and labour-market policy is cast in a subsidiary role. Within these limits, however, demand-side job-creation projects can assist in managing macroeconomic demand. They would be relevant especially in dealing with seasonal deficiencies in demand. Keynesianism also recognizes the existence of structural unemployment, and some role is foreseeable for training and retraining programs.

In contrast, post-Keynesian thinking emphasizes much more the scope of structural unemployment, as opposed to the demand-deficient variety, and the inflationary consequences of running the economy at very high levels of demand. Both concerns lead to a much larger role for labour-market policy than that envisaged by Keynesianism. The expression 'active labour market policy' has often been used to characterize post-Keynesian attitudes. The enhanced role is derived from two sources. First, post-Keynesians remain committed to full employment but argue that the use of high levels of aggregate demand is inevitably inflationary. A restricted level of demand might contain inflationary pressures, at the cost of some unemployment. If such unemployment could be eliminated by job creation or, preferably, training programs to equip jobless workers with useful and marketable skills, then the prospect of non-inflationary full employment is opened up. A rotating portion of the labour force would always be undergoing training. The skilled workers produced would prevent 'bottlenecks' in the supply of certain types of labour. In itself, this would reduce inflationary pressures. The existence of a pool of trainees would similarly reduce pressures on demand. And the increased productivity of a highly trained work-force means, theoretically, that the context could be one of a high-wage but low-inflation economy.

Second, active labour-market policies are well suited, at least in theory, to deal with structural and regional unemployment. Post-Keynesians believed that structural unemployment increased rapidly in the 1960s and 1970s and that it was not susceptible to demand-side solutions. Supply-side policies such as training and relocation could, however, contribute to a solution. Active labour-market policy could also encompass demand-side measures such as job creation, especially as a response to regional and seasonal unemployment.

In principle, monetarism represents a withdrawal of the state from direct intervention in the operation of labour and other markets. Its main aim is to control inflation, partly through reduction in the scale of state spending and intervention. With inflation under control, unemployment is expected to gravitate to its 'natural' level. Full employment, it will be recalled, is not an objective, unless defined arbitrarily as being equal to the natural rate. Since the theory considers it possible for actual unemployment to be higher than the natural rate, some role may exist for labour-market policy. This might consist of measures to assist the labour market to function efficiently and thus enable the rate to drop to its natural level. Examples might include providing information, assisting the geographical mobility of the work-force, providing assistance to specific groups who find it difficult to participate in the labour market, and – though this is stretching a point in terms of monetarist theory – providing training and retraining for workers affected by structural economic changes (the theory posits that employers and prospective employees should share the costs of training). The rationale for state involvement, then, becomes the transferability of many skills between employers. In this situation, 'free-loading' tendencies among employers may result in insufficient training.

Like post-Keynesianism, monetarism emphasizes supply-side labour-market measures. Monetarist policies, however, are essentially passive, minimalist measures, designed to promote the adjustment of labour supply to demand. The context is one in which the economy is driven by market forces and there is no state commitment to full employment. Monetarism also takes a more restrictive approach to unemployment benefits (see chapter 6) and to unions and collective bargaining (see chapter 7), since it regards these as obstacles to the proper functioning of the labour market and as driving the actual unemployment rate above its natural level.

Chapters 1 and 3 outlined the connection between the economic paradigms and the various types of state activity. Post-Keynesian and monetarist approaches paid more attention to accumulation, at the expense of the concrete legitimation measures which Keynesians had viewed as consistent with and contributing to accumulation. Implementation of post-Keynesianism and monetarism led the state to increased coercion and ideological legitimation to compensate for its declining efforts to win legitimacy by providing real benefits such as full employment. These shifts in emphasis are reflected in the options favoured by the labour-market policy of each paradigm. Demand-side activities such as job creation can best be viewed as adjunct policies to achieve full employment and hence contribute to concrete legitimation. Such projects find a role in both Keynesian and post-Keynesian thinking but are significantly de-emphasized in monetarism. Purely information services aimed at helping the labour market function better, and supply-oriented activities such as mobility and training which socialize the costs of employers' labour forces, contribute largely to accumulation. Such activities find favour in both post-Keynesian and monetarist labour-market thinking but receive slight emphasis in Keynesianism. Whether this apparent correspondence holds up will become evident later in the chapter. What will also become apparent, however, is the difficulty of any definitive classification of labour-market programs by type of state activity, by economic goal, or according to other criteria. Virtually all the literature concurs in characterizing the policy area as one of confused and overlapping goals and purposes. There is, however, evidence that suggests that the anticipated link between paradigms and the state's priorities can be traced in state policy and that this reveals the dynamics of state activity.

In an assessment of the content of labour-market policy, the following criteria may serve as a useful benchmark or constructed type. Labour-market policies can be viewed as a concrete legitimation activity to the extent that they form part of a full-employment strategy, are available to all sectors of the population who require assistance in obtaining suitable employment, are responsive to individual needs and/or the provision of demonstrable community benefits, and are financed from general revenues raised on the basis of a progressive taxation system. To the extent that labour-market programs do not form part of a full-employment strategy, are targeted rather than generally available, and present a contrast between their proclaimed objectives and the actual level of resources assigned to them, they can be regarded as ideological legitimation activities. Such programs serve to promote capital accumulation if they are designed primarily to serve the needs of employers for a good supply of trained labour power, do not aim at full-employment, are financed from regressive sources of revenue, such as UI contributions, and/or put major priority on allowing profit-making opportunities to the private sector in implementation of the programs.

The evolution of Canadian labour-market policy falls into three broad periods: rather limited activity until the mid-1960s; much greater activity, in which programs multiplied, through the early 1980s; and reorienting and refocusing of the policy package since 1984. Such periodization highlights shifting emphases but may exaggerate the differences and conceal periods of transition. I shall try to maintain a balance between elements of continuity, those that point to future options, and those that are new.

In the first two periods, training and job creation were addressed largely by separate programs, and so it makes most sense to treat the two activities separately. In 1985 the Canadian Jobs Strategy integrated the two areas, and from that point the analysis will be combined.

Early Policy

Prior to the 1960s, labour-market policy was underdeveloped, largely because of the dominance of Keynesian theory and federal-provincial conflicts over jurisdiction. Keynesianism emphasized macroeconomic policy as the chief instrument for addressing employment-related issues.

Training

Federal participation in occupational training was restricted by the constitutional division of powers, which made education and, by extension, training an area of provincial jurisdiction. In the mid-1960s, the federal government began to assert a role for itself derived from federal responsibility for the economy. This intrusion met considerable provincial resistance.[1] Prior to the mid-1960s, the federal role was limited largely to conditional-grant programs – most notably, the Vocational Training Coordination Act (1942) and its successor, the Technical and Vocational

Training Act (1960) (Paquet 1976). The paucity of funding for skills training, and some provinces' lack of interest, can be explained in large part by Canada's reliance on immigration to provide skilled workers (Doern and Phidd 1983: 504).

The 1960 legislation represented the 'federal government's first tentative attack on economic problems through manpower policy' (Paquet 1976: 6). Increased activity addressed structural unemployment associated with the early influence of post-Keynesianism. In form, the act resembled its predecessor, offering federal financial support for teaching institutions and contributions toward the costs of training the unemployed. Given Ottawa's constitutional responsibility for UI, the latter was an obvious area for federal activity. In addition, however, funds could be provided to train those in employment who were in danger of losing it. The sums of money involved, moreover, clearly indicated much higher priority than previously. Between 1961 and 1968 almost $1 billion was provided, over 70 per cent of it for capital expenditures toward construction of training facilities (Goldman 1976: 84–5). Operational support consisted of funding for apprenticeships and for ten other training programs – some aimed at students, others at the already employed. The largest, in financial terms, covered the unemployed. The programs involved both general education and more specialized occupational training.

Under federal-provincial agreements, the provinces retained control over the location, structure, and administration of training facilities. During the 1960s, Ottawa became increasingly dissatisfied with these arrangements, because of lack of federal 'visibility,' failure to obtain political credit for the activities, and disparities in provincial participation (Dupré et al. 1974: 37–46). Nonetheless, the programs stimulated creation of training facilities, provided training to many Canadians, and marked a major extension of labour-market policy.

Job Creation

The use of demand-side components of labour-market policy was limited in these early years. The main initiative was the Winter Works Programme, in effect 1958–68 (see Close and Burns 1971); federal contributions totalled some $267 million over the ten-year period. It was claimed that over 33 million person-days of work were provided – about 14,000 person-years of work per year. The program dealt ostensibly with seasonal unemployment occasioned by Canada's winter climate. Over time, the seasonal aspect diminished, and municipalities began to include anticipated federal contributions as part of their normal budgeting. The program was a 'sidelight' (Doern and Phidd 1983: 505) in the overall picture and in 1968 fell victim to an early exercise in financial restraint. The newly created Department of Manpower and Immigration had in any case begun to consider retraining seasonally unemployed workers rather than merely creating temporary jobs for them (Close and Burns 1971: 71).

In both training and job creation, the level of activity was quite low, à la Keynesianism. Job creation was aimed at seasonal unemployment and could best be regarded as a form of legitimation. The state did assist in capital accumulation through its involvement in training, accomplished largely via public institutions. There was little direct subsidization of private-sector training costs or opportunity for profit-making in implementation of the programs.

Active Policy

Development of a post-Keynesian view of economic management meant theoretical support for an enhanced role for labour-market policy. Doern and Phidd (1983: 506–7) trace articulation of this view to the first two annual reports (1964 and 1965) of the Economic Council of Canada. These 'endorsed the need for a middle-level and medium-term supply-side tool to augment the macro Keynesian "demand management" approaches which invariably operated only in a short term context. The key phrase was "manpower policy."' The necessity for such a strategy flowed from imperfections in the operation of the labour market (Dupré et al. 1973: 31–2), and its potential role was outlined by the Economic Council of Canada (1964: 170): 'High employment can be sustained without rising prices and a deterioration of the nation's balance of payments only if there is efficient use of manpower resources ... Labour market policy is concerned with facilitating fuller and more efficient use of manpower ... It must have the status of an important national economic policy integrated with general fiscal and monetary policy.'

In 1966 the Department of Manpower and Immigration was established to administer the new policy area. It concentrated initially on immigration, provision of labour-market services, and training. In the early 1970s a major job-creation component was added, and in 1976 the department was reorganized. The Canada Employment and Immigration Commission (CEIC) was created, with administrative responsibility for labour-market services, immigration, and unemployment insurance, as well as job creation and training, which are to be dealt with here.

Training

Despite its early focus on supply-side activities, the department soon became involved in creating demand for labour. Yet, as Table 5.1 indicates, training did remain dominant throughout the 1970s and into the 1980s. Federal dissatisfaction with the Technical and Vocational Training Act (1960) has already been noted. The replacement legislation, the Adult Occupational Training Act (1967), created the Canada Manpower Training Programme (CMTP), Ottawa's main training vehicle until the National Training Programme was set up in 1982. The CMTP was modified over time, but its basic elements remained fairly constant. The Department of Manpower and Immigration, and subsequently the CEIC, purchased institutional training mainly from provincial community colleges: academic upgrading, sometimes known as basic training for skill development; language training for immigrants; specialized training for particular skills; and apprenticeship training for a variety of trades. The department also financed industrial training-on-the-job projects. (See Table 5.2.)

Dupré et al. (1973: 123) explain the emphasis on institutional training: in federal-provincial negotiations the provinces obtained a continued federal commitment to maintain referrals to provincial institutions; operational problems plagued training-in-industry projects, given the large numbers of small plants and branch plants in Canada; the bureaucracy was inexperienced in dealing with industry on this type of project; and government fears that on-the-job training could easily become little more than a straight subsidy to industry. The 1970s saw some expansion in industrial training, partly in response to criticisms levelled at institutional training by the Economic Council of Canada in its Eighth Annual Review (1971). The government, however, remained sensitive to charges that such expenditures constituted an industrial subsidy (cf. Dupré et al. 1973: 128).

Table 5.3 presents a break-down of full-time institutional training under the CMTP by type of training. The bulk of the training, whether measured by training days purchased or by number of people who commenced training, was oriented to acquiring skills for particular jobs. A significant portion was devoted either to academic upgrading, to bring

TABLE 5.1
Expenditures and participants: training and job creation, 1968–85

	Training			Job creation			Totals	
	$ (m.)	(%)	No. (000) of participants	$ (m.)	(%)	No. (000) of participants	$ (m.)	No. (000)
1968–9	190	(100)	301.2					
1969–70	245	(80)	304.9					
1970–1	289.6	(75)	344.8					
1971–2	328.4	(61.4)	308.2	205.9	(38.6)	119.7	534.3	427.9
1972–3	343.5	(60.7)	316.2	223.5	(39.3)	115.8	567	432
1973–4	363.2	(76.6)	319.7	111.2	(23.4)	69.6	474.4	389.3
1974–5	401.2	(77.0)	291.6	120.3	(23.0)	59.7	521.5	351.3
1975–6	506.6	(74.3)	274.6	176.1	(25.7)	71.5	682.7	345.1
1976–7	547.7	(73.3)	297.2	200.1	(26.7)	46.7	747.8	343.9
1977–8	572.2	(67.0)	299.4	282.6	(33.0)	107.9	854.8	407.3
1978–9	637.3	(64.1)	286.5	356.8	(35.9)	105.9	994.1	392.4
1979–80	532.2	(58.2)	309	382.4	(41.8)	130.8	914.6	439.8
1980–1	770.0	(68.6)	307.8	350.2	(31.4)	131.5	1,135.2	439.3
1981–2	803.1	(69.3)	292.8	356.4	(36.7)	132.5	1,159.5	425.3
1982–3	925.9	(69.3)	271.8	410.7	(30.7)	107.1	1,336.6	378.9
1983–4	1,021.3	(49.3)	277.3	1,054.8	(50.7)	321.9	2,076.1	599.2
1984–5	1,089.8	(45.1)	259.4	1,325.1	(54.9)	302.0	2,514.9	561.4

SOURCE: Annual reports of EIC and CEIC

TABLE 5.2
Institutional/industrial balance of training expenditures and trainees

	Expenditures (%)		Trainees (%)	
	Institutional	In industry	Institutional	In industry
1968–9			88.4	11.6
1969–70			88.5	11.5
1970–1			92.8	7.2
1971–2			89.8	10.2
1972–3			87.2	12.8
1973–4	94.9	5.1	86.5	13.5
1974–5	90.7	9.3	82.9	17.1
1975–6	90.0	10.0	77.6	22.4
1976–7	89.1	10.9	79.6	20.4
1977–8	86.5	13.5	76.7	23.3
1978–9	86.7	13.3	72.4	27.6
1979–80	84.9	15.1	73.0	27.0
1980–1	85.2	14.7	72.8	27.2

SOURCES: Annual reports of EIC and CEIC

TABLE 5.3
Full-time institutional training: distribution by training type (%)

	Skill	Apprentice	Language	Academic upgrading (basic training for skill development) and similar
Full-time trainings days				
1969–80	37.3	9.33	8.1	45.2
1970–1	44.5	7.46	7.9	40.1
1971–2	46.2	7.62	7.0	39.3
1972–3	49.4	8.1	6.5	36.0
1973–4	50.0	8.8	6.0	35.2
Full-time trainees				
1974–5	44.2	22.9	4.7	28.2
1975–6	39.9	28.2	5.8	26.1
1976–7	39.3	30.9	4.5	25.3
1977–8	39.1	32.0	4.4	24.5
1978–9	40.1	31.7	3.5	24.7
1979–80	40.9	31.4	6.5	20.7
1980–1	37.1	33.7	9.2	20.0
1982–3	36.5	37.8	7.5	18.2
1983–4	37.5	34.7	7.6	20.2
1984–5	37.4	30.4	9.1	23.1

SOURCES: Annual reports of EIC and CEIC

the individual to such a level as to facilitate employment or provision of skill training, or to language training for immigrants.

During the 1970s, three potential goals commonly were advanced for a more active labour-market policy (Goldman 1976: 8–10). First, such policies aimed to promote economic growth through helping the labour market function smoothly and through increasing workers' productivity. Second, such policies could stabilize the economy by smoothing out cyclical or seasonal fluctuations in unemployment. Third, they might provide greater equity for individuals or regions by creating job opportunities. The first two goals are economic in nature and seem to contribute to accumulation and legitimation respectively. The third goal, partly economic and partly social, seems best categorized as legitimation, though of narrower scope that that conferred by pursuit of full employment.

The Department of Manpower and Immigration's early annual reports and policy statements tended to stress the goal of contributing to Canada's economic growth. Correspondingly, its programs consisted largely of training and other supply-side measures. But the goals of stabilization and equity gradually became more important, as seen in the addition of job-creation programs and in training policy. An automatic identification of training with economic growth and accumulation might be too simplistic.

Examples of the intrusion of other goals into training activities can be illustrated by the 1971–2 Special Employment Plan (Department of Manpower and Immigration Annual Report 1971–2: 1–2). Training initiatives were a relatively small part of the package, but the countercyclical or stabilization motive for the Canada Manpower Training-on-the-Job Programme (CMTJP) was clear. Its purpose was 'to encourage and assist employers to prepare for future expansion by engaging a substantial number of the unemployed employables in learning-on-the-job skills that ... [will] prepare them to take advantage of future employment growth.' The CMTJP allowed employers to hire and train workers who would otherwise be unemployed. Priority was given to those actively seeking work through a Canada Manpower Centre. Equity considerations were a central concern: youth, women re-entering the labour force, and welfare recipients received particular attention. Assistance for the disadvantaged or clients with special needs was to be an ongoing theme, and a significant percentage of the department's training resources was directed toward these clients.

Critics of Canadian training programs pointed to confusion about the purposes of training. Referring to the early 1970s, for example, Dupré et al. (1973: 126) argued that industrial training reflected equity and stabilization concerns and tended to provide countercyclical income maintenance: 'At that it is a particularly beguiling form of income maintenance: were the trainees in institutions, they would simply be excluded from the calculation of that most sensitive indicator – the unemployment rate. Because they are receiving on-the-job training, the trainees count as employed members of the labour force and accordingly make a positive contribution to reducing the unemployment rate.' It has also been argued (Muszynski 1985: 266) that a high proportion of federally purchased institutional programs consisted of training in basic skills – the academic skills that would prepare the client for job training. This, it was suggested, is more consistent with equity or legitimation concerns than with economic growth or accumulation.

Thus Canadian training programs were not aimed solely at economic growth nor entirely connected to capital accumulation. A 1976 joint evaluation of the CMTP by the Department of Manpower and Immigration and the Treasury Board conceded that the economic objective of training required greater emphasis and that provincial allocations should be related more closely to employment opportunities than to jobless rates. Operational changes gave economic reasons for training a higher profile and tied activities closer to employment opportunities (cited in EIC 1984c). These modifications, however, suggest that while training included equity concerns and consequently was partly a legitimation activity throughout the 1970s, accumulation provided a major rationale for training activity. Four points may be made in this context.

First, even if all basic skills training was based on equity considerations, the proportion of trainees involved declined during the 1970s (see Table 5.3). It increased again 1983–5, but not to the same levels. Even if immigrants undergoing language training are added, the proportion receiving training not directly related to employment was never more than a one-third after 1974–5 and did fall as low as a quarter. Skill or apprenticeship training related more directly to economic growth ranged between 66 and 75 per cent of trainees throughout the period.

Second, and contrary to Dupré's argument, not all industrial training is countercyclical. The Canada Manpower Industrial Training Program (CMITP) existed 'to meet the skill needs of employers and to improve the employability and earning capacity of workers through the expansion and improvement of employer-provided training' (EIC, n.d.). The first objective is economic- and accumulation-oriented. Table 5.2 indicates that the percentage of trainees in industry increased significantly between 1973 and 1976 and continued to do so thereafter. Figure 5.1 shows the extent to which expanded industrial training was related to stabilization concerns. The decision to expand industrial training clearly had other sources as well.

Third, the sensitivity of spending on training to cyclical fluctuations can be exaggerated (Figures 5.2 and 5.3). It is difficult to interpret the volume of training activity as a response to fluctuations in unemployment.

Fourth, the department attempted to gauge how its training programs benefited the chronically unemployed (see Table 5.4). While these figures understate the impact of the equity motive, since they relate only to the most severely disadvantaged of the department's clients, they

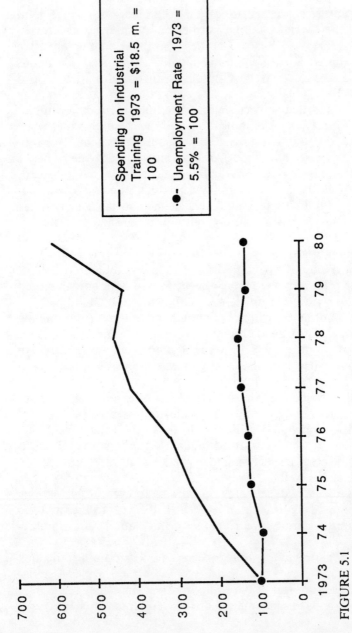

FIGURE 5.1
Federal spending on industrial training and the unemployment rate

Spending on Industrial
Training 1973 = $18.5 m. =
100

Unemployment Rate 1973 =
5.5% = 100

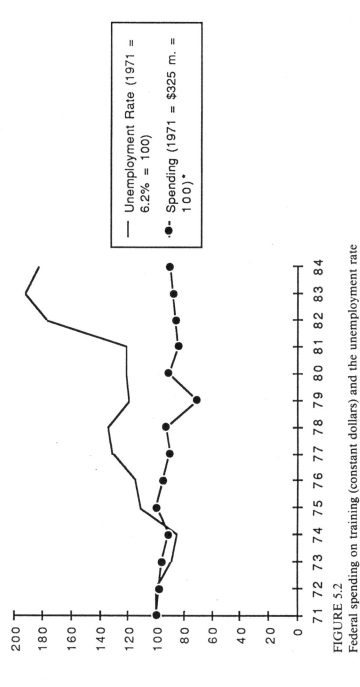

FIGURE 5.2
Federal spending on training (constant dollars) and the unemployment rate

Legend:
— Unemployment Rate (1971 = 6.2% = 100)
•— Spending (1971 = $325 m. = 100)*

*Gross national expenditure implicit price index: spending figures are for the fiscal year and are presented for the calendar year in which most of the fiscal year falls, i.e. 1971 for 1971–2.

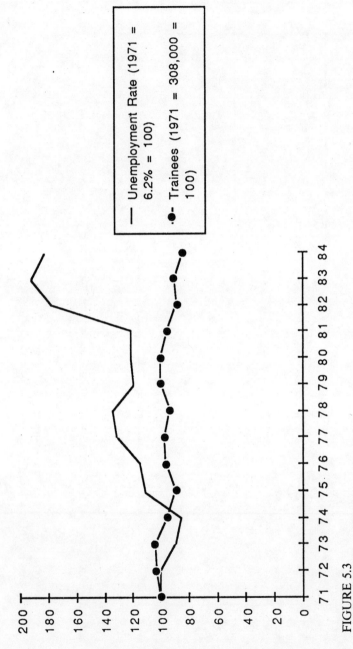

FIGURE 5.3
Number of trainees and the unemployment rate

TABLE 5.4
Degree of commitment to disadvantaged and special needs clients

Year	% of training expenditures	% trainees
1974–5	13.0	9.8
1975–6	13.7	10.2
1976–7	13.1	9.2

SOURCES: Annual reports of EIC and CEIC

show that the CMTP had not substituted equity considerations for economic ones.

Training did contain cyclical, equity, and legitimation aspects but remained centred on economic growth and accumulation. Whether it contributed effectively to these objectives is another matter. An evaluation of the CMTP revealed that only 10 per cent of those involved were trained in occupations in shortage in that year. A further 14 per cent were trained in occupations with both shortages and surpluses. Special-needs and female participants were disproportionately trained in surplus occupations. Further, when asked what they would have done in the absence of the program, 53 per cent of employers answered that they would have trained anyway and only 22 per cent indicated that they would not have been able to train and that this would have resulted in reduced operations or postponed expansion (EIC, n.d.). The incrementality of the program was thus quite limited. As a result, much of the money spent must have represented a windfall subsidy to employers rather than an essential support to their training efforts.

Training came under rigorous scrutiny in a series of reports in the early 1980s which sought to document or textualize the necessity for changes in policy orientation and were ideological preparation for departures in policy.[2] The outcome was a number of changes, beginning with the National Training Act (1982) and continuing through to implementation of the Canadian Jobs Strategy.

Reforms

In the early 1980s the Allmand Report (1980), the Dodge Report (1981), and the Economic Council of Canada's *In Short Supply* (1982) assessed Canadian labour-market policy. The reports criticized the effectiveness of the Department of Employment and Immigration's training programs.

The Allmand Report concluded that many of the department's activities 'tended to focus on the short-term reduction of unemployment
rather than on the long-term creation of productive employment (1980:
52). Too many programs were directed at occupations little in demand,
and much of the spending was related to provincial unemployment rates
rather than to demand for skills. This oversight was attributed partly
to lack of adequate data to predict training needs. The report called
(chapter 7) for increased priority for on-the-job training.

The Economic Council of Canada charged that training programs had
'tried to serve both efficiency and equity considerations to the detriment
of both.' It argued (1982: 84–6) that programs under the Adult Occupational Training Act had been highly sensitive to regional unemployment, especially in the Maritimes and Quebec. Training was therefore
concentrated in regions with relatively low employment growth. The
programs, particularly in institutional training, tended to concentrate
on the already unemployed and thus failed to develop those skills most
in demand.

The Dodge Report, *Labour Market Development in the 1980's* – the
most influential of the three documents (see Blair 1984: 82–5) – helped
shape the National Training Act and the National Training Programme
(NTP). It called for increased training, providing higher-level skills in
demand by employers (205–6). Consistent with government restraint,
it argued that better use of existing expenditure levels would meet training needs in the 1980s. The report foresaw job creation through wage
subsidy rather than the direct job creation typical of the 1970s. And, in
an early statement of a major theme, it recommended that job creation
should contain non-institutional, basic skills training. As a result, some
state-funded training would be privatized. Federal spokespersons argued
that provincial institutions were slow to respond to new demands and
opposed cancellation of courses for which demand might no longer exist
(Interview, EIC official).

Implementation of Dodge-style measures in the National Training
Act led a member of the Ontario Manpower Commission (Wolfson
1983: 147) to argue that 'there has been a marked departure in the federal
approach to the training system, moving from a focus on the needs of
the unemployed for training to the manpower requirements of employers. It is now the key instrument of manpower policy rather than
an adjunct of income maintenance policy.' Though previous training
had not catered predominantly to non-economic goals, the increased
emphasis on meeting employers' needs was unmistakable.

The National Training Act came into effect in August 1982, in the midst of the worst recession (till then) since the Depression. It was an inauspicious context in which to begin making federal training more flexible and more relevant to labour-market needs. Under the Adult Occupational Training Act (1967) training was to provide industrial workers with skills to increase their employability and/or earning capacity and to help satisfy industry's needs for suitable skilled workers. An internal evaluation (EIC 1984c: 1) noted that these objectives were virtually identical to those of the new National Training Act except that 'the order of the two objectives has been reversed indicating the change in emphasis brought about by the new national training policy.'

The new act provided for three types of support. First, Ottawa would continue to purchase training courses from provincial colleges and training schools but would give higher priority to meeting existing and future skill shortages and would concentrate funding on apprenticeship and skill training. In practice, more trainees registered in these categories, as compared to those in language and basic skills training, in 1982–3 and 1983–4, but in 1984–5 the proportion fell again to its lowest level in a decade.

Second, industrial training was to be restructured so as to reduce low-level skills training and focus on high-level skills and skills in demand. The government was prepared to sign contracts with employers and their associations to assist in training their workers. It would provide financial support of up to 100 per cent of direct costs plus wage subsidies for trainees. Both General Industrial Training (GIT) and Critical Trade Skills Training (CTST) were foreseen. These categories absorbed an increasing proportion of the total training budget during the brief-lived National Training Programme, rising from 13.6 per cent in 1982–3 to 16.4 per cent in 1984–5. Table 5.5 shows that these expenditures were focused more and more on economic efficiency. GIT and CTST moved away from catering to the needs of the unemployed, or those with special needs, and toward upgrading the skills of the already employed.[3]

Third, the federal government would financially assist training institutions through the Skills Growth Funds, which would target designated national occupations and seek to overcome employment barriers for disadvantaged groups. The department concluded that under the National Training Act 'training programmes are oriented to meeting economic rather than equity objectives. The legislation seeks to ensure that industry will have access to the skills required for expansion and technological change; while allowing individuals the opportunity to acquire

TABLE 5.5
Employment status of trainees entering GIT and CTST

	Employed	Employment-threatened	Special-needs	Unemployed
1982–3	42.8	5.4	9.5	42.5
1983–4	45.7	4.9	9.2	40.2
1984–5	49.4	4.8	8.2	37.6

SOURCES: Annual reports of CEIC

the skills they need to be more productive and to compete in the labour market. It also seeks to provide women, natives, and the handicapped with greater access to employment' (EIC 1984c: 12). The emphasis had shifted toward economic and accumulation objectives.

Consultants presented reports to the department in 1985 (ABT Associates 1985b) and gave a generally positive assessment of the CTST's relevance to employers' needs and economic objectives but were rather negative about institutional training, particularly about the program's contribution to eliminating skill shortages. In the Skill Training component of the National Institutional Training Program (NITP), fewer than 11 per cent of trainee starts were in occupations with shortages, and about 65 per cent were in occupations estimated by EIC to be in surplus (164). The study was inconclusive about participants' gains in employability and earnings.

Management's response to this report was fairly enthusiastic endorsement of the criticisms and a claim that the new Canadian Jobs Strategy (CJS) better met training objectives:

Through extensive scrutiny of decisions with respect to occupations in shortage, the systematic involvement of employers, employees and provincial institutions in the decision-making process, and the greater reliance on market forces to direct the decisions we will ensure a greater relevance of our training to the labour market. The evaluation was timely and thorough. It served as a tool in re-shaping the programme thrust under CJS and in doing so constitutes a milestone in the search for the most effective approaches to the task of providing the workforce with needed skills. Management is confident that in the next programme evaluation the merits of the current change in direction will be apparent.

The department appears to have focused on those aspects of the report that justified the Conservative government's new labour-market policy. The report, for example, had noted (146–7) that over 40 per cent of trainee starts were in the thirty occupations projected to show the greatest employment growth in the 1984–92 period. Further, the finding that the majority of training was done in occupations with a surplus was heavily qualified. The consultants reported, for example, that more detailed occupational classification might alter the ratio of training in surplus/shortage occupations. In addition, their comments were valid only at the national level – occupations in surplus at that level might be in shortage in various provinces or regions. Most important, they pointed out that 'record post-war unemployment rates meant that most occupations will be classified as surplus. The skill shortage objectives of NITP will be more difficult to achieve in a depressed macroeconomic environment' (184).

Such findings might have justified a more supportive assessment of the NITP within the department. The actual response reflects the policy paradigm of the new government, with the report being used to legitimate ideologically the new approach. Asked about the perceived failures of previous training programs, one official replied: 'Personally, I feel it was because of different political philosophies. The reason previous programmes were found not to work was because the philosophy became different – more private sector/less government. It definitely affected the way the CJS developed. If there is a change of government I wouldn't be surprised to see the CJS scrapped' (Interview, EIC official).

The Mulroney government claimed that its approach more closely integrated training and job creation. That claim will be assessed following a review of job creation in the 1970s and early 1980s.

Job Creation

Beginning in the early 1970s, the federal government expanded job-creation activity. A bewildering array of programs with different names, objectives, and criteria succeeded each other over the next decade. Amid the variety a number of themes stand out.

Some programs, such as Opportunities for Youth and Summer Job Corps, aimed to counter summer seasonal unemployment, especially among students. Others, such as the Local Employment Assistance Programme, were aimed at disadvantaged groups who were likely to remain unemployed even in good labour-market conditions. Yet others, like the Local Initiatives Programme and Canada Works, began by dealing with seasonal winter unemployment but evolved into year-round projects targeted either at high regional unemployment or at countering cyclical unemployment. The succession of programs and objectives reflected real difficulties in determining which of the various sub-types of unemployment was to be addressed by a particular program. The problem is well illustrated by a lengthy quotation from an evaluation of the Job-Experience Training Programme (JET) – a small experimental effort in the late 1970s aimed at winter unemployment among the young and out-of-school population:

The causes of high unemployment among youth have been well documented elsewhere [sic] – suffice it to say that the *main* culprits [in Canada] are generally seen as the overall slack in aggregate demand; the current demographic situation; and rising youth participation rates. Structural factors, such as lack of appropriate training/experience and the frictional manifestations of job exploration and high turnover among youth have compounded the demand-deficiency problem. The manner in which the linking of human capital requirements to employment opportunities can best be achieved is, however, less well-documented and it is the educational system that usually bears the brunt of most of the criticism in this area. The internal design of J.E.T. reflects a concern for both the supply and demand side of the current problem. The wage subsidy is seen as an incentive to employers to hire a youth – (i.e. a youth that would *not* have been hired in the absence of the programme). Thus, aggregate demand for youth is a concern. On the other hand, the pre-employment counselling and job orientation courses combined with the job experience itself are seen as a means of attacking supply side concerns that focus on 'transition' problems from school to work. (EIC 1979: 4)

Contrary to the rather confident opening statement, this passage reveals considerable uncertainty about the causes of and solutions to this aspect of unemployment. It illustrates a problem faced by all of the job-creation programs.

In addition to providing jobs, the early programs also aimed at provision of a defined community benefit, generally on a non-profit basis. In the late 1970s the criterion of public benefit was challenged by a desire to benefit the private sector. A number of tax-credit and wage-subsidy schemes, such as the Employment Tax Credit Programme and Job Experience Training, were introduced for private employers who hired additional personnel. The former was intended 'to stimulate incremental employment in the private sector.' However, doubts about the incrementality of jobs created under it raise questions about the extent to which it helped reduce unemployment.

Increasing use began to be made of unemployment insurance (UI) funds to promote work sharing and to avert layoffs. Use of UI funds for such purposes was made possible by amendments to the Unemployment Insurance Act in 1977. Direct job creation, permitted by section 38 of the act, was limited to UI recipients, and participation did not establish further UI eligibility after termination of the project. A number of pilot projects were conducted in 1979–80, and in the midst of the 1982 recession the program was expanded to provide 'a strong contra-cyclical response to the high levels of unemployment prevailing in the economy' (ABT Associates 1984). The evaluation study concluded that the program met its objectives. Projects were well targeted to areas and sectors of high cyclical unemployment, jobs created tended to be incremental, and, although the evidence was fragmentary, 'few private sector projects we studied directly profited from the projects' (9).

During the 1982–3 recession, New Employment Expansion and Development (NEED) was established to create jobs for UI 'exhaustees' and for recipients of social assistance. Its rationale stressed the cyclical nature of much current unemployment and the need to target job creation at those most in need: the long-term jobless who had used up their benefits. Targeting was seen as more cost-effective at providing assistance than more broadly based expenditures. But such expenditures would still function as 'extended stabilizers in the economy [by contributing] to maintaining the level of aggregate demand' (EIC 1984a: 3). The rate of unemployment, particularly for the long-term unemployed (fourteen weeks or more) had jumped dramatically. By 1982 over half a million Canadians were in the latter category, and a similar number would exhaust their UI eligibility during the year. NEED's objectives look like an effort to offset the delegitimizing effects of mass unemployment:

As a contra-cyclical job creation measure a central focus of the programme has been related to the alleviation of hardship as the intensification of the cyclical downturn worsened ... Following claim exhaustion, with no alternative employment opportunities available, workers have no option but to fall back on their own resources or else apply for social assistance. Consequently, at the individual level, the NEED programme has been targeted on those workers whose requirement for income assistance is likely to be critical.

Moreover, through the employment provided, workers are able to re-establish further UI eligibility and thus future income support from the UI system. In this sense, social equity – through spreading the burden of individual costs of unemployment during a period of reduced economic activity – is a major concern of the programme. (EIC 1984a: 2)[4]

NEED generated employment primarily through subsidization of wages and certain other project costs. Private-sector organizations sponsoring projects had to contribute at least 25 per cent of total costs. Enhancement of private property was permissible if outweighed by benefits to the community or project participants. The program was considered successful in its targeting and contracyclical objectives. Over 90 per cent of participants were either UI exhaustees or social assistance recipients, and the regional distribution of jobs created reflected the impact of the recession. Private-sector projects accounted for almost 20 per cent of the jobs created.

Were the jobs incremental? If they would have been created anyway, federal contributions were windfall subsidies for participating firms and thus highly specific accumulation assistance. A preliminary internal evaluation reported: 'The programme's basic effect in moving forward employment activity is consistent with its role in the contra-cyclical context within which it is operating ... NEED's effect is not so much the result of rendering profitable (through a subsidy) something which would not otherwise be so. Rather, in the main, the financial assistance encourages firms to undertake activities which would otherwise have been viable at a later date' (EIC 1984a: 36).

Such findings, if valid, tend to confirm that legitimation concerns were as much a part of private-sector as of public-sector projects. Yet the evaluators cautioned: 'In essence, since many firms were not able to give even an approximate time frame of when they would otherwise have undertaken the work, the actual extent of the incrementality under the programme remains largely unknown and difficult to judge. To the extent that firms would otherwise have undertaken the activity shortly after funding commenced, etc., incrementality could be quite limited' (EIC 1984a: 36). Ultimately, therefore, the impact of federal contributions to private-sector projects under NEED remains unclear.

In 1983, about a dozen existing job-creation programs were consolidated into four major programs[5] which remained in effect until implementation of the CJS. The objectives were contracyclical stabilization and adjustment, local employment growth, and human resource development (CEIC, Annual Report, 1983–4: 25–7).

Job Creation and Symbolism: Ideological Legitimation?

Job creation can be regarded as a state response to public concern about high unemployment and demands that the government 'do something.' To the extent that Keynesian or post-Keynesian thinking was dominant in the early 1970s, such programs may have served as useful adjunct policies in pursuit of full employment and may be regarded as concrete legitimation activities. The macroeconomic strategy of more recent governments, however, casts such programs as attempts to legitimate ideologically the overall economic strategy through demonstrating concern about unemployment. Table 5.6 compares current- and constant-dollar expenditures as a percentage of GNP and of total federal expenditures. Despite steadily increasing unemployment, constant-dollar expenditures remained lower than their 1971–72 level until 1983. Figure 5.4 compares constant-dollar expenditures on job creation and the unemployment rate. Despite some parallel fluctuations, and hence a contracyclical aspect, the expenditures were inadequate to the scope of the problem. Even in 1984, after a dramatic increase in spending, constant-dollar expenditure was just 70 per cent higher than in 1972. But unemployment was 82 per cent higher.

Much the same kind of picture emerges from the number of participants in job-creation programs (Table 5.7). By 1983–5, the number of jobs created, as a percentage of the total number of unemployed, was equivalent to that in 1971–3. In the intervening period it had been substantially less. Most job-creation projects are of relatively short term and affect the annual average unemployment rate much less than the second column might imply. Many programs circulate temporary work opportunities among a sizeable number of people without substantially easing unemployment. In conditions of high unemployment, participants are not normally able to re-enter the mainstream work-force once their projects terminate. But they may benefit psychologically and in other ways. And job creation if publicized and visible, may assuage potential disaffection in society. A recent assessment of federal employment development in Newfoundland prior to the CJS concluded that it had created a system that 'although not by design, results in the dissipation of social unrest which might arise if people did not have the

TABLE 5.6
Job-creation expenditures and the unemployment rate

	$ (millions)	Constant 1971 $ (millions)	As a % of total fed. expend.	As a % of GDP	Unemployment rate
1971	205.9	205.9	1.1	0.21	6.2
1972	223.5	208.5	1.1	0.21	6.2
1973	111.2	95.5	0.5	0.09	5.5
1974	120.3	89.0	0.4	0.08	5.3
1975	176.1	112.9	0.5	0.10	6.9
1976	200.1	112.8	0.5	0.10	7.1
1977	282.6	145.3	0.6	0.13	8.1
1978	356.8	169.4	0.7	0.15	8.3
1979	382.4	166.4	0.7	0.14	7.4
1980	356.2	137.0	0.6	0.11	7.5
1981	356.4	120.6	0.5	0.10	7.5
1982	410.7	124.7	0.5	0.11	11.0
1983	1,054.8	296.9	1.1	0.26	11.9
1984	1,325.1	355.4	1.2	0.30	11.3

SOURCES: Annual reports of EIC and CEIC

combined safety net of unemployment insurance benefits and job creation on which to rely' (Montgomery 1986: 41).

Overall, the actual priority and impact of job creation declined steadily between 1972 and 1982. Such activity as occurred can be viewed as largely symbolic. Between 1982 and 1984, priority increased again, but not, in expenditures at least, to levels commensurate with rising unemployment. Nor can it be viewed as contributing to full employment. This area of labour-market activity has again declined in importance since the Conservative government came to office.

This general overview of trends in job creation is certainly consistent with the view that it has changed its role. From being a policy aimed at contributing to full employment in the early 1970s, it has become mostly a symbolic response to unemployment – itself created in part by macroeconomic policies. If this trend is discernible after 1972, it has become much clearer since 1984. Before dealing with the most recent period, though, in which the lines between training and job creation become quite blurred, a number of other comments about job creation prior to 1984 are in order.

First, programs may have performed a legitimation role other than

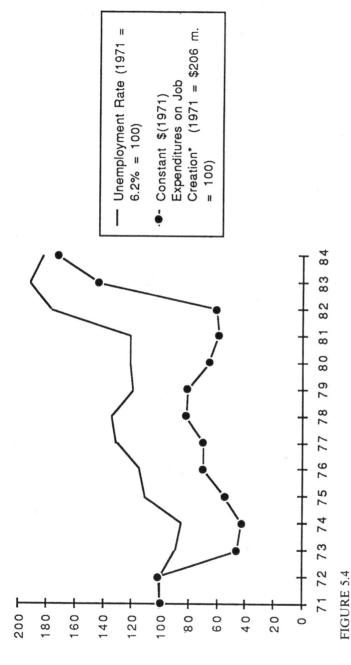

FIGURE 5.4
Constant-dollar* (1971) expenditures on job creation and the unemployment rate

*See note to Figure 5.2.

TABLE 5.7
Numbers of participants in job-creation programs

	Job-creation participants (000s)	% of labour force	% of unemployed
1971–2	119.7	1.4	22.4
1972–3	115.8	1.3	21.0
1973–4	69.6	0.8	14.0
1974–5	59.7	0.6	12.0
1975–6	71.5	0.7	10.3
1976–7	46.7	0.5	6.4
1977–8	107.9	1.0	13.0
1978–9	105.9	1.0	12.0
1979–80	130.8	1.2	16.0
1980–1	131.5	1.1	15.2
1981–2	132.5	1.1	15.0
1982–3	107.1	0.9	8.0
1983–4	321.9	2.6	22.2
1984–5	302.0	2.4	22.0

SOURCES: Annual reports of EIC and CEIC

by simply contributing to full employment or, later, seeking to legitimate high unemployment ideologically by demonstrating activity and concern. Huston (1973) argued, for example, that the Opportunities for Youth and Local Initiative Projects were designed specifically to reduce youth and student alienation and were in effect social control, integrating target individuals into society through paid 'meaningful activity.'

Second, Pal (1987: 41) has noted the increasing use of mandated employment, which aims to improve the job prospects and/or wage levels of designated groups (women, youth, handicapped, native people) through use of regulations and law. Pal (53–6) traces the development in the 1980s of concepts such as affirmative action, equality rights, and employment equity. Resulting legislation and programs involve positive discrimination in favour of hiring and promoting specified groups and monitoring of their conditions of work. The increased rights conferred are targeted rather than generally available. Many also do not cost the state much. In a time of macroeconomic restraint and of declining funds for employment programs that traditionally contributed to concrete legitimation, these measures can be viewed as a substitute or alternative approach.

Although the benefits are real and concrete, for the groups that benefit, they are probably more significant ideologically: in a context of scarce resources the state appears particularly concerned about the welfare of the least advantaged. In spite of some incompatibility with aspects of the new paradigm,[6] therefore, these initiatives have found some favour with neo-conservative governments. Recent studies of pay-equity legislation have pointed to its uneven and contradictory effects. Though such state activity represented a victory for women and for the movements that had pressed for gender-based wage gaps to be closed, details of the legislation reflected employers' pressure and fall far short of what was demanded. Armstrong and Armstrong (1990: 46) consider that 'the state gained legitimacy from the legislation while limiting its impact through the technical details.' Warskett (1990), while recognizing the importance of legislated equal pay for work of equal value, also criticizes its inability to deal with the wage gap and demonstrates the compatibility between the method of implementation and 'the inegalitarian and meritocratic logic of distribution in market society' (70). Similarly, Cuneo (1990) argues that defects and loopholes in the laws mean that victory is far from complete, and that the legislation may represent an attempt at co-option of the labour and feminist movements.

Third, changes in job creation allowed aspects of capital accumulation to intrude into a policy area formerly directed toward legitimation, most obviously through increased private-sector involvement and provision of wage subsidies and tax credits. By 1978 there was little doubt that orientation had shifted. In a discussion paper prepared for the November 1978 First Ministers' Conference on the Economy, the EIC cast labour-market policy in a role supportive of, and subordinate to, growth led by the private sector:

The Federal government's economic program ... is based on the fundamental principle that an efficient and competitive private sector should play the main role in assuring Canada's economic growth ... It follows from the above principle that the government's demands on total resources should be generally reduced so that the dynamism of business may be enhanced and the purchasing power of consumers increased ... In terms of the labour market this principle means that governments should intervene specifically to act as catalysts in promoting self-reliance. On the demand side, emphasis should be shifted to private sector employment development, helping industry employ Canadians, particularly young job seekers. On the supply side, continuing attempts should be made to increase incentives to work and remove barriers to unemployment which could arise through lack of appropriate skills. (Quoted in Muszynski 1985: 273–4)

The theme of 'helping industry to employ Canadians' found policy expression in wage-subsidy and tax-credit schemes. The Employment Tax Credit Programme seems to have been triggered by representations from the Canadian Federation of Independent Business (EIC 1982: 1) and looks like an attempt by the government to increase its support in the small-business sector. Small firms did participate disproportionately (12), though the measure was generally available. Within the government's budgetary process, a tax-credit scheme by-passed normal decision-making channels, providing an additional motive for the choice of this particular mechanism to assist hiring by small business (Interview, Department of Finance official). This temporary wage subsidy was intended to stimulate incremental employment. The 1978–80 period saw participation of more than 65,000 workers, 55 per cent of whom had relied previously on UI benefits or welfare. Gera (1987) finds the program reasonably effective in creating jobs in areas of high unemployment. But only a third of these jobs represented an incremental gain in employment, and the program did not increase the probability of future work for participants. Two-thirds of the jobs would have been created anyway, implying considerable private-sector subsidization.

Toward the Canadian Jobs Strategy

The Canadian Job Strategy (CJS) is the Conservative government's major labour-market initiative. Previous developments reveal the nature of the new government's inheritance in this policy area. Active labour-market policies dated back to the 1960s. The initial emphasis had been on training; the 1970s saw a greater role for demand-oriented measures. During the 1970s direct job-creation programs were developed and implemented. Except in the recession years of 1982–3, the early 1980s saw stronger emphasis on training and labour supply.

The 'rediscovery' of training was, in fact, a gradual process. After the impact of the economic crisis began to be felt, real expenditures on training, compared to those on job creation, were slightly better sustained (Douglas Smith 1984: Tables 5.4 and 5.5). In July 1981, the Dodge Task Force provided ideological foundations for the tendency, already apparent in practice, to downgrade job creation and to stress training. One result was the National Training Act (1982) and the National Training Programme. The new program emphasized development of high-level skills at the expense of basic skills training, on-the-job training (in industry) received a higher profile, and efficiency gained ascendancy over such goals as distribution and regional equalization (Davies 1986) – moving 'from a focus on the needs of the unemployed for training to the manpower requirements of employers' (Wolfson 1983: 147). Similar deference to the private sector could be observed in job creation.[7]

Entering office in the fall of 1984, the new government can hardly have been displeased with the general trend of labour-market policy. In keeping with neo-conservative concerns with supply-side factors, policy had already shifted toward training focused on employers' needs, direct job creation supportive of the private sector's requirements, and relatively restricted macroeconomic policy.

The new government's initial policy statements emphasized labour-market strategy. Following consultations with the provinces at the First Ministers' Conference on the Economy in February 1985, the government announced its approach to the policy area. The basic principles, agreed to by federal and provincial governments, were to provide

1 Training and job creation that is economic in orientation with emphasis on small business and support of entrepreneurship;
2 Programming that is innovative, flexible and responsive to regional and local needs;
3 A recognition that responsibility for training and employment development has to be shared between governments and the private sector;
4 A commitment to equality of access to training and employment development programs; and
5 Programming that is simple, understandable and avoids wasteful duplication. (Ontario 1987: 1–2)

According to federal representatives, the key principle was that 'federal support will be part of a collective effort with the private sector and the provinces. Simpler, more flexible, decentralized programmes and an integration of training and job creation will be features of the strategy' (Wilson 1985: 22). Additional funding of $900 million would be made available for the new strategy.

The full package, termed the Canadian Jobs Strategy (CJS) (EIC 1985), was unveiled with considerable fanfare in June 1985. The minister of employment and immigration, Flora MacDonald, claimed that the strategy was 'a complete redesign of the government's labour market programmes and a fundamental change in the way we develop and invest in our most important resource – the people of Canada' (1). Criticisms levelled at previous policy included: failure to co-ordinate or support provincial or private-sector efforts, lack of regional or community flexibility, complexity, concern with short-term countercyclical problems rather than fundamental structural issues, and separation of job creation from job training, which resulted in make-work projects that produced neither marketable skills nor real employment opportunities (3–4).

Six programs were announced to implement the strategy (EIC 1985; see also Montgomery 1986: 23–7; Daenzer 1987: 59–62). Skill Investment was designed to help employed workers acquire skills necessary to avert layoffs. Employers could train and retrain workers in times of technological and economic change. Options and levels of subsidy were available, including full-time leave for those retraining, on-and-off the job training schemes, and support for unions or employers to set up trust funds to finance future training needs. Job Entry aimed to assist young people and women having difficulty entering the labour market and consisted of training, placement assistance, and monitoring of participants' progress. Job Development differed from previous programs such as Canada Works in incorporating training during at least 25 per cent of the duration. Available options included wage subsidies and contributions to employers' capital and training costs. Skill Shortages provided employers with financial assistance to ensure themselves an adequate supply of specialized labour through training delivered in-house by the employer or purchased from public or private institutions. Innovations would aim at funding pilot projects that tested novel approaches to labour-market problems. Community Futures offered help to communities hit by major layoffs or experiencing chronic unemployment.

As an integral part of each program, the government made a commitment to employment equity, identifying four groups that required special measures: women, native people, persons with disabilities, and visible minorities (EIC 1985: 22). As noted earlier, such increased targeting can be construed as ideological legitimation. At the time the CJS was announced, institutional training agreements were still in force with the provinces. The government proposed to integrate institutional training within the CJS as new agreements with the provinces were negotiated.

Even if the CJS was not a 'fundamental change' from its predecessor, it included significant alterations (cf. Montgomery 1986: 37–8): the tighter connection between training and job creation and the overwhelming emphasis on training and on development of human resources rather than on community benefit. This focus was consistent with the individualism of neo-conservative ideology. Similarly, the new programs placed a far greater premium on private-sector involvement and direct assistance to business. These features have led some observers to contend that the CJS was restructuring the labour market so that individual employees would be helped to 'retool' and adjust to the type of economy being generated by greater international competition and technological change. By such an interpretation, labour-market policy was shifting from mixed objectives to almost exclusive assistance to capital accumulation.

Though much of the rhetoric surrounding introduction of the CJS made this interpretation tempting, subsequent implementation casts grave doubts on this view. Two major alternative theories exist. For some participants, the new departure looks much more like 'an exercise in expenditure reduction' (Interview, Manitoba official) – also consistent, in a different way, with the new government's ideology. Another, not mutually exclusive alternative is that the new strategy was mostly concrete legitimation: the programs assisted the disadvantaged, were heavily infused by equity concerns, and operated as an adjunct of social rather than of economic policy. Expenditure reductions might simply indicate lower priority rather than rejection. Evidence for and against the three interpretations will now be reviewed.

The CJS: Expenditure Reduction?

Labour-market expenditures have fallen in absolute and, especially, in relative terms since introduction of the CJS (see Table 5.8). Clearly expenditures in training and job creation did respond to the deep recession of 1982–4 but thereafter resumed their declining relative priority (Figure 5.5).

Most provincial officials believe that these expenditure reductions were the object of the exercise. An Ontario official recalled that just after the Conservatives came to office in Ottawa, the Neilson Task Force was established to evaluate all government expenditures. Its report contained, in this official's view, proposals to 'plunder' labour-market policy in order to effect financial savings. Neilson (1985) considered that the federal government was overinvesting in institutional training and recommended substantial cutbacks (17–18), particularly in Basic Training for Skill Development, which allegedly existed to rectify deficiences in provincial education programs (25).

TABLE 5.8
Expenditures on training and job creation

	% of federal expenditures	% GDP
1980–1	1.9	0.37
1981–2	1.6	0.33
1982–3	1.5	0.36
1983–4	2.2	0.51
1984–5	2.3	0.54
1985–6	1.4	0.30
1986–7	1.5	0.30
1987–8	1.25	0.25

SOURCES: Annual reports of CEIC; Budget Papers

Federal-provincial consultation took place in the context of the Neilson review. While all provinces subscribed to the February 1985 statement of principles, the provinces believed that there was little consultation about the design of the CJS programs, which they saw as deviating from the principles in a number of respects (Ontario, Skills Development, 1987: 2). A Manitoba official argued:

The CJS hasn't worked because it was an expenditure reduction strategy ... There was no consultation with the provinces about the design of the specific programmes. At a meeting of deputy ministers the Federal government presented some programme examples. The examples, to which some provinces agreed as examples, became the six programmes of the CJS. ... It seemed like the number 1 priority, at the time and in retrospect, was expenditure reduction. Many in the federal government felt that this was an area where they could get away with major reductions. Within the Department [EIC] there was a fight for self-preservation. A new package was prepared for a new government, putting its own stamp on the policy area. So the new programmes were targeted differently and were ideologically consistent with the new government (e.g. the stress on the private sector rather than provincial institutions).

Similarly, an Ontario official described the CJS as 'an unfit instrument' to fulfil the guiding principles outlined in February 1985, partly because of its budgetary implications.

A number of subsidiary themes illuminate the role of this policy area in the government's basic economic strategy. Four themes stand out.

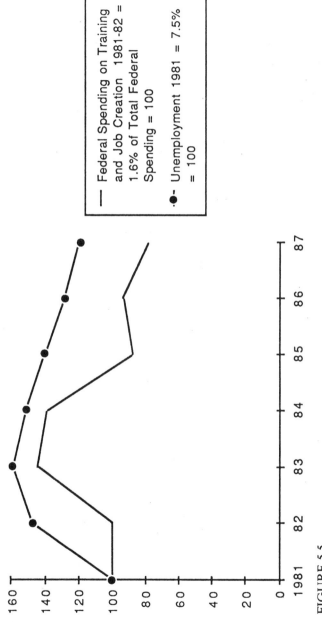

FIGURE 5.5
Priority of federal spending on training and job creation relative to unemployment, 1981–7

Legend:
— Federal Spending on Training and Job Creation 1981-82 = 1.6% of Total Federal Spending = 100

●- Unemployment 1981 = 7.5% = 100

First, the federal strategy de-emphasizes institutional training in provincial community colleges in favour of training in and by the private sector. It amounts, therefore, to partial privatization of training. Second, Ottawa is attempting to make greater use of UI and Canada Assistance Plan (CAP) funds to serve labour-market purposes. Third, there is some effort to legitimate ideologically expenditure cutbacks by emphasizing availability or accessibility of much larger amounts of money than are actually spent. Fourth, the form of delivery produces more direct payments to the private sector. Many critics of the CJS have argued that rather than being fees for services provided (i.e. training), these sums subsidize the private sector. Each of these themes suggests the state's increased desire to tailor its programs to support capital. Each has also produced federal-provincial tension, since Ottawa's initiatives undermine provincial training institutions.

The federal government's wish to increase private-sector training clearly posed a threat to provincial institutions which had formerly exercised almost exclusive 'selling rights' of training to federal authorities. The new priorities were reflected in the negotiations for new federal-provincial training agreements. The first to be signed was the Canada/Ontario Agreement on Training (6 March 1986), which enabled Ottawa to implement its own priorities while it also protected Ontario's community colleges. Direct Purchase was the same as in previous arrangements: federal authorities purchased training directly from community colleges. Under a new mechanism, Indirect Purchase, Ottawa provided funds to third parties which might purchase training from colleges or private trainers. Purchases might be arranged by Community Industrial Training Committees (CITCs) or by other third parties, such as employers or non-profit organizations. Indirect purchase would make training more relevant to local labour markets and to the private sector, which Ottawa liked.

Since the new mechanisms might undermine the training activities of provincially funded community colleges, the agreement contained safeguards to limit the damage. First, minimum levels were established for direct purchases over the three-year term of the agreement. Second, colleges were to be granted fair access to compete for training purchased by all third parties: they would receive notice of all third-party training proposals and inform third parties of training courses available in the colleges. Third, Ottawa would increase the real level of training in Ontario. Fourth, a joint assessment of the way the agreement was working would be made prior to deciding allocations between direct and indirect purchases in the final year of the agreement.

The Ontario agreement was fairly typical of the new generation of federal-provincial training arrangements. Did these agreements protect institutional training? As the examples of Ontario, Manitoba, and Newfoundland seem to indicate, experience varied.

Ontario's perception (Interview, Ontario official) is that the agreement achieved many of the province's aims. In comparison to other areas covered by the CJS, institutional training had fared reasonably well. Areas covered by Job Development, for example, experienced a 30 per cent reduction in spending. Even so, a consultant's report concluded that indirect purchases were not offsetting declines in direct purchase revenues and that colleges were not receiving projected revenues (Woods Gordon 1988: 5). The official expressed dissatisfaction that Ottawa had broken the agreement. It had failed to increase training funds in real terms. It had actively attempted to thwart and stall review procedures: 'They have decided to cut without the benefit of the information the review would have provided.' And, although 95 per cent of all training purchased by CITCs had been bought from colleges, Ottawa had failed to implement fair access with respect to private-sector training and had not notified colleges about proposals for training activities (see also Woods Gordon 198: 6). It had not provided explanations when it accepted higher-cost training proposals from the private sector in preference to those from public institutions.

Manitoba's perception (Interview, Manitoba official) was that its agreement provided little protection for institutional training. Indirect purchases by employers were not likely to make up the shortfall – most employers are small and have little capacity to train. The problem was compounded by bureaucratic problems at the federal level: funds tended to be disbursed on a local rather than a regional basis. The province had put together a training package with employers in a local area only to find out that the local office had spent its quota for that program. Meanwhile, in an adjacent area, funds for that purpose went unspent.

Representatives of Newfoundland's community colleges made similar arguments in briefs presented to the House of Commons Standing Committee on Labour, Employment and Immigration (*Proceedings*, 18 January 1988, 48A1–48A18). They stated that they were denied the possibility of initiating training under Skills Shortage/Skill Investment, and, given the region's underdevelopment, businesses were unable or unwilling to involve themselves in training programs even where skill shortages existed. As a result, one college had experienced a 25 per cent decrease in federal grants from 1987 to 1988 (48A6).

Employment and Immigration Canada (1987: 17) has rejected such criticism and denies that the shift to private-sector training is radical, although it concedes that 30 per cent of the agreements under the CJS are with the 'for-profit' sector, which makes up 40 per cent of all CJS participants. Clearly this situation represents a significant proportion of a declining expenditure item; the CJS appears to operate as an expenditure-reduction plan in an area perceived by the Conservatives as social policy. The shift to private-sector training maximizes accumulation potential by partially privatizing the provision of training. We shall return presently to the issue of quality control over such training.

The expenditure-reduction aspects of the CJS have, of course, been disguised by familiar techniques of ideological legitimation. The rhetoric surrounding it, especially at the time it was introduced, stressed its role in helping workers adjust to meet the challenge of international competition. Later, as its more modest role became apparent, it received a much lower profile in macroeconomic statements. For example, the 1987 budget statement referred to its equity component opening opportunities for those Canadians 'who face particular problems in finding employment' (Wilson 1987b: 16) rather than to its being a key tool for economic renewal. Rhetorically, therefore, the CJS has rather rapidly shifted from accumulation to legitimation. In more detailed publications the department has sought to combine these justifications: 'Under the Canadian Jobs Strategy, the federal government recognizes that it is only one player in labour market adjustment. We do those things that we do best – helping those most in need ... The emphasis on the individual in need and the great flexibility that is possible in developing solutions allow the CJS to be a powerful but flexible tool for economic adjustment. The distinction between the "social" and the "economic" orientation is ultimately artificial' (EIC 1987: 23–4).

The second aspect of ideological legitimation is the time-honoured one of claiming to spend, or 'make available,' more money than is actually spent (see Table 5.9).

The CJS: Social Policy?

There are grounds for regarding the CJS as a form of social spending, albeit heavily targeted. Many of its programs are directed at the severely

TABLE 5.9
CJS expenditures ($ million), 1985–6

Program	Projected*	Actual†	Actual as % projected
Skill investment	100	7	7
Job entry	350	180	51
Job development	700	327	47
Skill shortages	50	60	120
Community futures	150	68	45
Innovations	100	2	2
Total	1,450	644	44
Institutional training	650	686	106

*EIC (1985: 30). The document notes: 'Funds provided for old programming now being replaced by the Canadian Jobs Strategy have been allocated to the new programs'; and 'Institutional Training, under the National Training Act, continues to be governed by existing federal-provincial agreements until the end of the ... fiscal year.'
†CEIC and Department of Employment and Immigration, *Annual Report, 1985–6* (Ottawa 1986).
‡*Annual Report, 1985–6* lists additional expenditure of approximately $101 million. If included, this brings the actual grand total to $1,432 million – or 68 per cent of the amount projected in EIC (1985).

employment-disadvantaged or seek to provide equitable opportunities for women, native people, and other groups.

With expenditures being reduced, however, concentration on the long-term jobless discriminates against others who may well require assistance. Participants in Job Development must have been unemployed for twenty-four of the previous thirty weeks, and women using the Job Entry scheme must have been out of the work-force for a minimum of three years. This selectivity runs counter to the notions of equity that are part of the CJS's rationale. In response to criticisms, eligibility criteria were reviewed and a number of changes introduced effective 1 July 1988. Specifically, the '24 out of 30' criterion would be waived 'on an exceptional basis,' and the requirement of three years' homemaking activities for women was removed (EIC 1988: 15–16).

The quality of some of the training provided under the CJS, examined in the next subsection, reinforces the perception of a social program. Testimony from the National Action Committee on the Status of Women (House of Commons Standing Committee on Labour, Employment and Immigration, 3 November 1987: 43: 7–10; see also McKeen 1987) contrasted the implicit recognition of the need for a well-educated work-force with the nature of training that women were receiving: 'It does not appear that the CJS is providing women with the training necessary to become part of a highly skilled and technologically sophisticated workforce ... Although employment equity is claimed as a guiding principle in the CJS, the vast majority of women are receiving training in the traditional pink-collar occupations – namely, clerical sales and service.' The CJS appeared to be functioning as the training equivalent of a 'make-work' project. The committee also noted that private-sector delivery served to diminish the quality of training: training subsidies could be used to lower costs and enhance profit or to maximize benefits for trainees. As a result, the CJS often provided little more than 'wage subsidization to employers.'

Further support for the social-policy designation came from provincial officials, who noted Ottawa's penchant for using UI and CAP funds to finance CJS activities. Among the advantages foreseen for this strategy, two stand out. First, participants who had been on UI received allowances rather than wages and were not requalified for UI benefits. Second, for participants who had been on social assistance, it was a means of diverting CAP funds into training. By linking CAP funds to CJS purposes Ottawa hoped to bring provincial funds into an area of federal responsibility and, according to one Ontario official, to count such monies as part of its own contributions to the CJS, thereby cutting expenditures.

All of these points illustrate the social-policy and concrete legitimation aspects of the CJS. But the selectivity of the approach, the accent on private-sector delivery of training, and the context of declining expenditures make it clear that the CJS may have served as a vehicle for managing declining attention to concrete legitimation.

The CJS: Adjusting to International Competition?

The rhetoric surrounding introduction of the CJS suggested that federal training policy would radically increase workers' skills in the face of growing international competition.[8] Three factors tend to undermine this view: the cuts in expenditure already noted, the doubtful quality of much of the training, and the reductions in spending specifically targeted on high-level skills in private-sector training (as opposed to payments for training of more questionable quality).

The quality-of-training issue cannot be definitely resolved. Much of the evidence is impressionistic or anecdotal, but much of the training seems of poor quality. Responsibility for attesting and monitoring the quality of training rests with the provinces. 'Attesting' refers to advance examination of third-party training plans in order to ensure their quality; 'monitoring,' to checking whether training takes place as specified. Regular procedures exist for quality control of training performed in provincial institutions. But what of assessing private-sector training? The federal-provincial agreements recognize provincial responsibility for this function and provide for this to occur. But provincial officials report that they receive copies only of some training plans, which, given federal reluctance or refusal to pay for more intensive assessment, are given only a very simplified paper review (Interview, Manitoba official). According to a consultant's report for Ontario's Ministry of Skills Development, the province received only 27.6 per cent of the training plans which Ottawa was required to file with it for attestation – not sufficient to ensure high-quality training (Impact Group 1987: 24–5). Similarly, only about 2.5 per cent of training contracts were monitored.

This situation of course does not prove that the training provided is of poor quality. It means simply, since federal monitoring is confined to finances and program management, that no one knows how good the training is. This ignorance demolishes the argument that the CJS aims to improve the skill level of the Canadian work-force. If this were the objective, monitoring and assessment would play a major part in the strategy.

Similarly, one would expect such a strategy to focus on high-level skills to enhance the productivity of private-sector workers. According to the estimates of Ontario's Ministry of Skills Development, spending on this category of training, which used to be covered by the CTST, has actually fallen by half since introduction of the CJS (Interview, Ontario official).

Thus much of private-sector training expenditure under the CJS looks suspiciously like subsidization of that sector. Such activity is consistent with increased emphasis on furthering accumulation but cannot be rationalized as improving productivity so as to enhance competitiveness.

Summary

It was anticipated that the transition from the Keynesian to the monetarist policy paradigm would be accompanied by a changing role for labour-market policy. Keynesianism had assigned the policy area a limited but useful adjunct role in the state's pursuit of full employment.

Post-Keynesian thinking laid major stress on labour-market policy as a means of achieving non-inflationary full employment, emphasizing supply-side measures contributing to accumulation. Under the monetarist paradigm, labour-market policy conceivably might help move actual unemployment closer to the natural rate, but its role would be limited and subordinate to market forces.

To an extent even greater than in most policy areas, economic and social concerns, equity and efficiency, and legitimation and accumulation are tightly entwined. Nonetheless, it seems reasonable to advance a number of tentative conclusions.

First, if the area is regarded as primarily one of social policy, then its declining priority accords with the notion that economic crisis led the state to sacrifice or reduce its concrete legitimation activities. Relative decline in this area, combined with repudiation of a full-employment commitment at the macro level, makes programs such as job creation, and some types of training, placebos ('ideological legitimation') designed to help manage public discontent occasioned by the return to high unemployment. Their transformation from real, if limited, adjuncts to a full-employment policy into largely symbolic exercises reveals the state's increased ideological efforts to gain legitimacy.

Second, if the area is viewed as contributing to capital accumulation, then the last decade or so has seen the emergence of a preferred and narrow method of providing such assistance. Training and job creation have increasingly emphasized direct benefits to the private sector, frequently through tax benefits or wage subsidies – often, given lack of incrementality of jobs or training, little more than windfall gains for the recipients. Such measures therefore constitute direct state assistance to capital. Under the CJS, these trends were carried further with the private sector's greater role in training and little assessment or monitoring of the quality of training. This arrangement amounts to partial privatization of training.

Third, if accumulation means that the state directly provides capital with a general service – in this case, adequate quantities of suitably trained personnel – then the effort was abandoned in the mid-1980s. This is entirely consistent with the market-based accumulation strategy favoured by the monetarist paradigm. The metaphor of 'rise and fall' seems particularly suited to the changes reflected in the abandonment of the National Training Programme and its replacement by the CJS. The latter's inadequacy in contributing to accumulation through provision of a highly trained work-force means that, like some of its predecessors, it too is heavily imbued with symbolic politics.

6   The Role of Unemployment Insurance

In 1940, as a result of a constitutional amendment, unemployment insurance (UI) became an exclusive responsibility of the federal government. A contributory UI scheme was immediately established, with contributions from employers, employees, and the government in the ratio 40:40:20. Just over 42 per cent of the work-force was covered (cf. Pal 1988b: 38–41 for a summary). Numerous amendments and changes of regulation occurred over the following decades, in the direction of 'almost unbroken expansion and liberalization' (Pal 1988: 35). This trend culminated with enactment in 1971 of the new Unemployment Insurance Act, with substantially more generous terms and conditions than its predecessors. Amendments and changes since 1971 have generally restricted and tightened provisions – a reversal of the trend between 1940 and 1971.

Let us first locate UI within the framework of policy paradigms and the state's role in capitalist societies. In his analysis of the US fiscal crisis, O'Connor (1973) used two categories in examining state expenditures: those on social capital expanded surplus value and hence were indirectly productive; those on social expenses were considered entirely unproductive. O'Connor's example was the welfare system which, he asserted, was 'designed chiefly to keep the peace among unemployed workers' (7). He therefore classified welfare spending as a legitimation rather than accumulation activity. He categorized unemployment insurance, however, as a species of social insurance 'which expands the reproductive powers of the workforce while simultaneously lowering labour costs' (7). In this way, he argued, social (and unemployment) insurance contributed to the extraction of surplus value, increasing the rate of profit, and should be considered as an aspect of the state's accumulation function. O'Connor's reasoning seems to reduce bona fide legitimation activities to a residual level.[1] His analysis was probably influenced unduly by characteristics of the American 'welfare state.' US unemployment insurance and other social insurance programs may be geared predominantly to employers' interests, and unemployment insurance is far from providing an adequate safety net for jobless Americans (Ashton 1986: 165–7). But in countries with more generous and broadly accessible social programs, whether financed out of general revenues or by way of social insurance schemes, it seems quite misleading either to deny their legitimizing effects or to insist that their legitimation role is wholly subordinate to the state's attempts to contribute to capital accumulation.

Whatever the situation in the United States, Canadian UI seems predominantly a legitimation program. This is confirmed by steadily increasing coverage and accessibility after 1940 and by the circumstances surrounding its establishment. Cuneo (1979, 1980) has noted that UI, and the form in which it was introduced in Canada, formed part of a two-pronged response to pressures for protection against unemployment. To radical and communist advocates of non-contributory and universal benefits for the unemployed, the state's response was coercion and repression (Cuneo 1980: 48–51). To advocates of contributory UI, the response, after long delay, was to concede. The system that resulted was not particularly generous, excluded the majority of the work-force, and contained elements of coercion and ideological legitimation. The latter consisted of token labour involvement in administration; coercion was represented by procedures to protect the system against abuse: disqualifications, fines, and imprisonment.

The legislation nonetheless conferred concrete benefits on over 40 per cent of Canadian workers. Coverage was gradually extended to almost the entire work-force. It seems reasonable to cast UI mainly as concrete legitimation. It also did other things, but provision of income maintenance in the event of unemployment, along with the pooling of risks through a state-organized system, clearly served to legitimize the capitalist market economy and the state itself.

The long delay in establishing UI has been attributed variously to federal-provincial jurisdictional disputes and to the ideological hegemony of business. For Pal (1988: 151–2), the constitutional problem was a genuine obstacle. For Struthers (1983: 209–10), the jurisdictional issue served as a useful excuse for inaction. More important was the dominance of an ideology that recognized only the needs of a capitalist labour market (6–9). Two world wars and fears of social disturbance following the second served to push aside the lingering dominance of this ideology (cf. 213; Cuneo 1979: 149). The fears of business were assuaged by the rather conservative nature of the scheme. Pal (1988b: 102–9) explains the system's design in 'state-centred' rather than 'society-centred' terms: state bureaucrats' 'actuarial ideology' was relatively impervious to pressure from either business or labour. Since, however, 'this led to a similarly of views between employers and officials' (109), Pal perhaps exaggerates the state's autonomy. The ideological similarly between state officials and business leaders gave the later tacit guarantees unavailable to labour interests. The state bureaucracy could engineer a class compromise which conferred limited but real benefits on labour without seriously endangering business's fundamental concerns. For business, once the inevitability of UI became apparent, the design was reassuring. For labour, implementation of any sort of UI represented an advance.

Adoption of a UI plan and its subsequent development were assisted by the growing influence of Keynesianism, just as resistance was expressed in terms of classical economic theory. Since the latter enjoyed a renaissance during the 1970s and 1980s, accompanied by vociferous criticism of the UI system and attempts to restructure it, this is an appropriate point at which to outline the views derived from each paradigm.

Classical economics and, more recently, monetarism oppose UI because it interferes with the free operation of markets. Provision of UI benefits, however financed, improves labour's bargaining power vis-à-vis capital (Pal 1988: 20). Recognition of this fact accounts for business's caution not only about UI but, indeed, about full employment per se (Kalecki 1943; Sawyer 1985: chapter 7). Increased bargaining power finds expression in higher wage levels than would occur in the absence either of full employment or, as the case may be, of UI. According to Robinson (1986: 119–319), monetarist economists argue that higher wage levels actually lead to increased unemployment: firms cannot afford to employ all potential workers at high wages, jobless workers receiving UI benefits can afford to reject work and wage rates they might otherwise have been forced to accept, and additional people are attracted to join the labour market by the prospect of receiving UI benefits once their qualifying period of work is over. For these reasons, monetarism, like its classical forbears, favours a very limited, if any, system of UI.

Given the initial necessity to make concessions to labour, and the political impracticability of abolishing established systems of UI, this theoretical orientation tends to find expression in demands for reductions in benefits and tightening of conditions. Reductions in benefit levels arguably ease the pressure on wage levels and reduce public expenditure and/or deficits. Such proposals are often accompanied by the argument that unemployment will then fall because lower wage levels will increase opportunities for work. Alternatively, or as well, it is argued that all unemployment is voluntary and that recipients of UI benefits are 'work shy scroungers' (cf. Robinson 1986: 447). Regardless of the ideological packaging, such proposals aim at a transfer of bargaining power from labour to capital.

The Keynesian approach consisted of using monetary and especially fiscal policy to achieve full employment. Given likely fluctuations in economic performance, however, spending on UI benefits could serve as an 'automatic stabilizer.' To the extent that macroeconomic policies achieved full employment, little need be spent on benefits. In a recession, however, these could help sustain aggregate demand and assist an economic recovery (Sherman 1976: 190–1). In the post-Keynesian variant, UI would offer financial support to assist workers adapt to accelerating structural changes in the economy. The financial compensation rendered by UI benefits would need to be tied to an active labour-market policy. Attempts to operationalize this conception of UI can be found in Canadian labour-market policy in the 1970s and 1980s.

Certainly the growing strength of the Keynesian paradigm had spurred introduction of UI in 1940:

Keynesian economics provided another powerful incentive for Ottawa to assume national responsibility for the jobless. Once the Department of Finance accepted the view that mass unemployment was avoidable through centralized control over fiscal and monetary policy, centralized control over the victims of unemployment followed logically. Governments, it seemed, could spend their way out of depressions, but only through efficient and coordinated policies. Since the goal of this expenditure was to put the unemployed to work, it made sense to entrust their care to the government which had both the financial power and administrative expertise to achieve this end. (Struthers 1983: 212–13)

From 1940 until 1971, the government extended UI coverage and eased conditions under which benefits might be claimed. Prior to the

1971 legislation, however, this trend can be most clearly discerned in the percentage of the work-force covered, which grew from 42 per cent in 1940 to around 80 per cent in 1970–1. It also became marginally easier to qualify for benefits. Under the 1940 legislation, 180 daily contributions in the previous two years, 60 of them in the previous year, were needed to qualify. By 1961, the criterion was thirty weekly contributions in the previous two years, eight of them in the year preceding a claim. Allowing for a shorter working week, no dramatic improvement emerges from the comparison. The same holds when benefits are considered as a percentage of average weekly wages and salaries. In 1961, average UI benefits amounted to only 30.4 per cent of average weekly wages. In 1949, the figure had been 31.4 per cent (all figures from Pal 1988: 47–51). The case for wholesale liberalization prior to 1971 therefore should not be exaggerated, but extension of coverage to a large majority of the work-force indicates the direction of the Keynesian-era incremental changes. The 1971 act was to bring this process to fruition and represents the apogee of Keynesianism's influence on this policy area.

The Unemployment Insurance Act, 1971

The Unemployment Insurance Act of 1971 introduced the most dramatic change to the UI system since its inception in 1940. Dingledine (1981) traces the beginnings of the 1971 reform as far back as 1961, when John Diefenbaker's government established a committee of inquiry (the Gill Committee) to review and analyse the existing act – primarily the relation between UI and other social security programs – with a view to improving its efficiency. In 1962, the committee submitted 244 recommendations expressing considerable dissatisfaction with the existing system.

It was not until 1968, however, that a Liberal government, under increasing pressure to adopt the Gill Committee's recommendations, assembled a research team from the public service and the university community to investigate new directions for UI policy. Johnson (1981: 618) credits this team with developing the main pillar of the 1971 act – the 'social efficiency' scheme: 'a unique unemployment insurance programme that combined objectives from three different policy areas ... labour market and manpower policy, social welfare policy, and insurance principles [which were] twisted into a more efficient and socially useful package of unemployment insurance.'

However, other forces were at work. The Trudeau government had swept to power in 1968 on the rhetoric of creating a 'Just Society' and promises of new and progressive social policies. Social reform in the 1960s was stimulated by widespread social unrest, youth and student rebellion, and an upsurge of labour militancy. By its second year, the new government had not introduced new measures of significant redistributive potential. According to Johnson, the Liberals felt forced to choose between introduction of a new guaranteed annual income or progressive reform of existing UI in order to maintain legitimacy. The ministers responsible believed that reform of UI would be the cheaper alternative, and the government accordingly set out to overhaul the system. The result – a major liberalization of the existing program – reflected the fact that 'policy makers were coming to see unemployment insurance more within the context of social than economic policy' (Pal 1985: 78).

The first public stage in the process was the tabling of a White Paper on Unemployment Insurance in June 1970. Legitimation, accumulation, and coercive concerns were all reflected in the White Paper and the subsequent 1971 legislation. The White Paper aimed at greater social equity and was based on an optimistic assessment of future economic growth (Pal 1985: 3). Many of the income maintenance provisions were considerably more generous than those of the previous legislation; benefits were higher, entrance requirements were relaxed, near-universality was introduced, sickness and pregnancy coverage was offered, and regional unemployment patterns were included in the eligibility formula.

Approximately 96 per cent of the paid labour force would be covered, as opposed to only 80 per cent previously. Benefit payments increased from 40 per cent (50 per cent for those with dependants) of insurable earnings to 66 $\frac{2}{3}$ per cent (and 75 per cent). Average weekly benefit payments in 1972 were 41 per cent of average weekly wages/salaries, compared to 29 per cent immediately prior to 1971 (Grubel et al. 1975a: 176). Benefits could be claimed after eight weeks of insurable employment, as opposed to thirty insurable weeks in a 104-week qualifying period. The new program recognized time lost because of illness, injury, quarantine, pregnancy, and retirement as eligible for benefit payments (UIC 1977: A12–A20).

Income-redistribution and economic-stabilization components of UI reflected heightened emphasis on legitimation, especially when unemployment exceeded 4 per cent. For example, the system allowed for extended benefits in cases of high regional unemployment (UIC 1977: A18).

The tone of the White Paper, and provisions of the legislation, made it clear that UI benefits were being viewed as an instrument of social policy. Bryce Mackasey, the minister responsible, derived his enthusiasm for the reforms probably from a perception that they would advance social justice (Johnson 1981: 624). Mackasey's advocacy was to persist despite mounting criticism over its unexpectedly high costs and even after he was no longer the minister responsible (627–8).

Despite the emphasis on legitimation, considerations of accumulation and coercion were also present. The reformed UI system aimed to provide 'an efficient pipeline' to a variety of labour-market programs and services designed 'to help the unemployed requalify for jobs under changing technological conditions' (Department of Labour 1970). All applicants would be interviewed twice, permitting officials to channel applicants into appropriate jobs and/or training and enhancing the system's contribution to labour supply. Such motives were post-Keynesian. Interviews could also help to identify abusers and hence constituted an element of coercion within an otherwise more liberal system (cf Pal 198: 113–14).

Developments since 1971

On the basis of arguments presented in earlier chapters, one would anticipate the state's cutback in concrete legitimation activities to be reflected in the UI system from the mid-1970s onward, accompanied perhaps by increased emphasis on accumulation and attempts to legitimate the changes ideologically. The following constructed type will be useful. Any UI scheme has a legitimation effect which is likely to be maximized to the extent that it is financed from a progressive general taxation system, is administered by some form of working-class or trade-union self-management, covers all workers, and pays benefits on a generous and redistributive basis. Such a scheme is likely to satisfy accumulation needs, and thus be acceptable to business, to the extent that it is financed by regressive contributions, is administered by companies or business associates (with bipartite or tripartite administration as a second alternative), covers only contributors, pays benefits on a limited or selective basis, and, when in surplus, can be used to promote labour-market flexibility and adjustment (see Therborn 1986). In an effort to determine where the balance lies we shall consider, in turn, the financing of UI, the legislative and regulatory framework within which it operated, and the use of UI funds for 'developmental' purposes.

Financing

Under the 1940 legislation, employees, employers, and government each contributed in the ratio 40:40:20 to a UI fund out of which benefits were paid. The 1971 act linked financial contributions to a five-phase benefit structure (Dingledine 1981: 63–8). The first three phases consisted of sickness and maternity benefits and up to twenty-five weeks of UI benefits. Provided national unemployment was beneath 4 per cent, all benefits in these phases were to be financed by contributions from employees and employers. If unemployment exceeded 4 per cent, the federal government was to pay the portion of benefits attributable to the higher rate. Ottawa was to pay the total costs of benefits in the later two phases – essentially extended benefits of various types: some available for claimants with a major attachment to the labour force and others payable when the national jobless rate exceeded the norm or in regions of above-average unemployment. The five-phase scheme was simplified to three phases in 1977.

More significant for the government's contribution to costs, in 1975 the 4 per cent threshold was scrapped and replaced by an automatically adjusting rate based on an eight-year moving average of the monthly unemployment rate. Table 6.1 records the impact of this formula on the threshold rate. While the formula did afford federal finances some relief, it failed to 'catch up' to the actual unemployment rate. In the early 1980s, a no-threshold system was implemented; it transferred costs away from the government to the contributions of workers and employers. Table 6.2 summarizes the scope of direct government contributions throughout the various changes in financing formula. The table clearly indicates both the government's increased share of costs following the 1971 legislation and its success in reducing and stabilizing such costs in the later 1970s.

Should the UI account be in deficit, monies are advanced from general government revenues and are to be repaid from employer/employee contributions. In effect, the latter are specially designated taxes. The contributions are more fiscally regressive than general taxation. One of the issues, then, in the shifting portion of UI borne by general revenues

TABLE 6.1
National unemployment rate compared to UI threshold

	National unemploy-ment rate (%)	Threshold formula (%)
1972	6.2	4.0
1973	5.5	4.0
1974	5.3	4.0
1975	6.9	4.0
1976	7.1	5.6
1977	8.1	5.8
1978	8.3	6.2
1979	7.4	6.6
1980	7.5	6.8

TABLE 6.2
Government's share of cost of UI program

	As % of program costs	As % of GDP
1970–1	24.8	0.18
1971–2	19.4	0.19
1972–3	44.2	0.81
1973–4	42.4	0.72
1974–5	38.0	0.58
1975–6	51.2	1.00
1976–7	38.4	0.69
1977–8	43.4	0.82
1978–9	47.4	0.93
1979–80	30.9	0.47
1980–1	21.6	0.33
1981–2	18.6	0.28
1982–3	19.1	0.48
1983–4	24.9	0.70
1984–5	25.7	0.65
1985–6	24.9	0.60
1986–7	23.8	0.55

SOURCES: Annual reports of EIC

and contributions is the extent to which the program is redistributive. The 1971 act increased the share paid out of general revenues and, as a result, the redistributive element. From the late 1970s, however, this trend was reversed and 'normality' restored. Financing benefits through progressive taxation enhances the concrete legitimation aspect of any comprehensive system of UI. Increasing reliance on regressive taxation from the late 1970s is therefore consistent with a state cutback in its concrete legitimation initiatives.

The 1971 act also contributed to redistribution by making the program more universal, increasing benefit payouts, and offering special provisions to regions with chronically high unemployment. This was recognized by the Economic Council of Canada (1976: 39): 'It [unemployment insurance] is a means of achieving a more equitable distribution of the national wealth by providing transfer payments to persons most exposed to uncertain or seasonal jobs. It has the effect, it may be argued, of transferring to persons most prone to involuntary unemployment, many of whom have less than average education, some of the income security that others now enjoy as a result of past public transfers of wealth implicit in the education and training systems.'

Although the Comprehensive Review (UIC 1977) endorsed UI's income-redistribution functions, redistribution appears to have declined as a result of legislative amendments. Osberg (1979) cautioned that UI would be redistributive only if any deficit in the fund were financed from general revenues rather than contributions. The trend in the late 1970s was to increase the share coming from private contributions. Similarly, reduction of benefits from 66.6 per cent of insurable earnings to 60 per cent tended to have greater relative impact on lower-income claimants.

As Table 6.3 indicates, however, overall costs of UI, and hence the benefits it conferred, expanded. Costs of UI experienced two major jumps. The first followed the more generous system introduced by the 1971 act and is reflected in the 1972–3 figures – more than double those of 1970–1. In the same period, unemployment itself had increased only marginally. Clearly, therefore, expansion of the scheme represented an increase in concrete legitimation activity by the state, especially because more of the costs were coming from general revenues. The second jump was associated with the 1982 recession (see Figure 6.1). In comparison to the system's generosity in 1972, expenditures lagged behind unemployment: UI became less generous, especially after 1975. This trend is even more apparent in government contributions to UI from general revenues as compared to the unemployment rate (Figure 6.2). Figures 6.1 and 6.2 show that the decreasingly generous program was being financed more regressively, because of legislative and regulatory changes to the act during the 1970s, which are examined in the next section.

TABLE 6.3
The cost of UI, 1970–87

	Cost of UI program ($ millions)	As % of GDP*
1970–1	730	0.81
1971–2	949	0.97
1972–3	1,991	1.83
1973–4	2,161	1.70
1974–5	2,305	1.52
1975–6	3,334	1.94
1976–7	3,529	1.78
1977–8	4,124	1.89
1978–9	4,462	1.85
1979–80	4,192	1.52
1980–1	4,811	1.55
1981–2	5,371	1.51
1982–3	9,317	2.49
1983–4	11,285	2.78
1984–5	11,209	2.52
1985–6	11,540	2.41
1986–7	11,792	2.31

SOURCES: Annual reports of EIC
*GDP figures for calendar year commencing with 1970

Legislative and Regulatory Framework

The 1971 UI act placed a cash ceiling of $800 million on the government's share of total benefit payments. It quickly became apparent that this was an underestimate,[2] and over $450 million extra had to be authorized through governor general's warrants in the first year of operation. In early 1973, Bill C-124 removed the ceiling on cash advances to the UI account.

A second bill introduced in 1973 was designed to 'tighten' up the system in order to slow the increase in program expenditures. Bill C-125 introduced new provisions to curb abuses allegedly encouraged by the existing legislation. The proposed amendments aimed to discourage workers from voluntarily leaving positions without just cause, from losing jobs because of misconduct, and from failing to seek new work actively once unemployed. The bill was also to have empowered the Unemployment Insurance Commission (UIC) to decide arbitrarily potential disqualification cases, such as those involving non-acceptance of

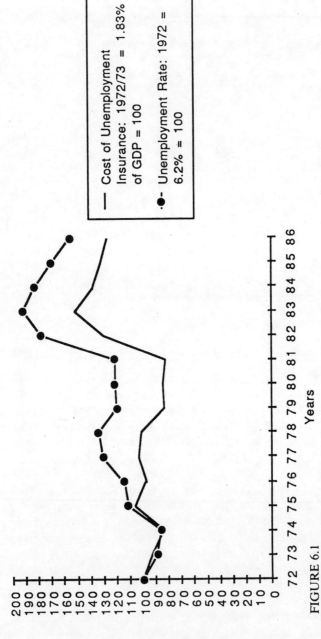

FIGURE 6.1

Costs of UI compared to the unemployment rate, 1972–86

(*Note:* Costs are for fiscal years beginning with 1972–3.)

Legend:
— Cost of Unemployment Insurance: 1972/73 = 1.83% of GDP = 100

•– Unemployment Rate: 1972 = 6.2% = 100

Years

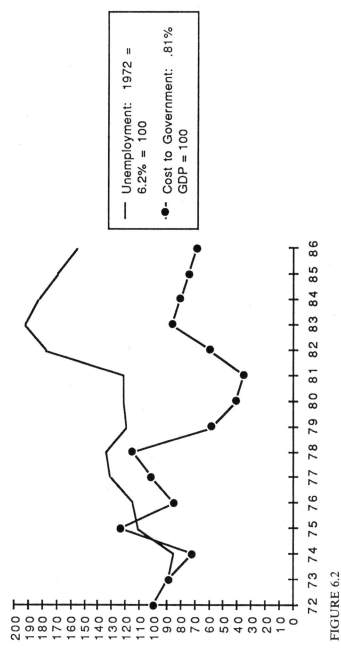

Legend:
— Unemployment: 1972 = 6.2% = 100
•—• Cost to Government: .81% GDP = 100

FIGURE 6.2
Cost to government of UI (as % of GDP) compared to the unemployment rate, 1972–86
(*Note*: Costs are for fiscal years beginning with 1972–3.)

'suitable' employment. It was claimed that the bill would reduce expenditures by $100 million. The New Democratic Party opposed the bill, and in October 1973 the minority Liberal government withdrew it. The attempt to tighten controls and reduce costs continued by administrative means (Pal 1988: 45), as indicated by a substantial increase in disqualifications of those applying for and receiving benefits.

In 1974 the Liberals regained their parliamentary majority and intensified the effort to reduce expenditures. In 1975, in the wake of a significant amendment to the official mandate of the UI program, the UIC implemented several administrative control measures. The new formulation was 'to offer temporary income support to unemployed workers while they found new jobs, and to assist the unemployed in becoming reabsorbed into the labour force as quickly as possible' (Dingledine 1981: 75–6). This was the first major restatement of the program's objectives since 1971 and demonstrated renewed and perhaps more earnest interest in the integration of UI and labour-market policy.

The government's concern with aligning UI with labour-market policy reflected the growing strength of post-Keynesian ideas, which favoured an active as opposed to a passive or compensatory approach to unemployment. These ideas, however, were also conducive to measures that the UIC wished to take in order to respond to a fiscal crisis. By the end of 1974, the cumulative deficit of the UI account was over $400 million, in spite of an increase of over 55 per cent in employee's premium rates since 1971. The UIC's response was to advocate stronger links with the labour market and a more active role in job placement.

Underlying the logic of tighter linkages was a more coercive approach to program restraint. The Special Job Finding and Placement Drive Programme (SJFPD) can serve as one example. Introduced in 1975, it operated in co-operation with the Canada Manpower Centres (CMCs) and required claimants to preregister with CMCs as a condition of benefit payment. In addition, claimants were required to undergo CMC interviews and employment counselling and, in some cases, to enroll in training courses. It can be argued that the SJFPD was both a cost-cutting and a coercive strategy rather than an active labour-market plan to relieve unemployment. For example, of over 400,000 claimants exposed to the program in 1975, 8 per cent were placed in jobs by CMCs, less than 1 per cent were placed in training courses, and over 30 per cent were disqualified or disentitled from benefits on the grounds that they were not actively seeking employment or had declined 'suitable' job offers (*Hansard* 1975: 8569). The power to disentitle claimants arbitrarily had been denied to the UIC on the withdrawal of Bill C-125 in 1973. By 1975 such powers were nevertheless being exercised. The SJFPD, by rationalizing the disqualification of almost 150,000 claimants, contributed significantly to the 75 per cent reduction in the UI account's deficit, from $418 million in 1974–5 to $97 million in 1975–6.

Other administrative controls set in place in 1975 increased the UIC's powers to control benefits and ultimately to reduce expenditures through cutting benefits. An expanded system of identical UI/CMC occupational coding provided the UIC with a more precise instrument to identity 'suitable' employment for claimants and with easier means of justifying claimants' disentitlement on the grounds of refusal. Also the UIC's system of verifying claimants' employment/earnings was made more efficient by extension of National Revenue audits of employers' records and by introduction of controlled employment-reporting procedures for union hiring halls (Dingledine 1981: 76). Similarly, Gonick (1978: 26) reported that the system of benefit control set in place in the mid-1970s established a quota: 'According to official documents issued by the Commission, its benefit control system, set up to interview and monitor claimants, aimed to cut off around 40 per cent of those who would otherwise collect.'

In December 1975, Bill C-69 further significant amending legislation, was passed. Robert Andras, minister of employment and immigration, identified two main objectives. First, the bill was an attempt to 'complement measures outlined in the June 23 budget and is in accordance with our efforts to provide a more rational allocation of government resources' (*Hansard*, 1975: 8567). Several amendments further tightened the administration of benefit control. Disqualification periods doubled for claimants who were deemed to have left their employment voluntarily, who were fired due to misconduct, or who refused to take suitable new work. Other provisions reduced benefits to claimants over sixty-five years of age and claimants with dependants, allowed for voluntary termination of claims, eliminated advance payments of benefits to claimants deemed to have a 'major attachment' to the labour force, and increased the government threshold from a national unemployment rate of 4 per cent to one of 5.6 per cent. According to Andras, these measures would reduce government costs by approximately $660 million in 1976, while increasing total employee/employer contributions by approximately $490 million through higher premiums (*Hansard* 1975: 8567–70). These measures led to a cumulative surplus in the UIC account of $204 million in 1976–7. Although total benefit payments had risen, the government's contribution declined (see Tables 6.2 and 6.3). The effect, therefore, was more and more to finance UI from regressive contributions rather than from somewhat more progressive general taxation.

Second, Bill C-69 was to introduce amendments 'directed toward improving the influence of the Act on the relationship between supply and demand of workers' (*Hansard*, 1975: 8567): 'In view of the importance this government is placing on job creation in the current budget, it is appropriate that one of the proposed amendments to the Unemployment Insurance Act ... will permit the extension of coverage to sponsors of job creation programs like the Local Initiatives Programme and the Local Employment Assistance Programme' (8569). Use of UI funds to 'act on the relationship between supply and demand of workers' was a major step toward integrating the program and labour-market policy.

Bill C-27, passed in August 1977, further integrated UI and labour-market policy. The Employment and Immigration Reorganization Act made several major amendments to the UI system. First, it integrated the Department of Manpower and Immigration and the UIC. A new Canada Employment and Immigration Commission (CEIC) was created and charged with administering the labour market, employment services, UI, and immigration. In addition, the Department of Employment and Immigration was established to form a bridge between the CEIC's activities and policy-making and the government's overall economic and social strategies.

Second, Bill C-27 further tightened administration of benefit control. It increased the qualification period significantly and introduced a new three-phase benefit structure (down from the previous five phases), which more closely linked the number of weeks of insured employment and the duration of benefit entitlement. The savings effected by these measures made a major contribution to the 1977–8 UI surplus of $414 million (in spite of a record benefit payout of $3.9 billion) and the 1978–9 surplus of $741 million (Dingledine 1981: 95, 104).

Third, Bill C-27 authorized developmental use of UI funds – as training allowance for claimants participating in UIC-approved training courses, in special job-creation projects, or in approved work-sharing. The minister claimed that developmental uses would often provide for more 'productive' allocation of resources: 'There are instances ... when the productive impact of the [UI] programme is inhibited by factors such as obsolete or inappropriate skills, or the absence or shortage of employment opportunities in a particular area. In these circumstances the role of the [UI] programme to facilitate job searches has, inevitably, a diminished applicability. I believe, therefore, that there is a need to work out programme alternatives that would permit a more productive use of time while on claim' (*Hansard*, 1977: 2592).

The minister's notion of 'a more productive use of time while on claim' refers, of course, to a claimant's participation in job training, job creation, and/or job-sharing. The legislation empowered the CEIC to use surplus funds from the UI account to finance job training programs that it now administered. Enhanced state activity would facilitate capital accumulation: rather than simply compensating unemployed individuals, the system would supply employers with a trained work-force. Trainees would in effect pay for their own training by drawing from their benefit-period entitlement. Job training, therefore, though remaining supported largely out of the state's general revenues, was increasingly subsidized by contributors' premiums.

Further amendments to the system were enacted in 1978. Bill C-14 further tightened the operation of UI. Some individuals working part-time were henceforth excluded. High-income claimants would now have to pay back up to 30 per cent of all UI benefits received in a taxation year – mainly an exercise in ideological legitimation, for the amounts collected were quite small (Kesselman 1983: 62) and ranged from 0.5 per cent to 0.8 per cent of total program costs. Any redistributive effect was therefore minimal. The benefit rate was reduced from 66.6 per cent to 60 per cent of average weekly insurable earnings to encourage the 'voluntarily' unemployed to seek and accept work more readily. At 66.6 per cent, the income-replacement ratio was judged to constitute a disincentive to work. Both measures – paybacks and reduced benefits – seem inspired by monetarism and show its growing strength in the late 1970s. Bill C-14 also transferred the costs of extended benefits from the government to contributions, increasing the regressive financing of UI. The minister estimated that the amendments introduced by Bill C-14 would reduce the net program cost by $935 million in fiscal 1980–1 (*Hansard*, 9 November 1978: 984). Dingledine (1981: 101) considered that the reduction for 1979–80 was $655 million, with the government's share declining by $675 million and the private sector's rising by $20 million. For 1980–1, the reduction was $935 million, with the government's share declining by $885 million and the private sector's by $50 million (101).

Bill C-3 (1980) further reduced the government's share of total UI costs. Some administrative costs were shifted to contributions, increasing the private sector's share of total costs by $246 million for 1980–1 (Dingledine 1981: 11) and reducing the government's overall contribution to the early 1970s level of around 20 per cent. (See Table 6.2.)

By 1980, erosion of the 1971 act had reached the stage where the government was apparently comfortable with the program's benefit structure and with its own share of costs. Amendments for most of the 1980s did not appreciably tighten the program, even though a number of reports and studies, reviewed later in this chapter, could have rationalized such action. Several bills introduced somewhat progressive reforms, in response to massive unemployment of the early 1980s.

Bill C-3 (1980), however, shifted additional program costs onto the private sector and away from general revenues, although it eased restrictions on part-time workers. According to Bill C-14 (1978), part-time workers had required at least twenty hours of insurable employment per week in order to receive benefits, a restriction particularly discriminatory toward women, who dominated the part-time labour force. The new minister, Lloyd Axworthy, introduced amendments that reduced the eligibility requirement to fifteen hours per week, or one-fifth of maximum insurable earnings.

Axworthy also signalled the government's intention to consider a major overhaul of UI. As a preliminary step, a task force on UI was established. It released its report, *Unemployment Insurance in the 1980s*, in 1981 – the first of several in-depth investigations, discussed below. The general tenor of their analysis and recommendations was to further restrict and tighten the system, but the actual legislation marginally eased the system's operation. For example, Bill C-156 (1983) eased restrictions on eligibility and payment of benefits in the case of maternity applications, as well as extending maternity benefits to adoptive parents. Bill C-116 (1988) liberalized maternity provisions by extending benefits to fathers in special cases and to women in the case of premature births. Bill C-50 (1987) entitled claimants with separation earnings, such as pensions from previous employers, or severance pay, to full benefits. All of these amendments had been suggested by *Unemployment Insurance in the*

1980's; the report's more restrictive recommendations were not implemented. Collectively, these pieces of legislation indicate a hiatus in the legislative retreat from the principles of the 1971 act, even though the reports on UI prepared the ideological groundwork for further assaults.

The growing prominence of the monetarist paradigm and its hostility to the market-blocking effects of UI benefits make the failure further to restrict the system seem surprising. Three factors may render it less so. First, the severity of unemployment in the early 1980s made it politically inopportune to cut off claimants, tighten eligibility further, or reduce benefit levels. Monetarist arguments that all or most unemployment was voluntary were unlikely to be received favourably. Second, legislative changes in the 1970s had secured the government's financial position as a 'junior partner' in UI. The large increase in costs required greater contributions from general revenues, but these did not, as a share of total program costs, or as a percentage of GDP, reach the levels of the mid-1970s (see Table 6.2 and Figure 6.2). Most of the increased costs were borne by the regressive contribution system.

It was argued in earlier chapters that macroeconomic policy pursued a strategy of high unemployment after 1975. Changes to the financing of UI in the late 1970s are consistent with the government's distancing itself from the expenditure effects of this strategy by transferring much of the cost to the regressive special-purpose tax known as UI premiums. Compared with the position in the mid-1970s, therefore, the state's expenditure budget was relatively insulated from the effects of high unemployment.

Third, the growing use of UI funds for 'developmental' purposes may have meant that the system increasingly performed an accumulation service for capital. This argument is considered below. To the extent that it is valid, it may have impeded further restriction of the system for most of the 1980s.

Following the re-election of the Conservative government in 1988, pressure on the UI system once again intensified. On 11 April 1989, Employment Minister Barbara McDougall announced that the government intended to save $1.3 billion annually by making benefits harder to get and to keep. Qualifying periods were to be increased, benefit periods reduced, and penalties for those who quit their jobs voluntarily made heavier. The government claimed that savings would amount to 12 per cent of the total UI budget and that they would be redirected to training and work-experience programs. Public reaction to the legislation, Bill C-21, was sharply divided, with business spokespeople providing support, while labour, anti-poverty, and women's groups were the major sources of opposition.

In June 1989, Finance Minister Michael Wilson announced the government's intention to cease contributing to the UI fund. Savings of $1.9 billion were anticipated in 1990. The shortfall in funds was to be made up by higher premiums, but critics allege that a deficit of $3 billion is to be expected by 1992 (Finn and McBane 1990). If their projections are correct, then further increases in premiums are to be anticipated.

Bill C-21 resumes government's efforts of the 1970s to reduce costs, integrate UI and labour-market programs, and make the system less accessible. As noted above, the policy changes involve the anticipated mixture of increased coercion and attention to accumulation while cutting back on the concerns with legitimation embodied in the 1971 legislation.

Developmental Uses of UI Funds

Bills C-69 (1975) and C-27 (1977) authorized use of UI funds for 'developmental' purposes: job creation, work sharing, and training. Pal (1983) argues that these uses reflected a major shift of emphasis away from welfare goals and toward those of labour-market policy. Developmental use of contributions enabled the CEIC, at a time of fiscal restraint, to fund new programs or substitute them for old ones, thereby reducing unemployment, through work sharing or job creation or, in the case of training, subsidizing the private sector's training costs.

Any use of UI funds, even for income maintenance, is more regressive than use of general revenues for the same purpose. When UI funds were used instead of general revenues for labour-market programs, lower-income groups carried a disproportionately large share of the burden. This reduced the intraclass income-redistribution effect of UI, at a time when the state's labour-market programs demonstrated increased sensitivity to the needs of capital. On the assumption that employers pass on much of the cost of contributions to workers in the form of lower wages and benefits, developmental expenditures in the form of wage subsidies, job-creation grants, tax incentives, and work-sharing benefits contribute to capital accumulation. Training expenditures, if effective, socialize the costs of a trained labour force and thus contribute directly to capital accumulation. Table 6.4 indicates that the bulk of developmental expenditures of UI have been spent on training. Considered as a percentage of total UI costs, the amount spent on training is quite small, ranging from 0.5 to about 4 per cent of total costs. Some $1.7 billion, however, was made available from the account – a significant share of total training costs (Table 6.5).

In April 1989, the government announced a new Labour Force Development Strategy (LFDS) which would extend developmental uses of UI funds. Bill C-21 was expected to realize $1.3 billion in savings, of which $775 million would be appropriated for training purposes. These funds will be administered on the advice of a Labour Force Development Board (LFDB) dominated by business and labour representatives (*Globe and Mail*, 15 January 1991). At the time of writing it remained unclear how the new strategy would work in practice (but see Mahon [1990] for a preliminary view). However, it does seem clear that the LFDS will strengthen the trend to use UI funds for accumulation purposes and that the LFDB bears the hallmarks of a consultative ideological legitimation device.

Ideology, Monetarism, and UI

The argument presented to this point can be summarized as follows. UI, at least as it evolved in Canada, can be considered predominantly a concrete legitimation measure. Its legitimizing effects are enhanced to the extent that it is financed from progressive taxation and minimized by financing from regressive sources. The 1971 UI act completed the edifice of the post-war Canadian welfare state, perhaps going further than its sponsors intended. Almost immediately the provisions of the program began to be curtailed and tightened, as the state's priorities shifted away from concrete legitimation and toward activities and programs that promoted accumulation. This theory, it has been argued, is demonstrated in the more regressive financing of the system; the use of UI funds for developmental, especially training purposes; reductions in benefit levels; and more rigorous qualification criteria. This process has at times involved greater coercion, as indicated by extensive use of disqualifications and heavier penalties for quitting or being dismissed from a previous job.

These changes have been accompanied by an intensified ideological debate. Many monetarist precepts have both been implemented and used to legitimate retrenchment. Incorporation of the monetarist view

TABLE 6.4
Developmental uses ($ million) of the UI account

	Work sharing (section 37)	Job creation (section 38)	Training (section 39)
1977	0.03	–	20.4
1978	1.3	–	107.2
1979	0.2	0.9	140.7
1980	–	0.5	161.6
1981	–	–	172.3
1982	83.2	23.7	211.8
1983	83.1	106.7	230.7
1984	32.4	115.2	227.2
1985	25.2	132.6	234.5
1986	21.7	96	236.9
1987	17	87	224
1988	17	102	238
Total	281.1	664.6	2,205.3
Percentage	9	21	70

SOURCES: Annual reports of CEIC; CEIC, Annual Statistical Bulletin

TABLE 6.5
Share of training costs paid from UI account

	Share from UI account (%)
1977	3.5
1978	16.9
1979	21.0
1980	21.0
1981	20.8
1982	22.9
1983	22.6
1984	20.8
1985	16.4

SOURCES: CEIC, Annual Statistical Bulletin

of UI into a number of state documents in the 1980s signals both the greater influence of that paradigm and its utility for the state in ideologically legitimating its actions. The documentation or textualization of the monetarist orientation seems to lay the basis for further retrenchment, should circumstances make this opportune or necessary from the point of view of the state or business élites.

Many of the arguments against the 1971 UI system found expression in articles by academic economists. The 'work disincentive' literature provided the theoretical underpinnings for numerous regressive amendments in the 1970s. It advanced the general argument that UI offered material incentives that encouraged voluntary unemployment. Three main themes ran through this critique of the program set up in 1971: its relative generosity had increased the measured rate of unemployment, it encouraged prolonged periods of job search, and it had encouraged greater labour-force participation (Green and Cousineau 1975; Maki and Sax 1975a; 1975b; Siedule, Skoulas, and Newton 1976; Rea 1977; Bodkin and Cournoyer 1978; Grubel and Walker 1978a; Lazar 1978).

As early as 1977 the *Comprehensive Review of the Unemployment Insurance Programme in Canada* (UIC 1977) took note of studies that linked the system's generosity to work disincentives and rising unemployment. The review stated: 'All the economic studies share the view that unemployment insurance removes the necessity for some people to stay at work and for the others to return to work quickly' (E9). The review, however, did mention several critical limitations of these studies. Examples included: rigid and artificial assumptions (for example, that unemployment is all voluntary and all leisure), statistical and data problems that 'cast considerable doubt on the reliability of the findings,' and questionable methods which weakened inference (E-10, 12, 19, 20, F-19, 20). In fact, the study examined in most detail (Rea and Jump 1975) prompted the review committee to conclude that 'the combined results from the Rea and Jump studies indicate that the 1971 unemployment insurance programme changes had a negligible net impact on the unemployment rate' (E-17).

In spite of awareness of the studies' major limitations, the review concluded that 'it is undeniable that unemployment insurance contributed to work disincentives ... the greater the income protection provided by the unemployment insurance programme, the greater is the potential disincentive effect' (E-31–2). On the basis of the questionable causal link between the 1971 act and rising unemployment, the review endorsed the regressive legislative amendments and recommended further administrative controls to 'reduce the incentive to claim, increase the incentive to remain at work and to return to work more quickly' (E-34).

Even after having reported that 'U.I.C. administrative statistics on detected misuse do not indicate a concentration of misuse among 8–11 weekers' (E-34), the review urged legislative attention to the 'questionable' rights of claimants deemed to have a minor attachment to the labour force (8–11-weekers) and those with irregular work patterns to UI benefits.

The literature that focused on the supposed work disincentives has been heavily criticized, but such criticism has been ignored by government. The fact that conclusions drawn from the literature have been used to erode the income-maintenance component of UI since 1971 is certainly pertinent to understanding how the government actively employed ideology to justify cutbacks in its concrete legitimation activities. In this case, it has employed the results of academic research in a highly selective manner. It may prove instructive to indicate briefly how criticism of the state-sponsored 'work-disincentive' contradicts the basis of UI policy formation in the mid-1970s.

Ironically, the best source of criticism of the work-disincentive hypothesis is the literature itself.[3] Typically, the studies are self-deprecating and littered with disclaimers regarding unrealistic assumptions and ungeneralizable methods. The architects of the *Comprehensive Review* were aware of these fundamental weaknesses but nevertheless used the studies for policy justifications.

The critique can be divided into two categories: methodological, and policy conclusions. Lazar (1978: 569) attempted a replication of three major studies (two of which were used in the review) which posited a direct relationship between the 1971 act and rising unemployment. Even although his findings were consistent with the studies replicated, he concluded: 'Although the empirical evidence accumulating in Canada tends to confirm the theoretical supposition that the improvements enacted in the Unemployment Insurance Act have raised the unemployment rate and hence, must be considered in the formulation of the targets for macroeconomic policy, it is important to emphasize that the induced changes attributed to the revisions, in this paper and others, may be overstating the adverse impacts because other dramatic changes in the economy have been largely ignored.'

Kaliski (1975) questioned a number of methodological elements in the widely cited study by Grubel et al. (1975a), also used in the review, as well as a number of the policy conclusions derived from those apparently faulty methodological elements. Rea and Jump (1975) noted that once the impact of UI on aggregate demand and hence employment generation was considered (which many state-sponsored studies neglected to do), the unemployment-inducing tendency of UI was largely offset: 'The *net* impact on the measured unemployment rate was to increase it only *marginally*, less than half of one percentage point, a magnitude significantly smaller than the increase in voluntary unemployment mentioned by other studies' (cited in UIC 1977: F-17).[4]

These studies generally posited that increased labour-force participation, prolonged periods of job search, and voluntary unemployment all hurt the labour market by increasing the measured rate of unemployment. But the studies merely assumed that the consequences were negative. The UI act was designed to allow claimants a reasonable period in which to locate employment for which they were best suited. Its architects believed that this helped achieve labour-market efficiency. The *Comprehensive Review* recognized this objective of the UI program: 'To the extent that unemployment insurance fulfills one of its prime objectives of facilitating a more effective job search and preserving skills, some of the effects of increased voluntary unemployment are positive' (UIC 1977: E-31). In spite of arguing that 'this is a priority area for empirical investigation' (E-31), the review proceeded to endorse regressive measures intended to 'reduce the incentive to claim, increase the incentive to remain at work and *to return to work more quickly*' (E-34).

In regard to prolonged job searches induced by UI, Grubel and Walker (1978a: 16) point to the methodological barriers that block any attempt to establish empirically that such a relation is detrimental to labour-market efficiency: 'It is essentially a theoretically open question whether ... the existence of unemployment insurance lowers the average unemployment through increased labour market efficiency or whether it raises the rate through the effect on prolonged job-search.' In other words, extended job searches encouraged by generous UI benefits may reduce unemployment through increasing labour-market efficiency. Grubel and Walker claim (17–19) that UI induces greater unemployment in a number of other ways. In each case, however, 'there exist no reliable methods for establishing the size of the group of people' (17); 'it is impossible to establish the magnitude of the induced unemployment due to increased labour force participation separately from other types of induced unemployment' (18); and 'the magnitude of induced unemployment due to industry mix effects is particularly difficult to measure' (18). This is all rather unsatisfactory. It is also quite typical of the work-disincentive literature as a whole.

None of the empirical or theoretical weaknesses of this literature, however, prevented its use by the state as a rationale for cutting back the generosity of the UI system. In a period when emphasis on accumulation was a major state priority, monetarist analyses were simply too useful to be ignored on such grounds. Incorporation of monetarist arguments in important state documents – the reports of a UI task force (1981), the Macdonald Commission (1985), and the Forget Commission (1986) – served in turn to enhance the prestige of these ideas and, as a result, increase their utility as tools of ideological legitimation.

The task force report *Unemployment Insurance in the 1980s* (1981) echoed earlier arguments on the work-disincentive effects of the UI system (36–9). In addition, however, it highlighted another possible negative effect of UI on the labour market: UI benefits and services, especially those geared specifically to regions of chronic high unemployment, discouraged labour mobility to regions of relatively low unemployment. As a 'corrective' measure, the task force recommended several amendments intended to remove impediments to mobility. Viewed differently, such amendments penalized the unemployed for remaining in their home region and for being unable to find jobs. The recommendations specifically intended to reduce the negative impact on mobility were higher entrance requirements for claimants applying for benefits on the basis of the regional rate of unemployment; shorter benefits, particularly for claimants with briefer job attachments (e.g. seasonally employed); reduction in the spread of benefits available in low- and high-unemployment areas; and ending of the cycle of dependence on UI for people in high-unemployment areas by directing funds toward establishment of long-term jobs (101).

These recommendations encouraging labour mobility reflected growing emphasis on the integration of UI and labour-market policy. Since reliance on monetary policy to fight inflation increases regional variations in unemployment (see Reeves and Kerr 1986), implementation of the recommendations would also have brought this policy into closer alignment with macroeconomic policy.

The task force's lip service paid to the income-redistribution component of UI was undermined by other recommendations, such as further reductions in the portion of costs borne by general revenues. For critics of the task force, like the Social Planning Council of Metropolitan Toronto (1982: 68), such proposals signalled that 'this policy is part of [the government's] general strategy to reduce government spending on social programmes ... [and] ... a reflection of the federal government's abandonment of responsibility for maintaining low levels of unemployment.'

The Royal Commission on the Economic Union and Development Prospects for Canada (Macdonald Commission) released its final report in three volumes in 1985. Many of the monetarist tendencies apparent in the task force's report found further expression in the Macdonald Report. In dealing with increases in measured unemployment throughout the 1970s, the commissioners relied heavily on claims that the 1971 act had unemployment-inducing characteristics. Ignoring literature that questioned the validity of these arguments, the report claimed (vol. 2, 595): 'The 1971 revisions of the Unemployment Insurance Act, which increased the generosity of the unemployment insurance scheme in several respects, are generally considered to have increased unemployment by some 1 to 2 percentage points.' The commission concluded that the 1971 act contributed to an increase in the duration of unemployment; increased the volume of temporary layoffs; reinforced the concentration of temporary and unstable jobs in high-unemployment and low-wage regions; and provided too generous a subsidy to Canadians whose labour-force behaviour was characterized by repeated unstable employment.

The report conceded that such effects had, at least in part, been offset by the restrictive amendments and tighter administration in the late 1970s. But it nevertheless recommended further retrenchment to reduce the benefit rate to 50 per cent of earnings (from 60 per cent [1979]); raise the entrance requirement to 15 to 20 weeks of insured work over the preceding year (from 12 weeks [1979]); tighten the link between the maximum benefit period and the minimum employment period: for example, establish a ratio of two or three weeks of work to qualify for one week of benefits; and eliminate regional differentiation. These changes were intended to 'encourage steadier job attachments, more intensive job search during periods of unemployment, and a higher proportion of job search while employed' (vol. 2, 612) and would reduce the program's cost by some 35 to 40 per cent, or about $4 billion (613).

The commission recommended that these savings 'should be used to facilitate labour-market adjustments through the creation of a Transitional Adjustment Assistance Program' (vol. 2, 613). In effect, the enormous surplus in UI funds that would be created by its recommendations should be directed toward developmental purposes such as wage subsidies and training allowances, thereby substituting revenues from UI payroll deductions for general tax revenues. The commission made it clear (617) that it was not advocating extension of the current developmental uses of UI but rather facilitating 'labour-market adjustments through the creation of a Transitional Adjustment Assistance Programme with the following features: a greater emphasis on industrial training; portable wage-subsidies attached to the TAAP beneficiary (worker) allowing greater programme flexibility and some degree of competitive advantage for older beneficiaries; a greater emphasis on mobility grants; special projects financing; e.g., employee purchase schemes relating to closures; and tie-in financing with unemployment insurance benefits' (616–17).

These proposals would promote market-driven efficiency within the labour market. In referring to the historical tendency of labour to migrate from regions of low wages and/or poor employment prospects to developing regions of relatively high wages and/or more positive employment prospects, the commission argued (vol. 2, 609):

Unemployment insurance can be expected to slow this adjustment process, as it makes location in regions with poor employment prospects relatively more attractive than it would be otherwise. In 1971, the unemployment insurance programme was regionally differentiated: shorter qualification periods and larger benefit entitlements periods were introduced in regions with high unemployment rates. Thus it is likely that the unemployment insurance programme has retarded migration from high unemployment regions even further since 1971.

Finally in 1986, the Commission of Inquiry on Unemployment Insurance (the Forget Commission) advocated a major reform of both the objectives and operation of the UI system. Critical of the apparent inequities and complexities of the current regime, and its conflict with the principles of social insurance, the report recommended that 'the role of Unemployment Insurance would become one of strict income replacement. Income supplementation and other aspects of the current programme would be transferred to programs specially designed for these purposes' (315). Forget suggested that UI had moved well beyond its original objective of providing temporary assistance between jobs. This, however, should be its main purpose:

Unemployment Insurance plays essentially a transitional role, that of partial income replacement for a specific period during an interruption of earnings. It should serve as a lifeline rather than holding them in a pattern of dependence. The many additions to its functions over the years have subverted its essential nature and created unacceptable inequities. This has occurred largely because of the lack of other, more appropriate programs or agencies. Unemployment Insurance should return to its original purpose and other initiatives should now be adopted to assume the functions of income supplementation for low-income families. (307)

The Forget Report was unenthusiastic about developmental use of UI funds. It argued (92), for example, that their use 'for job creation is not appropriate for an insurance program, no matter how worthy or successful a project may be. These projects should be funded directly by the federal government and should be available to all citizens, but not through unemployment insurance and not restricted to recipients of Unemployment Insurance benefits.' The report recommended that section 38 (job creation) of the UI act be rescinded. It generally favoured use of UI funds for work-sharing arrangements during temporary downturns (162) and recommended that provision for work-sharing be retained but that procedures and administrative costs be streamlined.

The report highlighted four apparent problems regarding use of UI funds for training. First, this practice tended to favour some forms of training over others and was therefore discriminatory. Second, benefits that extended beyond the training period to support job search violated the insurance principle of the program. Third, employment training funded through employer/employee premiums violated the insurance principle and the main objective of UI. Fourth, training expenses such as transportation, child care, books, and equipment should not be deducted from benefits, because to do so was to consider these benefits as earnings.

The report came under intense criticism, not least from labour representatives on the commission who issued a ninety-page dissenting minority report (427–516). The dissenters (505) found the report essentially monetarist on unemployment: 'At the root of the Forget's proposal for massive benefit cuts is a general perspective and analysis in which unemployment is seen as predominantly an individual rather than a societal problem. It is this perspective that leads to proposals to penalize those who are chronically or seasonally unemployed and to eliminate regional benefits. In its stark form, the argument is that chronic, seasonal and regional unemployment are all the fault of the individual who is unemployed.'

Strong opposition from at least four sources led the government initially to decline the opportunity to act on Forget's recommendations. According to Pal (1988: 11): 'Any revision to unemployment insurance, especially one as radical as Forget's, engenders tremendous counter-pressures from affected provinces, regions, unions, employers, and social advocacy groups. Unemployment insurance is by now so deeply and widely embedded in the Canadian political economy that fundamental change would seem virtually impossible.'

Although Pal is correct to point to the powerful coalition of class and other interests that rallied to the defence of UI, he may have underestimated the power of business. Business pressure against the 1971 legislation has been unremitting, and the long series of restrictions chronicled earlier in the chapter bears testimony to the state's adoption of the business agenda. The introduction of Bill C-21 in 1989 showed that the incremental assault on Canada's UI system was far from over.

Summary

In 1971, in the final stages of the Keynesian era, a relatively generous UI scheme was enacted. The act can best be understood as a concrete legitimation initiative by the state. In the years that followed, the UI program was subjected to incremental changes which reduced its generosity, accompanied by episodic increases in coercion toward claimants and by significant efforts to legitimate ideologically further program reductions. To date, however, sufficient support has existed for the system to prevent its emasculation. Debate about the program may be cast in monetarist terms. But the persistence of UI shows that the Keynesian era lives on, truncated and threatened, but testimony to the failure of ideology entirely to undermine concrete legitimation benefits, once conferred.

In the balance of class forces, labour and associated interests have been powerful enough to prevent the complete destruction of the UI system. This in no way, however, obscures the general direction of change throughout the 1970s and 1980s. Business's ultimate agenda regarding UI may not have been implemented at a stroke and, indeed, may be far from completion. But the state's actions over most of the past twenty years have significantly addressed business's concerns and testify to business's growing influence over state policy. Labour's victories on these issues have been very much defensive exercises in damage limitation.

7 The State and Industrial Relations

The state's direct involvement in regulating the relation between labour and capital has its origins in labour's resistance to the unrestricted right of capital to manage its work-force. From the point of view of capital, a 'labour problem' came into existence. Pentland (1968: 2) characterized this problem as consisting of 'how to make other people work effectively while turning over a good part of the fruits of their labour to the elite.' In conflicts that arose between labour and capital, each side sought to make use of the state to bolster its own position. In capital's case, such assistance would be additional to the legal structure which defended the rights of property in general. The conflict between capital and labour drew the state into such matters as regulation of their relationship, specification of certain standards pertaining to the work process, and, through its monopoly of legally sanctioned coercion, arbitration of last resort. This chapter deals with these aspects of state policy under the general category of industrial relations policy.

The typology of activities used elsewhere in the book also provides a useful framework within which to analyse the development of industrial relations policy: 'Under the rubric of accumulation, labour constitutes an indispensable factor of production with whose general availability, quality, discipline, and price the state may have to concern itself in the service of economic efficiency and growth. But the "labour problem" is a problem of legitimation insofar as class conflict threatens the justificatory foundations of the liberal state in equity and community' (Craven 1980: 160).

Analysis of the interplay of these state activities can be divided into three areas: policies relating to the work process and environment; regulation of the interaction between labour and capital; and the imposition of outcomes on the labour-capital interaction, either through coercively ending disputes, or through wage policies, which substitute a legislated for a negotiated settlement. The historical stages in the evolution of state activity in this policy area correspond to the dominance of particular economic paradigms: the pre-Keynesian era, prior to 1944; 1944 through the late 1960s, when Keynesian economic ideas, including those about the proper role of unions and collective bargaining, were prevalent; and from the early 1970s to the present, with post-Keynesian and monetarist conceptions of the economy and corresponding changes in attitudes toward unions and collective bargaining, the end of the postwar boom, and the return of economic crisis and instability.

Early Industrial Relations Policy

Policies addressing such issues as the terms, conditions, and environment of work provide early examples of the state responding to labour pressures in ways that legitimated the economic and political systems. State actions typically involved restriction of employers' rights, usually by establishing minimum standards. Quite a broad range of policies and legislation fall into this category: regulations governing minimum wages, legislation on permissible hours of work, provision for vacations with pay and statutory holidays, health and safety protection, laws prohibiting discrimination against female and minority workers, employment security provisions encompassing notice of dismissal and severance pay, and provision for recovery of wages from employers (Crispo 1978: 782–5).

Introduction of such legislative protection for the labour force was a response to the 'flagrant degrading and dehumanizing' treatment of employees in the period prior to the emergence of a labour movement (Crispo 1978: 281; Manga, Bruyles, and Reschenthaler 1981: 117–18).[1] Consciousness of such conditions was fostered by embryonic labour organizations in Canada, especially among skilled workers, and by the example of European states' responses to working-class organization. In contrast to regulation of labour-capital bargaining and confrontation, in which the federal government has played the leading role, the jurisdiction and the initiative with labour standards rested at the provincial level (Baggaley 1981: 45). The most industrialized province, Ontario, led the way, with the first Factory Act (1884), Employers' Liability Act (1886), Workmen's Compensation Scheme (1914), and establishment of a division of industrial hygiene (1920) (Manga, Bruyles, and Reschenthaler: chapter 7). British Columbia was first to set a minimum wage (1918), a measure adopted swiftly by most other provinces, although implementation was sometimes postponed or confined only to women workers, or to urban workers in the case of the prairie provinces. Such legislation usually promised more than it delivered. The inspectorates appointed to administer the Factory Act were staffed inadequately (Baggaley 1981: 19–20), the wording of the legislation was often vague, and the onus of proof was placed on the worker (Manga, Bruyles, and Reschenthaler 121). Considerations of capital accumulation were certainly present in the design of this type of legislation (see Piva 1975: 37–56; Guest 1980: chapter 4). Similarly, the priority given to occupational health and safety tended to be a function of labour shortages. Whenever labour became a scarce and valuable factor of production, as in wartime, federal-government contracts contained clauses which required 'the employer to maintain a safe and healthful workplace' (Manga, Bruyles, and Reschenthaler 121). As labour became more plentiful, this concern slackened.

In general, though, legislation and policy on employment standards can be regarded as part of the state's legitimation activities. Concerns for sweated female and child labour and about overcrowded and unsafe factories tended to merge with concerns over other threats to 'the fabric of society,' such as intemperance and deserted wives and children. Labour legislation of the type discussed above, like efforts to stamp out such social ills, 'was an attempt to protect the social order' (Baggaley 1981: 23). Rather inadequate enforcement mechanisms highlight their cosmetic nature.

On the initiative of the federal government, an authentically Canadian system of industrial relations was developed which emphasized conciliation and prevention of industrial disputes. Side by side with this system of legislation went fairly widespread use of state coercion against recalcitrant workers (cf. Jamieson 1968). Most observers have focused on the coercive aspects of state policy in this period. Bob Russell (1987), however, has shown how the legislative system of industrial relations did perform a legitimation role. This was built on in the industrial relations system established as part of the post–Second World War 'settlement.'

The development of a legislatively defined system began with the Trade Unions Act (1872), which released unions from the threat of prosecution for criminal conspiracy. Subsequent legislation in 1875–6 legalized peaceful picketing. Though clearly an advance for the unions, this type of legislation did nothing to compel recognition of unions by employers and left such questions to be determined by the rather asymmetrical power relations of the market (Woods 1973: 39–42).[2]

Legislative attempts to provide for voluntary conciliation of worker-employer disputes can be identified in some provinces as early as the 1870s. These efforts, apparently inspired by similar legislation in Australia, seem to have had little success and were soon repealed (Smucker 1980: 242). Construction of a voluntary conciliation system, with some elements of compulsion, really began early in the twentieth century with a series of dominion enactments.[3] The essence of the new approach (Woods 1973: 56–64) was state intervention, at the request of either party, in an actual or anticipated industrial dispute. Once intervention was requested, a compulsory investigation of the dispute occurred during which suspensions of work were prohibited. The findings of a conciliation board were not binding on the parties, though there was provision for moral suasion through publication of the board's findings. By this means it was assumed the force of public opinion could be brought to bear on the parties.

Although a 1925 judicial decision[4] allocated the bulk of the jurisdiction over industrial relations to the provinces, all provinces except Prince Edward Island passed legislation enabling the dominion's Industrial Disputes Investigation Act (IDIA) to apply to them. Consequently the IDIA approach constituted Canadian policy toward industrial disputes between 1907 and 1944. The act did little to address the problem of employers' refusal to recognize and negotiate with unions which bedevilled Canada's fragile and fragmented labour movement in these years. Employers were compelled to participate with unions during investigation of a dispute, but this 'recognition' could prove merely tacit and temporary. The ban on work stoppages during an investigation also hindered the exercise of labour's maximum sanction.

The full-employment conditions of the Second World War, and the labour militancy associated with it, enabled Canada's trade unions to extract a modicum of state support in establishing an ongoing bargaining relationship with employers (MacDowell 1978). Growing acceptance of the Keynesian paradigm, which saw in unions a partial mechanism for sustaining levels of aggregate demand, helped to rationalize the state's concessions to the increased strength of organized labour. The initial response came in 1944 through a dominion order-in-council (PC 1003)[5] and will be dealt with below.

In addition to these types of state activity, there were a number of initiatives designed to determine the outcome of conflict between labour and capital. These included direct repression of industrial conflict, wage controls, and ad hoc emergency back-to-work legislation.

The coercive apparatus of the Canadian state affected the outcomes of labour-capital conflict. In addition to such dramatic events as the 1919 Winnipeg General Strike (see Masters 1956), repressive policies were widely used against radical and militant workers' organizations, often accompanied by a more conciliatory policy toward skilled workers and more moderate labour organizations (Cuneo 1980: 48–9). The Royal Canadian Mounted Police and its predecessors performed, among other duties, a labour-control function (Brown and Brown 1978). The legislation and common law which the RCMP and other police forces in Canada have enforced has been described as going 'to great lengths to protect employers' property and freedom to use their property pretty much as they saw fit, while providing little or no protection of workers' freedom to protect their jobs and livelihoods' (Jamieson 1968: 471–2).

Wage controls are classified as one of the state's accumulation activities, since their purpose and, if successful, their effect are to weaken labour's bargaining position and to freeze or, more likely, reduce the share of wages in the national income (Miliband 1969: 81; Nuti 1972: 433–8). The greatest significance of wage controls as an element of labour policy came after the onset of economic crisis in the 1970s. In that period, post-Keynesian economic theory recommended this policy instrument as a key tool in the fight against inflation. The issue was also present in this earlier period, however, largely as an ad hoc response to wartime inflationary pressures. Canada's entry into the Second World War resulted in unprecedented state intervention into the economy, including regulation of wages (see Woods and Kumar 1976). After tentatively agreeing to wage controls in the first years of the war, organized labour became increasingly hostile to them, because of early recognition that tying wage increases to rises in the cost of living would 'chain labour forever to its present inadequate share in the wealth of the country' (local trade union resolution, cited in Logan 1948: 529); the policy's failure to cover low-wage industries; the policy's detrimental effects on collective bargaining; and the discrepancies in the sacrifices demanded of labour and business (MacDowell 1978: 13). There was concern as well about labour's lack of input into government decisions, especially those affecting workers. With removal of wage controls in November 1946, however, the issue faded until the late 1960s.

Canada's wartime experience with wage controls illustrates the tensions that may exist between accumulation and legitimation aspects of labour policy. Dissatisfaction with wage controls helped to fuel labour's demands for reforms in collective bargaining. The 1944 reforms which Prime Minister King felt it politic to concede were in part the result of this inherent contradiction between different aspects of labour policy.

Keynesian-Era Industrial Relations Policy

In work process, the period was characterized by incremental adjustments to the range and level of employment standards in such well-established fields as minimum wages, vacations, maternity leave, severance pay, and unjust dismissal. The next major initiatives were to come in the 1970s and are dealt with in the next section.

The Keynesian era commenced with PC 1003, establishing a new legislative environment for industrial relations which is often regarded as an imitation of the US Wagner Act. Aspects of the Wagner Act's approach to labour-capital relations were certainly mirrored in the Canadian legislation, including acceptance of trade unionism and collective bargaining as a right (provided there was evidence of a certain level of worker support) and establishment of enforcement machinery (Woods 1973: 64–70, 86–92). But Canada's post-war legislation also contained provisions for compulsory conciliation and mediation before strikes could occur, banned strikes during the duration of collective agreements, and otherwise restricted the way unions could operate.

Growing acceptance of Keynesian theories helped reconcile Canada's political and economic establishments to an enhanced role for trade unions: unions could assist in sustaining levels of aggregate demand. But unprecedented working-class pressure, both industrial and political, produced the concessions represented in the 1944 order-in-council and in post-war legislation (cf. Panitch and Swartz 1988: 18–20). Cold War coercion against radical unions and unionists also played a role in ushering in the new system.

The legal framework that did emerge was not an unqualified victory for labour, a possible indication that élite commitment to Keynesianism was to be highly qualified. The new industrial relations system contained elaborate certification procedures, legally enforceable contracts, no-strike provisions for the duration of contracts,[6] and liability of trade unions and their members if illegal strikes occurred. The legislation did, however, guarantee the right to organize and to bargain collectively, forced employers to recognize unions once certain conditions were met, defined unfair labour practices, and provided remedies under the law for violations.

Although the balance of class power had shifted in labour's favour during the war, unions had still lacked sufficient power to force employers into recognition and bargaining unassisted by the state. Pressure on the state to help establish a bargaining relationship ultimately had proved successful. But the price for this assistance was extensive state regulation and continuation of compulsory conciliation and 'work stoppage delay' (McBride 1983: 508–9). The restrictions curtailed severely labour's right to strike (Woods 1973: 93).[7]

Legislative concessions to labour took place in a context of developing international Cold War between the United States and its allies on the one hand and the Soviet Union on the other. These developments strongly affected Canadian labour. A number of processes which can be considered part of the tacit post-war settlement were reinforced by the Cold War milieu.

First, Canada's social democratic party, the Co-operative Commonwealth Federation (CCF), underwent a process of ideological moderation. The radical overtones of the Regina Manifesto, with its promise to eradicate capitalism, were gradually replaced by acceptance of Keynesianism and ideological convergence with the established political parties (Zakuta 1964; Cross 1974).

Second, CCF activists within the trade unions waged a truly ferocious battle against communist and other radical rivals for leadership of the labour movement. These efforts were assisted by the violent anti-communism of the post-war years. It is clear, too, that the social democrats received extensive assistance from the political authorities in both Canada and the United States (Lang, n.d.; Abella 1973; Green 1986; Lembcke and Tattam 1984). Ultimately their efforts were largely successful. Most unions under radical leadership were either taken over, expelled from membership in trade union federations, or destroyed. Accompanying greater tolerance of trade unions based on Keynesian ideas, then, was coercive restructuring of the union movement. The end result was that the Keynesian era was able to proceed with ideologically acceptable and, on social and political issues, rather docile trade unions.

With the expiry of the War Measures Act in 1945, labour relations returned largely to provincial jurisdiction (although emergency powers legislation remained in force until 1954). Despite this, a Canada-wide system of collective bargaining continued to exist because most provinces adopted legislation patterned after PC 1003. Saskatchewan, under a CCF government, deviated in the direction of less restriction: public servants were granted the same right to trade unionism as other workers, and there were no compulsory conciliation procedures. In general, however, any deviations from the pattern were in the direction of greater restrictiveness (Pentland 1968: 327–35); examples included restrictions on picketing, secondary boycotts, and sympathy strikes in Alberta, British Columbia, and Newfoundland; prohibition of strikes in essential services in Alberta; government supervision of strike votes in British Columbia and Manitoba; regulation of the internal affairs of trade unions in British Columbia, Newfoundland, Ontario; limits on the ability of unions to provide funds for political parties in British Columbia, Newfoundland, and Prince Edward Island; and decertification of allegedly communist-led unions in Quebec. In general, however, the basic pattern of PC 1003 – a mixture of the IDIA and Wagner approaches – was established.

A noticeable change came with development of special provisions for public-sector collective bargaining in the 1960s and early 1970s. Saskatchewan's Trade Union Act (1944) had treated public servants and other public-sector workers the same as private-sector workers. Except in that province, no public servants enjoyed collective bargaining rights until 1964 (Crispo 1978: 57–60). A decade later, public-service employees in all jurisdictions enjoyed some form of bargaining rights.[8] The principal variations centred around the extent to which public servants received the right to strike, the scope of collective bargaining, and differential treatment of public-sector workers. Workers in the federal public service and provincial employees in British Columbia, New Brunswick, Newfoundland,[9] Quebec, and Saskatchewan enjoyed the right to strike. Excepting Alberta, Ontario, and Prince Edward Island, this right applied also to public-agency workers. The scope of bargaining rights was generally narrower for public servants than for private-sector workers, though there was considerable variation among jurisdictions (Gauvin, Marchand, and McKerral 1975: 62–87).

Growing differences in policy toward public-service labour relations have tended to undermine the Canada-wide industrial relations system developed after the war. Creation of special legislative frameworks to deal with particular segments of the labour force has been termed a 'redirection of public policy' (Woods 1973: 19). Groups generally excluded from collective bargaining include agricultural workers, domestic servants, and managerial employees with access to confidential information (Crispo 1978: 40–2). Those increasingly covered by special legislation include, in addition to public servants and public-agency employees, construction workers, firefighters, health-care workers, police, and teachers (Gauvin, Marchand, and McKerral 1976).

The economic crisis of the 1970s and the displacement of Keynesianism first by post-Keynesianism and later by monetarism were reflected in attacks on the collective bargaining rights of unions generally, and of public-sector unions in particular. The 'post-war consensus' had perhaps been especially fragile concerning the rights of unions which, however moderate, represent a challenge to the rights of property owners. These developments are, however, best left to the next section.

In the late 1960s, the first tentative moves were made toward controlling wages. In 1969, Ottawa established a Prices and Incomes Commission which, for the next several years, advocated introduction of voluntary prices and incomes restraint (Berger 1973; Hawthorne 1973). The federal government's interest in incomes policy came at a time when greater militancy on the part of organized labour, in conditions of relatively full employment, was increasing its share of the national income (Wolfe 1977: 260–3). For the government, already influenced by post-Keynesian ideas, incomes policy might limit wage costs without the anticipated high economic, social, and electoral costs of allowing unemployment to rise. Despite labour opposition, the Prices and Incomes Commission was encouraged by business and government to continue its work. In 1970 it terminated its activities because of the 'tensions [which] developed in the relations between [it and] the organized labour movements' (Berger 1973: 15). Its failure took the issue off the political agenda for several years. It was to return with a vengeance in the later 1970s and early 1980s.

The other way of regulating the outcomes of labour-capital interaction – emergency back-to-work legislation – also mushroomed during the 1970s and 1980s. Even in the late 1960s, however, this type of legislation was becoming more common. Greater use of this policy instrument (Table 7.1), by both federal and provincial governments coincided with extension of collective bargaining to public-sector workers and, particularly in the later period, with deepening economic crisis and the perception, common to both post-Keynesian and monetarist paradigms, that trade unions bore major responsibility for the economic ills afflicting the country.

TABLE 7.1
Back-to-work legislation, 1950–69

	Federal	Provincial	Total
1950–4	1	–	1
1955–9	1	1	2
1960–4	2	1	3
1965–9	2	8	10

SOURCE: Royal Commission on the Economic Union and Development Prospects for Canada (1985) (Macdonald Report), vol. 2, 680

The 1970s and 1980s: Economic Crisis and New Paradigms

The economic crisis that began in the mid-1970s has been accompanied by a variety of labour-policy initiatives. One of the state's direct responses has been to determine the outcome of labour-capital and labour-state conflicts by wage controls. On one occasion, 1975–8, it applied them generally; on the other, from 1982, only to public-sector workers. The first attempt could be rationalized in terms of post-Keynesian theory and was presented as an anti-inflation measure. The second had effects that met monetarist concern to control the deficit and restrain government spending, although 'pure' monetarists would frown on the method. In addition to imposing wage controls, federal and provincial governments have made extensive use of back-to-work legislation.

These actions have tended to create a legitimacy problem in the state's relations with organized labour. Given the unpopularity of trade unions in Canada, a perception that governments have played on and helped to create, the antagonistic relation between state and labour might contribute to a broader legitimacy which the state may enjoy with some other sectors of the public. But there has also been some attempt, at both federal and provincial levels, to restore its legitimacy with labour through other policy initiatives. Two of these deserve particular mention: improvements in work process, and creation of consultative mechanisms designed to increase labour's participation and voice in economic policy. Despite being somewhat undermined by its own wage control and emergency legislation, and by similar actions on the part of the provincial governments, the legitimacy initiatives have had some success.

The legislative framework for labour-capital interaction remains recognizable as the system in place from the 1940s to the end of the 1960s.

But it is under assault in a number of provinces, most notably British Columbia. And it has been undermined in all jurisdictions by regulation of the outcomes of a 'free' bargaining process. Panitch and Swartz (1985) dubbed this regular suspension of the system 'permanent exceptionalism.'[10] We turn first, however, to attempts to regulate the outcomes of collective bargaining.

Though it was billed as the Anti-Inflation Programme, virtually all the actors connected with the decision viewed the federal government's measures of 14 October 1975 as wage control (Maslove and Swimmer 1980: 11). The program covered federal and crown corporation employees, public-sector workers in participating provinces,[11] workers in larger private-sector firms, and professionals. Allowable wage increases varied according to a complex formula which permitted exceptions on certain grounds. In general, the program permitted increases in its first year in the 8–12 per cent range. In the subsequent two years, permissible rises were progressively reduced. From 1975 to 1978, then, the incomes of most Canadian workers were controlled and their collective bargaining was correspondingly curtailed.

A second round of wage controls, from 1982 onward, was aimed specifically at the public sector. In February 1982, a federal-provincial conference on the issue had failed to reach agreement. But in June of the same year Ottawa announced a two-year wage-control policy, under which federal employees would be limited to 6 per cent in the first year and 5 per cent in the second. Two provinces had already taken their own initiatives: Alberta had imposed guidelines in January, and in February British Columbia had imposed a 10 per cent limit on public-sector wage increases for two years. Within a year the other provinces and territories had adopted some form of wage restraint for public-sector workers. In some cases, such as British Columbia, the legislation was renewed and extended well beyond the period covered by federal law.

While categories of public-sector employees covered by restraint varied, along with the wage limits to which they were subject, these policies severely undermined the already circumscribed collective bargaining rights achieved by these workers in the 1960s and early 1970s. Except in the 1975–8 period, and despite occasional exhortations to voluntary restraint, governments seemed content to allow rising unemployment to take care of wage bargaining in the private sector.

But some categories of private-sector workers, along with many in the public sector, continued to be affected by the second major type of intervention in collective bargaining – use of ad hoc emergency legislation to end disputes. Table 7.2 documents the increased incidence of this type of legislation in the 1970s and 1980s, and Table 7.3 describes this legislation more fully in the period 1975–83. Provincial employees are clearly the most likely to be affected. In effect, the frequent resort to emergency legislation represents a retreat from the earlier extension of collective bargaining rights to these groups.

The contradiction between this type of state intervention and winning legitimacy for the system was explicitly acknowledged in 1983, by André Ouellet, minister of labour, in his remarks to the Macdonald Commission:

Governments in Canada have been intervening, perhaps too often, to terminate labour disputes and impose settlements by *ad hoc* legislation. Governments have, of course, felt obliged to intervene in these cases, but what has perhaps been overlooked in this incremental process is the long-term effect on the labour relations system and the role it is meant to play. The frequency and predictability of government interventions in both strikes and wage settlements may have created a contradiction. On the one hand, the political process has sanctioned a wage determination system that is based on free collective bargaining which guarantees the right to strike. On the other hand, *ad hoc* measures have been taken that may have paralyzed the system and removed various rights essential to its smooth functioning. That system is our principal method of determining wage differentials and working conditions ... The threat of economic sanction makes it work. Without that threat, the whole system would have to be redesigned. (Ouellet 1983: 4–5)

Despite these warnings, the spate of emergency legislation continued unabated and was paralleled by considerable activity to redefine the rules under which labour and employers' organizations interact.

In the years since 1970, the rather untidy, varied, and partial extension of collective bargaining rights to public-sector workers has continued to undergo a process of definition. In the early 1970s, bargaining rights were extended in some areas, but since then the general trend has been toward restriction. In addition to imposing wage controls and ad hoc emergency legislation, some provinces have sought roll back collective bargaining rights and union security, and not only – though most visibly – in that sector. In a detailed examination of measures enacted between June 1982 and December 1987, Panitch and Swartz (1988: Appendix II) classify the legislation as 'restrictive (temporary),' 'restrictive (per-

TABLE 7.2
Back-to-work legislation, 1960–84

	Federal	Provincial	Total
1960–4	2	1	3
1965–9	2	8	10
1970–4	4	9	13
1975–9	6	16	22
1980–4	1	18	19

SOURCE: Macdonald Report, vol. 2, 680

TABLE 7.3
Back-to-work legislation, 1975–83

	Public sector	Private sector	Total
Federal	2	4	6
Provincial			
Quebec	11	0	11
Ontario	7	0	7
British Columbia	3	1	4
Other	5	1	6
Total	28	6	34

SOURCES: Labour Canada, *Legislative Review*, No. 1–16

manent),' and 'reform' (Table 7.4). Clearly the overall picture, at least for this period, is one of restrictiveness.

Not all of the action has taken the form of legislation. Since entrenchment in 1982 of the Charter of Rights and Freedoms within the Canadian constitution, the judiciary has increasingly been called upon to pronounce on industrial-relations matters (see Panitch and Swartz 1988: chapter 4). At issue has been the constitutional validity of legislative limits on the right to strike and to bargain collectively. The Supreme Court of Canada has ruled (57–8) that freedom of association under the Charter of Rights does not include either the right to bargain collectively or the right to strike. Legislation limiting or abrogating these rights is, therefore, constitutional.

In the 1980s, the federal government moved to undermine the right to strike of its public servants by increasing the number of jobs designated 'essential to the safety and security' of the public. Swimmer (1987)

TABLE 7.4
Labour legislation, June 1982 to December 1987

| | Restrictive | | Reform |
	Temporary	Permanent	
Federal	3	1	1
Provinces and			
territories	10	31	15
Total	13	32	16

SOURCE: Panitch and Swartz (1988: Appendix II)

notes that a 1982 Supreme Court decision gave the Treasury Board a virtually free hand in determining which jobs could be designated essential. Beginning in 1986–7, the Mulroney government augmented this approach with a strategy of confrontation with unions in federal crown corporations. Demands for concessions were backed by the use of scab labour and prompt resort to back-to-work legislation which contained increasingly draconian penalties for violators (Panitch and Swartz 1988: 70–7). Such trends were also characteristic of many provinces.

Acting in the name of fiscal restraint, British Columbia's government in July 1983 introduced a package of more than thirty bills, several of which had a major impact on public-sector labour relations. Among the provisions were some permitting the government to alter or abrogate existing contractual provisions in staff contracts; elimination of job security, including that based on seniority; and indefinite extension of wage controls. Most of this package became law, and the government seemed well on schedule to drastically reduce the size of the public sector and the rights of those employed within it. A massive protest movement and a two-week strike in November 1983 produced a partial victory[12] for government employees: they won exemption from the lay-off provisions of the Public Sector Restraint Act. This protected provisions mandating layoff by seniority which were part of the existing collective agreement.

In 1983, the province's Employment Standards Amendment Act reduced employment protection for both unionized and non-unionized workers, and in 1984, amendments to the provincial Labour Code declared political strikes to be illegal, made union certification more difficult and decertification easier, gave the cabinet extensive powers to declare particular projects essential services or economic development projects which would make strikes in them illegal, further restricted secondary picketing, and forced union workers to work alongside non-union workers on union sites (Annis 1987: 138).

In April 1987, further sweeping changes were introduced to British Columbia's labour legislation. The Industrial Relations Reform Act (Bill 19) and the Teaching Profession Act (Bill 20) had the stated purpose of ending 'confrontation between labour, management and government, to promote industrial peace and to encourage investment in British Columbia by repairing the province's reputation for strikes and lockouts' (Smith and Dobuzinskis 1987: 20–3). Bill 19 replaced the Labour Relations Board and mediation services by an Industrial Council headed by a powerful commissioner, weakened union shops and allowed circumvention of union hiring halls, eased conditions under which unionized companies could set up non-union firms, outlawed secondary picketing, increased opportunities for individuals to opt out of unions and to have unions decertified, and forced unions to hold votes on company's 'final offers.' Bill 20 extended collective bargaining rights to teachers but, in effect, forced the British Columbia Teachers Federation to sign up its own members by 1 January 1988 or cease to exist; created compulsory professional bodies, parallel to the union, to deal with teachers' professional interests; removed principals and vice-principals from membership of the union; and created a district structure for union membership. Districts might opt, instead of for the union, for local associations outside the framework of the act.

Given the earlier offensive against collective bargaining rights, these laws amounted to a radical restructuring effort to weaken labour (see Shields 1991). Some employers thought the legislation too crude and the level of labour opposition to it sufficiently worrying that they began tacitly co-operating with a B.C. Federation of Labour boycott of its procedures. James Matkin, president of the Business Council of British Columbia, commented: 'We are now seeing the use of less laws, in fact no law at all ... You don't need a lawyer if you don't go to the Industrial Relations Council. Its a funny formula for improving labour relations – draft a law that's ignored ... [there is] general lack of respect for the labour bill. Unions can get away with ignoring the law if an employer doesn't file a complaint' (*Globe and Mail*, 30 May 1988). Employers' reaction seems here to be influenced by the acts' threat to legitimacy. Nevertheless, the legislation remains on the books, available for use should these fears decline and circumstances permit.

In Alberta, a series of restrictive measures was introduced to an already tight industrial-relations system. In 1983, the Labour Statutes Amendment Act banned strikes by nurses and hospital workers and substituted compulsory arbitration which had to take into account such factors as ability to pay, government guidelines, and general fiscal policy. In effect, it was an ill-disguised formula for allowing the state to impose collective agreements in the health-care sector. Later the same year, Alberta passed legislation allowing unionized construction companies to set up non-union subsidiaries with relative ease. The situation in the construction industry has, however, been clouded by a series of contradictory judicial decisions (Panitch and Swartz 1985: 54–5).

This approach did not produce 'labour peace.' The well-publicized Gainers strike in 1986 was followed in the winter of 1988 by a prolonged illegal strike by Alberta nurses. In response to both disputes, the government signalled legislative changes. The initial response to the Gainers dispute came in the form of Bill 60 to amend the province's labour code (see Fricker 1988). The contents of the bill, however, hardly indicated a change of direction as far as restrictiveness. In a response to the proposals, the Alberta Federation of Labour (1988) charged that creation of compulsory consultative procedures and work councils, bans on support pickets, easing exemptions for payment of union dues, and enabling scabs and past employees to vote in union certification drives were all intended to weaken trade unions' rights. Other provisions imposed major restrictions on unions' ability to time strike activity and would enable determined employers to delay strike action for up to five months after commencement of bargaining. Noting references in the legislation to a 'competitive world market,' the federation alleged that this implied a willingness to reduce Alberta's legislative and employment conditions to the level of competitors such as South Korea and Taiwan. Bill 60 was subsequently divided into two: Bill 21, dealing with Employment Standards, and Bill 22, dealing with Labour Relations. While some changes were made in response to public submissions, the basic principles remained unchanged.

Other examples of major restrictive measures by provinces include the so-called Michelin Bill enacted by Nova Scotia in 1979. Passed at the behest of the Michelin Tire Co., the legislation provided that where a manufacturer's operations are situated at two or more locations in the province, and where at the employer's request the Labour Relations Board rules that the plants are interdependent, then all employees at all locations constitute the bargaining unit. The effect was to make it much more difficult to organize any Michelin employees.

Quebec, too, provides several examples of the tougher legislative environment for labour (see Tanguay 1986). In 1982, legislation imposed temporary wage reductions of up to 20 per cent and longer-term wage restraint, rewrote public-sector collective agreements' provisions regarding job security and working conditions, and effectively banned strikes until 1985. Subsequent legislation in 1983 authorized draconian penalties unless an illegal walkout ended immediately and set aside operation of the Charter of Rights and Quebec's own human rights charter. In 1984, construction workers had their working conditions imposed by decree, in effect losing their right to strike. In 1985, the right to strike was severely curtailed for hospital workers and somewhat restricted for other public servants, and in 1987, emergency legislation to prevent a planned series of health-sector strikes included the now-familiar threats – heavy fines, loss of seniority, and suspension of collection of union dues – for non-compliance.

Elsewhere there are examples of measures to grant employers greater latitude in opposing unionization drives (Manitoba in 1976, Saskatchewan in 1983), increasing the majorities necessary for certification or strike votes (Manitoba in 1976, Alberta in 1981, Saskatchewan in 1981), or clarifying the status of unions as entities capable of being sued (Newfoundland in 1977, Saskatchewan in 1983).

Some legislative changes were more favourable to labour: check-off of union dues on demand (Quebec in 1975, Alberta in 1977, Ontario in 1980), prohibition of use of professional strikebreakers (Quebec in 1977, Ontario in 1983), and legislation to impose first contracts and thus overcome employers' resistance (Ontario in 1985). In Manitoba, amendments to the Labour Relations Act in 1984 strengthened the role of the tripartite Labour Board, eased restrictions on union certification, and improved procedures for grievance arbitration. Subsequent legislation, endorsed by the Manitoba Federation of Labour, introduced – as a possible alternative to strikes – procedures for arbitration that involved selection between the final offers of each party. The procedures could be invoked by the union unilaterally, but by management only if the union consented.[13]

Such reforms, however, are rare compared to the volume of restrictive legislation. The overall direction of change has been away from concerns with legitimation and quite markedly toward emphasis on capital accumulation through coercion. While a comprehensive analysis of the impact of the Canada–United States Free Trade Agreement is still premature, Canadian trade unions predict increased restrictive pressure on labour laws because, despite the legislative changes of the 1970s and 1980s, Canadian legislation on industrial relations still provides a more favourable environment for unions than the equivalent acts in the United States.

American labour law makes organizing more difficult than in Canada, prohibits almost all public-sector employees from striking, and provides little employment standards protection. Twenty states, mostly in the south and midwest, have 'right-to-work' laws, which typically permit workers in unionized plants to opt out of union membership and payment of dues. In such states, minimum-wage legislation tends either to be non-existent or to set very low rates. Under free trade, the unions believe, Canadian firms are likely to argue that they will be unable to compete with low-wage competition from the 'right-to-work' states, where union density ranges from 6 per cent to 22 per cent of the work-force. The legislative assault on Canadian labour has so far had much less impact on its ability to organize and operate than has been the case in the United States (see Bob Russell 1991). The favoured remedy, the unions anticipate, is likely to be pressure to bring Canadian industrial-relations legislation into line with American (Lynk 1988a, 1988b). The trend toward state support for accumulation would then only intensify.

Side by side with such assaults on labour's rights, however, a number of initiatives – on consultative mechanisms, work standards, and employment equity – somewhat reassured labour and furthered the legitimacy of the system. One example consists of attempts to create new forums for tripartite or bilateral consultation. Waldie (1986) has traced early labour-government co-operation in Canada – episodic and generally linked either to gaining labour's co-operation for reconstruction after a war or to obtaining wage restraint during one. Labour's participation in consultation was accompanied generally by a suspicion that it was being entangled or co-opted into the formation of a consensus over which it would have little influence.

Motivated by a perception of crisis in Canadian industrial relations and by the search for a role for itself, the federal Department of Labour had begun, in the period prior to wage controls, to canvass creation of new legitimation mechanisms to promote a more consensual labour-capital relationship. These activities were paralleled by similar moves in some provinces (Fournier 1986: 303–11; see also Yates 1990). At the federal level, an early manifestation was the creation, in early 1975, of the Canada Labour Relations Council (CLRC), a tripartite advisory body. Among the council's terms of reference was consideration of 'ways and means to promote industrial peace by exploring methods and developing procedures by which labour and management may better reconcile their differences through constructive collective bargaining, thereby reducing conflict in their own and the public interest.' McVittie (1984: 14) notes that the CLRC's existence was always imperilled by its linkage, in the federal government's thinking, with the possibility of a voluntary incomes policy. The death knell of the CLRC was sounded by imposition of wage controls in October 1975. Canada's largest labour federation, the Canadian Labour Congress (CLC), spearheaded a vigorous campaign against controls. The government was accused of planning to establish some form of corporate state in which previously autonomous interest groups would be submerged and converted into agencies of social control (Morris 1976). In March 1976, to express its opposition to such developments, the CLC withdrew from bodies such as the CLRC on grounds that its participation constituted encouragement of trends toward corporatism. The episode typifies the contradiction between capital-accumulation aspects of labour policy, represented by wage controls, and legitimation aspects, represented by the search for new co-operative forums in which labour and business, together with the state, could interact.

In an abrupt about-turn in May 1976, the CLC, without dropping its opposition to wage controls, began to advocate creation of corporatist political structures (Panitch 1979; Giles 1982; McBride 1983). Though unsuccessful in achieving its ambitions, the new policy did lead to a search for new methods of co-operation with business and government. Despite the delegitimizing aspects of government policy, this new spirit of collaboration, frequently de-emphasized by the CLC leadership because of radical criticism within labour's ranks, led to labour's participation in a number of bipartite (with business) and tripartite agencies.

The CLC participated, for example, in the 1978 attempt to devise an industrial strategy through twenty-three sectoral consultative task forces established to make recommendations to the provincial and federal governments. In addition, a high-level CLC delegation served on the Second Tier Committee, which was established 'to identify and make recommendations about factors and policies that cut across sector lines' (Canada, Department of Industry, Trade and Commerce, 1978; Brown and Eastman 1981). Similarly, the CLC participated in the Major Projects Task Force which reported in 1981. In return for lending legitimacy to the exercise, and presumably forestalling labour resistance, it obtained concessions (Mahon 1983: 168–9). Mahon described the process as a series of state initiatives 'to restore international competitiveness by reducing labour costs, while attempting to maintain labour peace through establishment of "consultative mechanisms"' (165).

The federally orchestrated drive toward tripartite collaborative structures represented the state's attempt to make its capital accumulation and legitimation activities mutually reinforcing, as they had been perceived to be in the Keynesian era. The attempt was characteristic of the post-Keynesian paradigm in operation. And while labour's internal opposition to the CLC leadership's corporatist strategy forced reversal of that strategy at the 1978 CLC convention, piecemeal involvement in consultative structures, rather than decision-making ones, proved a more elusive target for opponents.

The 1983 Speech from the Throne attached tremendous importance to the forging of a 'national partnership for prosperity' in which labour would be admitted to full partnership with 'an equal voice in the resolution of issues like technological change and productivity improvement' (Mahon 1983: 164). The offers of new consultative opportunities for labour, a far cry indeed from the government's attitude to the ambitions of organized labour for a say in government policy,[14] were nevertheless qualified in almost every line by the imperatives of capital accumulation: increased international competitiveness and greater productivity.[15] Unsurprising, some sections of organized labour saw in these overtures an opportunity to escape from the impotence that had been their lot. Others remained profoundly distrustful, an attitude reinforced by wage controls and emergency legislation and perhaps by recognition that while consultative mechanisms designed to improve the 'atmosphere' of government-labour relations might confer benefits on the government, whose policies would to an extent be ideologically legitimated, there was little in them for labour.

Meanwhile, adjustments have continued to the range and level of employment standards in such long-established fields as minimum wages, vacations, maternity leave, severance pay, and unjust dismissal. A number of 'newer areas,' however, have also achieved considerable prominence: occupational health and safety, quality-of-working-life experiments, and employment equity or affirmative action. Greater pressure for an expanded definition of occupational health and safety and improved enforcement produced legislative results during the 1970s (Manga, Bruyles, and Reschenthaler 1981: 123–7; Reasons, Ross, and Patterson 1981: part III). A number of provinces have rationalized and strengthened legislation and enforcement mechanisms and have tried to involve labour and management in the policing of workplace conditions (see Tuohy 1990).

This legislative response has operated somewhat independent of the crisis-associated tensions central to other aspects of labour policy. At least in the federal case, however, increased emphasis on occupational health and safety, together with other legitimation items, was associated with labour's hostility to the 1975 imposition of wage controls. The Department of Labour was given 'almost carte blanche to initiate programmes which would appease organised labour' (Swimmer 1981: 159). In response, the department developed a fourteen-point program (Swimmer 1981: 160–1) which included establishment of an Institute for Occupational Health and Safety, substantial revisions to the Canada Labour Code in the employment standards area, a task force to study paid education leave, grants to unions to conduct labour education, greater worker participation in health and safety issues, and a Quality of Working Life program to study and assist the development of ways to increase industrial democracy and humanize the workplace. In Ontario, a Quality of Working Life Centre was established to disseminate information to workers and employees and to stimulate experiments in new working arrangements. Reviewing the limited evidence available, the report of the Macdonald Commission (1985) commented that Quality of Working Life Programmes 'can help to improve employee morale and job satisfaction, and promote organizational effectiveness and productivity. To the extent that this is so, these programmes should come into wider use, since employers and employees will find them to their common benefit (vol. 2, 709).

The unfavourable economic climate seems to have inhibited workers from seeking implementation of some of their new rights (*Globe and Mail,* 28 November 1983) such as that to refuse dangerous work, and many of the measures may have been intended to be largely symbolic. One observer has concluded that 'there is a higher government priority for programmes which pay symbolic lip service to occupational health and safety than for those aimed at enforcing health and safety legislation' (Swimmer 1981: 180).

Nonetheless, these measures, together with the search for tripartite co-operative boards, agencies, and consultative committees, represent a major attempt to salvage legitimacy from the damage wreaked by other, stop-gap responses to the economic crisis. Even in this sphere, however, one can note attempts to reconcile the accumulation and legitimation activities mentioned previously. This is symbolized in the administrative reform of 1979 in which the cabinet developed an expenditure 'envelope' system (Doern 1981a: Appendix A). The Department of Labour was included in the economic, rather than social affairs envelope, on grounds that 'a harmonious work environment is essential to the economic well being of Canada' (Swimmer 1981: 162). Or, as the 1983 Throne Speech put it, 'This government believes that the maintenance and improvement of workers' rights are fully consistent with, and indeed essential to, increased productivity ... A fundamental aspect of productivity is a secure, safe environment for workers.' Thus rather than labour policies aimed at legitimation serving as supports of the political and economic system in a broad sense, they have in recent times become much more narrowly instrumental.

Yet another legitimacy-generating state activity has been that of employment equity. The Abella Royal Commission (1983) conceptualized this as the equalization of economic opportunities for women, native people, the disabled, and visible minorities. Legislation that has emerged in a number of provinces, however, has tended to be focused more on pay equity. Such legislation primarily affects the public sector (for example, in Manitoba, New Brunswick, and Prince Edward Island), although in Nova Scotia and Ontario parts of the private sector are also covered. Typically, pay-equity legislation requires evaluation of specific jobs and gradual elimination of disparities in wages.

The federal Employment Equity Act (1986) applies to crown corporations and larger federally regulated employers (primarily firms in banking, transportation, and communications). It requires these employers to submit annual reports and to implement employment-equity programs. In addition, the Federal Contractors Programme specifies that suppliers with 100 or more employees, bidding on a contract worth $200,000 or more, must certify their commitment to implementing employment equity. Failure to do so may result in rejection of bids, and successful bidders are subject to compliance reviews. Within the federal public service, and some provincial civil services, somewhat more comprehensive programs are in place. The federal program covers women, native people, and the handicapped and is designed to eliminate barriers, correct underrepresentation of target groups, and rectify past discrimination (Swimmer and Gollesch 1986). In Ontario a similar program has been in place since 1974. A recent annual report on employment equity in the Ontario public service (Ontario Women's Directorate 1986) pointed to steady progress in a number of areas: average pay 79.1 per cent of that earned by men (compared to 71.6 per cent in 1974), 13.1 per cent of senior executives (compared to 3.9 per cent in 1975), and so on. The figures do indicate steady progress for women. In this sense, employment equity does confer real benefits. Yet change remains painfully slow. And, given the much later introduction of these programs in most jurisdictions, they may perform more of an ideological than a concrete legitimation role.[16] In conditions of slow, no, or negative growth in public-service employment, targets or quotas cannot be met (Swimmer and Gollesch 1986: 248).

Summary

It was anticipated that developments in industrial relations policy would closely follow the pattern indicated by a shift of paradigms and a change of emphasis in state activities. Pre-Keynesian economic thinking had regarded unions as an illegitimate challenge to the rights of property. Prudence might dictate tolerating their existence, but they were regarded as necessary evils to be held in check as much as possible. Under this approach, owners of capital would be free to accumulate capital without unwarranted interference from workers' organizations. Keynesianism took a rather more benign view: recognizing unions created social legitimacy for the free-enterprise system, and their participation in free collective bargaining could sustain demand at full-employment levels while simultaneously creating conditions for profitable capital accumulation. Post-Keynesians perceived unions as a cause of inflation and sought to entangle them in voluntary incomes restraint. Where this failed, the approach was prepared to tolerate the delegitimizing effects of imposed wage controls. In the monetarist view, unions assumed a still more negative profile. They were viewed as obstacles to market forces and, thus, to capital accumulation. In addition, the paradigm linked them to high unemployment, which was seen as caused by union-induced inflation. State policy in industrial relations in a number of historical periods, which generally coincide with the dominance of one or other of these economic paradigms, conforms to the predicted trends.

In the pre-war period, accumulation concerns were predominant and coercive methods often used. We can, however, detect in the Industrial Disputes Investigation Act and enactment of employment standards legislation attempts to create legitimacy and siphon off social and industrial discontent.

The rise of Keynesianism was associated with extension of collective bargaining. This change cannot be interpreted simply as extension of this paradigm's ideas to industrial relations. Industrial militancy during and just after the Second World War required the state to adjust to the greater power of organized labour. But the influence of the new ideas undoubtedly played a role. In addition, the prospect of a more humane society could be used in restructuring and deradicalizing the trade union movement with which the state would henceforth deal. In this project, the state found willing collaborators in many CCF union leaders who were eager to oust their more radical rivals. As the Keynesian era wore on, increasing contradictions were signalled by revival of industrial militancy and the state's increasing resort to back-to-work legislation. Consistent with the growing prominence of post-Keynesian interpretations of inflation, some major efforts were made, late in the period, to establish voluntary incomes controls.

The onset of economic crisis and the rise of monetarist ideas have in turn been associated with a much more restrictive approach to the unions. As the imposition of wage controls indicates, policy instruments have been far from purely monetarist in inspiration. But the more frequent use of back-to-work legislation, and piecemeal whittling away of legislative rights in the provinces, are indicative of a desire to tame Canadian unions. In some provinces, most notably British Columbia, these measures have amounted to a wholesale assault on trade unions. In the midst of the harsher climate, we can nevertheless detect, at the federal level and in some provinces, attempts to create new mechanisms of legitimacy which would also promote or at least be consistent with accumulation. Examples include increased attention to health and safety and to employment equity and attempts to create collaborative forums to improve relations among labour, business, and the state. Such efforts by the state are testimony to labour's continuing power within the balance of class forces. Indeed, the state's regular resort to coercion in recent decades can be viewed in this way. Even regular suspension of the 'rules' is different from their outright demolition, and incremental legislative changes are distinguishable from a systematic restructuring of industrial relations (McBride 1987b). In this area, as in unemployment insurance, efforts to rewrite the post-war settlement have encountered stiff resistance, and the ultimate outcome is far from clear.

8   Conclusion

Four major policy areas that are central to the state's response to economic crisis have been examined. In various ways the policy areas bear directly on the high unemployment that has been a feature of Canadian life since the mid-1970s. As far as possible, the conceptual apparatus outlined in the early chapters has been used in analysing policy. The approach has emphasized the policy paradigms that influenced state officials and the link between the paradigms and the types of activity in which the state has engaged. Much of this book has been concerned with identifying the shifting balance among the Canadian state's priorities. While it is hoped that this study can make a contribution toward the ongoing development of a theory of the capitalist state, it does not itself construct one. Some reflections on the most promising directions in the development of such a theory are, however, advanced later in this chapter. The principal findings for the substantive policy areas are as follows.

The Findings

Macroeconomic Policy

A discernible trend away from Keynesianism and toward monetarism was punctuated by a period of sometimes confused conflict between advocates of post-Keynesian policy remedies and adherents of monetarist policies. The process of paradigm change was thus rather untidy. As these changes occurred, the commitment to full employment, always less than trenchantly upheld by the Canadian state, foundered. Inflation, and later the deficit, were proclaimed to be the key economic problems.

Measures directed toward these problems themselves created unemployment – an effect that was understood if generally unacknowledged by Canadian politicians. In shaping and justifying the new priorities and policy measures, the monetarist paradigm proved increasingly useful.

The end of full employment meant that a central legitimizing component of the post-war economic consensus was removed. Increasingly, macroeconomic policy – fiscal, monetary, and incomes – emphasized accumulation over legitimation. It appeared that the preferred regime of accumulation would be one driven primarily by market forces. Since the ultimate aim of fiscal and monetary policy seemed to involve a reduced role for the state, this end-result may be said to have enjoyed the state's sanction.

The new approach was ideologically legitimated through its gradual implementation and by a variety of other means identified in chapter 4. An additional important component of ideological legitimation was the demonstration of concern about the plight of the unemployed. Labour-market policies, examined in chapter 5, which presented an image of concerned activity, played a significant role in this process. Indeed, the prominence of the themes of 'jobs,' 'training,' and 'job creation' in government pronouncements is testimony to the potentially dangerous impact of unemployment on the legitimacy of the state and the broader economic system. To be seen to be doing something about unemployment was as important to the state as evading either an analysis of its causes or an exploration of alternative means of responding.

Labour-Market Policy

During the Keynesian era, labour-market policies had played a limited support role in contributing to the maintenance of relatively full employment and could be considered a concrete legitimation activity. As post-Keynesian thinking became more influential, active labour-market policies, particularly training, came to be viewed as a key instrument for achieving non-inflationary full employment. These policies placed increased emphasis on accumulation through providing employers with a ready-trained work-force. As the monetarist paradigm became predominant, labour-market programs could be expected to lapse once more into a minor role, supportive of the broader economic strategy. In this capacity they might contribute to lowering actual unemployment to the NAIRU or to lowering the natural rate itself. In either case, unemployment would be less than it otherwise might have been. Continued participation in the provision of training would enable the policy area to contribute to accumulation as well. In practice, efforts partially to 'privatize' training through increasing the private sector's role in the training process meant an enhanced emphasis on accumulation. The private sector was enabled to provide itself with trained personnel and might also expect to make a profit from providing the training.

Throughout the period of this study, labour-market policy was 'sold' on a concrete legitimation basis: its capacity to create jobs or to increase the employability of individuals or groups. But closer examination suggested a somewhat different role. First, accumulation concerns became steadily more pronounced, as reflected in partial privatization of both training and job creation. Public subsidies were provided to the private sector either to hire more workers or to conduct training. Since there seems to have been little incrementality or monitoring, such subsidies can be regarded as little more than windfall contributions to capital accumulation. Second, the broader context of increased attention to accumulation was declining overall priority to labour-market policy, especially when this is considered in conjunction with the size of the unemployment problem to which it was supposedly addressed.

This combination of factors suggests that much of labour-market policy was a symbolic response to unemployment. Labour-market programs operated so as to legitimate ideologically other and unemployment-causing policies by presenting the appearance of a genuine response to the problem. Since a large amount of money was spent, the response cannot be judged entirely symbolic. But the level of spending lagged well behind the scope of the problem, and, as noted above, increasingly expenditure was targeted toward private-sector accumulation.

Unemployment Insurance

In view of the limited real impact of labour-market policy, it is reasonable to argue that compensation for unemployment, rather than its prevention, has constituted the basic Canadian approach. Indeed, since the overall macroeconomic strategy has been one of tolerating high unemployment, any other response would have been illogical.

The expansion of the UI system in 1971 was a high-water mark in the construction of the post-war Keynesian welfare state. The relative generosity of the 1971 reforms expanded the state's concrete legitimation activities. Since 1971 there have been repeated drives to erode the system, to finance it by more regressive means, and to subject claimants to greater regulation. The effect has been to increase the coercive and social-control aspects of the program. But despite numerous investigations and reports, which provided material that might have been used to legitimate ideologically further attacks on the system, it remains relatively intact and continues to perform a legitimation role. How severe might the socio-political impact of the 1982–3 recession have been in the absence of a reasonably adequate UI system?

In any case, the tenacity with which the system has been defended indicates limits to the new ideology's ability to undermine support for concrete legitimation programs. These limits are also observable in other areas, such as health and pensions, which lie beyond the scope of this book.

Industrial Relations

The tendency toward state cutbacks in concrete legitimation activities and increased emphasis on capital accumulation was also apparent in this sphere of state activity. The state dictated outcomes to the process of labour-capital interaction through imposition of wage controls and ad hoc back-to-work legislation. In addition, legislation steadily eroded trade unions' rights and thereby inhibited their ability to deal effectively with employers.

The Canadian State in Comparative Perspective

In the face of economic crisis, the policy package assembled by the Canadian state featured restrictive policies. These represented an enhanced response to the interests of capital, at the expense of those of subordinate classes which has previously been addressed by the state's orchestration of concrete benefits. Full employment, arguably the most important concrete component of the post-war legitimation package, was sacrificed. To meet pressure resulting from removal and reduction of concrete legitimation measures, the state more and more resorted to ideological legitimation and to coercion. The relative success of this strategy suggests that while the state's attempts to promote both accumulation and legitimation involve it in a contradictory process, the contradictions are far from insoluble even under difficult economic conditions. Legitimation has both concrete and ideological or symbolic elements. To some extent these elements are substitutable. Moreover, other measures such as coercion are available and capable of being applied in a graduated fashion.

In adopting such a strategy, the Canadian state was far from unique. But comparative evidence indicated that such a response was not automatic or inevitable. Faced with broadly similar economic problems and constraints, other states devised different policy responses and experienced different outcomes. Some states managed to maintain full employment, though perhaps with increased difficulty.

Is high unemployment an inevitable effect of the economic crisis of the 1970s and 1980s? It does not appear so. Why then has high unemployment been the Canadian experience? The short answer, and a central conclusion of this book, is that we have had high unemployment because the Canadian state has chosen to have it. The strategy implemented by the Canadian state inevitably produced high levels of unemployment. But other strategies were available and were not chosen. Why did the state in Canada choose such a strategy? The answer to that question depends on the relationship that is presumed to exist between the state and the dominant elements in society. Properly speaking, this falls into an area of state theory which has not been the focus of this investigation. But an answer to the question is sketched in the next, and final, section of the book.

Reflections on Theories of the State

Two issues in the theory-of-the-state literature can be addressed in this section. In the first case, the comments represent an issue for further research, since the present study has not attempted a systematic consideration of it. This issue concerns the degree to which the state acts autonomously from society and the dominant elements within it. The second issue concerns the extent to which the previously noted shift in paradigms has resulted in establishment of a new hegemonic ideology.

On the first issue, a growing body of literature attempts to 'bring the state back in.' This amounts to the argument that the explanation for policy changes lies within the state itself, and in its pursuit of its own interests, rather than in those of society or one of its components, such as capital. Reviewing the material covered in this book with the 'state-centred' versus 'society-centred' explanations in mind, it is difficult to avoid a preference for the 'society-centred' variety. Explanations that posit that the state's action represents a response to the articulated needs of capital seem especially plausible. The reasons are outlined below.

First, in adopting the monetarist paradigm, the state has taken on itself the 'blame' for the economic crisis. Inflation and the other economic maladies of the 1970s and 1980s essentially are attributed to the excessive role of the state. But once one steps outside the monetarist paradigm, it is by no means clear that this diagnosis is accurate. It is easy to see why the monetarist analysis of the causes of the crisis suits capital – itself a possible target of blame. But if, as most state-centred analysts do, one assumes bureaucratic self-interest on the part of the state machinery, why has the state been so willing to engage in the self-flagellation that adoption of the monetarist paradigm implies? The most logical response is that it has been induced to do so by the power of capital.

Second, the broad solution to the economic crisis is inconsistent with the notion of a 'self-interested' state. The broad solution is to enhance the power of the market, and hence of capital as the dominant actor within the market. This involves reducing the state's economic and social role. In other countries where a similar strategy has been implemented, it is argued that diminution in the state's economic role is balanced by a much stronger role in other areas. The title of Gamble's (1988) book, *The Free Economy and the Strong State*, nicely sums up this formulation. The increased scope for coercion and ideological legitimation initiatives documented earlier indicates that there might be some basis for the formulation in Canada and, in principle, could be explained in either state-centred or society-centred terms. But the idea that a strong state is developing in Canada is offset by other elements in the monetarist prescription which lie outside the scope of this study. Briefly, though, the decentralization of power envisaged in the Meech Lake Accord – a perspective that survived the accord's demise – and the increased economic, social, and political integration with the United States inherent in the Free Trade Agreement, suggest that if there is to be a strong neo-conservative state, it will not be located in Ottawa nor, probably, elsewhere on Canadian soil. Such an agenda is better understood as emanating from Canadian capital rather than from the state itself.

Third, the consistency of the flow of benefits to capital and the wealthy in the new policy strategy is remarkable. It is true, of course, that outcomes may be unintentional and that a correlation may exist between what capital proposed and what the state did without this proving causality. Nevertheless, given such a pattern, consistent over time and across different policy areas which themselves fall into various jurisdictional combinations, the notion that the state is responding to the power of capital seems more reasonable than the idea that it is not. Certainly it would seem more profitable to organize a future research project around the likelihood that there is a causal relation between the power of capital in Canadian society and the actions taken by the Canadian state, rather than around the supposition that the state proceeds independently.

It would still remain, of course, to specify how such a relation was manifested and to what degree the state might demonstrate some autonomy from the needs of capital. Even those holding to a society-centred position can concede some role for bureaucratic self-interest, federal-provincial conflicts, and so on. In the present study, we have touched on conflict between Ottawa and the provinces over training, noted provincial resistance to federal cutbacks in unemployment insurance since they would increase provincial social assistance costs, and encountered an interpretation of the Canadian Jobs Strategy which suggested that it was a bureaucratic survival strategy designed to avert still greater cutbacks in labour-market policy. Clearly such factors have a role to play in the evolution of particular policy areas.

In other cases, though, the state's apparent autonomy from capital may be better explained by the resistance, real or anticipated, of other social forces. For example, the Canadian state has failed, or declined, to roll back more extensively the unemployment insurance system, as well as some other concrete legitimation activities that lie beyond the boundaries of this study. State policy, then, can be relatively autonomous of capital either because of the state's own specific interests or because of the balance of forces within society. It might be supposed that such autonomy from capital would be enhanced if capital itself were divided, or if the policy area under consideration were not central to capital's interests.

Comparative evidence suggested that in countries where labour was strong, the state seems to have retained considerable ability to resist capital's agenda. In these countries, full employment and other concrete legitimation policies have survived the economic crisis. The structural power of capital may constrain the state in capitalist societies in that capital's interests will always weigh heavily on politicians and officials. But such outcomes suggest that capital's structural power does not entirely determine state policy. Politics, including factors associated with the 'instrumentalist' interpretation of state power, such as activity by business interest groups, the class background of state officials, and influence over political parties and office-holders, also seems crucially important. The outcome of the ideological struggle to establish the state's agenda is not preordained but is rather the outcome of more or less intense societal and political conflict.

There is no doubt that in countries like Canada the outcome of the ideological battle has registered some rather important policy victories for capital. But – our second issue here – do these victories imply a new ideological hegemony? The prominence of ideological legitimation is certainly one indication that a process of seeking to establish hegemony, what is often termed a hegemonic project, has been under way for some time. In Canada the project has been unattended by an association with the sort of formidable leadership which, in Britain for example, has led to the project's personification in the term *Thatcherism*. But the project has been just as substantial in Canada, involving the sacrifice of full employment, cutbacks in welfare state programs, reduction in the state's economic role, a Free Trade Agreement with the United States, attacks on the trade union movement, and glorification of market forces.

Such ideas have clearly become dominant among the business and state élites. Their successful, if incomplete, implementation suggests that they have shaped the political agenda. But 'hegemony' would imply that the new ideas had become internalized by the subordinate classes whose active consent to the new policy agenda had thus been ensured. There is little evidence that the new ideas have achieved such a status, and much that they have not. Trade unions are under assault but have not bowed; social programs have been attacked but have also been defended; high unemployment exists but is unpopular; and the Free Trade Agreement and the Meech Lake Accord both encountered significant opposition. The very effort put into ideological legitimation testifies to the failure, so far, to establish a new hegemony. If hegemony existed, there would be much less need for overt ideological legitimation.

Ideological and political conflicts over such issues serve to remind us of Marx's adage that although they do not choose the circumstances in which history is made, people do make their own history. And one of the ways they do this, of course, is through political action. Any theory of the capitalist state that fails to incorporate fully this point is unlikely to be of much value. The point does not seem to have been ignored by Canadian capital. In this context, it has been argued here that unemployment is not a 'circumstance' but rather a consequence of the political process. To understand unemployment, therefore, we require not an 'economics' of the subject but rather a political economy of it. And if the problem is one that is politically produced, the practical implications of the finding should be clear.

Notes

Chapter 1

1 See the useful survey of these, and other approaches, in Aucoin (1979).
   A different version of policy paradigms is used by analysts in the regulation school of political economy (see Jenson 1989).
2 Compare the following definition of ideology (Hamilton 1987: 38) with
   the previously cited one of paradigm: 'An ideology is a system of collectively held normative and reputedly factual ideas and beliefs and attitudes advocating a particular pattern of social relationships and
   arrangements, and/or aimed at justifying a particular pattern of conduct,
   which its proponents seek to promote, realise, pursue or maintain.'
3 The various types of unemployment are discussed in chapter 3; for further details see Hughes and Perlman (1984: chapter 2).
4 This term is used in Moon and Richardson's (1985) study of British job-
   creation policies.
5 'To understand the concept of legitimation one must understand what
   people *believe to be true*. To understand the legitimation component of
   the state's interventions, we must deal with motives, beliefs, forms of
   consciousness, all of which means resorting to ... evidence which is
   squarely "ideological" in nature – what people said as well as what people did ... what people held to be true must be taken with considerable
   seriousness, not because this is truth in a scientific sense, but quite simply because they believed it to be true and acted upon it' (Whitaker
   1977: 29–30).
6 In addition to the fiscal crisis literature of the period, there was also a
   growth industry in discussions of 'overload' and 'ungovernability.'
7 With reference to labour, Hall (1984: 40) notes that legitimation includes
   'the use of ideological techniques designed to justify the prevailing economic conditions and to redirect popular apprehensions of responsibility

for these conditions away from capital and the state toward labour organizations.'

Chapter 2

1 See Olsen (1991a, 1991b) for a critique of power resource theory.
2 This paragraph is reproduced from McBride (1983: 503–4). All quotations are from Canadian Labour Congress (1976).
3 The same factors would seem to explain the existence of a 'liberal welfare state regime' in Canada. The degree of the central bank's autonomy would appear to play only a marginal role in the Canadian case. In formal terms, the minister of finance has the power to issue written and public directives to the Bank of Canada; informally the Bank may possess much more autonomy than this situation would suggest. No such directive has been issued, probably as a result of anticipated reactions in the market (i.e. from the financial community). The central bank's autonomy is less of an institutional than a class power obstacle. In any event, given the dominant ideological composition of Canadian governments, the potential for disagreement with the Bank should not be exaggerated.

Chapter 3

1 For a sampling of post-Keynesian analyses see Eichner (1979).
2 The most prominent monetarist economist is Milton Friedman. For a useful discussion of the monetarists as a group, see Woolley (1982).

Chapter 4

1 In itself, this definitional change reflects the influence of the monetarist paradigm.
2 Maslove (1981) points to a single exception to this pattern, albeit an important one, the child tax credit.
3 For a detailed summary of the legislation see Maslove and Swimmer (1980) 33–8.
4 MacEachen's November 1981 budget, however, attempted to terminate a number of the tax breaks from which business derived significant benefits. On the resulting furore and restoration of the tax breaks see McQuaig (1987: chapter 8).
5 On the activism of the 1980–4 Liberal government see Doern (1981b, 1982).
6 The partial deindexation of the income tax in 1985 removed a major tax

expenditure which might be considered largely a concrete legitimation measure.

7 There were other reasons for gradualism. One of these is that business and state élites were proceeding to some extent by trial and error rather than on the basis of a blueprint whose results were entirely predictable or guaranteed.

Chapter 5

1 See Dupré et al. (1973) for an extended discussion of federal-provincial relations re training.

2 More generally, extensive use has been made of consultative mechanisms in labour-market policy (cf. Blair 1984: 17).

3 In 1984 the Conservative government reduced expenditures on GIT. Two reasons were advanced: the need for general fiscal restraint, and an evaluation that revealed that 'most employers who received GIT financial support did not require federal assistance' (CEIC, Annual Report, 1984–5). Given the importance attached to capital accumulation by the monetarist-inclined Tories, this cutback appears surprising. The National Training Programme, however, can be interpreted as a last attempt at post-Keynesian active labour-market policy. In this, as in many other areas, monetarism and the new government favoured 'downsizing' and 'refocusing.'

4 Even this program contained aspects indicative of continuing concern with accumulation. It aimed to select projects that would contribute to subsequent economic activity, enhance productivity, or stimulate regional development. Also, the projects would contribute to workers' retention of skills and industrial discipline (EIC 1984a: 3–4). Further, the private sector would sponsor particular projects: 'In a major development over earlier direct job creation measures, NEED has placed a very strong emphasis on a joint partnership with provincial and territorial governments and the private sector to obtain (a) *concerted action* in responding to prevailing unemployment problems; (b) *additional leverage* from federal expenditures as a result of funds from these two other sources; and (c) the *strategic targeting* of the programme on projects which would be of benefit to the economy' (ibid., 8). Although NEED's life was limited, the emphasis on provincial and, especially, private-sector involvement was to be a major feature of subsequent job-creation programs.

5 Canada Works was designed to help stabilize the labour market and to alleviate workers' dislocation. Summer Canada included projects that addressed summer unemployment among students. Private-sector employers and other organizations were eligible to create projects. Local

Employment Assistance and Development (LEAD) was targeted at areas of high unemployment. Private-sector involvement was encouraged so long as it did not result in unfair competition or displacement of existing workers. Career-Access was a wage-subsidy program designed to help the disadvantaged obtain work. Eligible employers included private business, other organizations, and governments. Job Corps was aimed at severely employment-disadvantaged individuals and consisted of financial contributions toward wages and other costs.

6 From a broader neo-conservative perspective, use of such measures is problematic. Affirmative-action programs and the like are anethema to some sections of the social and political base of neo-conservatism.

7 In 1983, Employment Minister John Roberts placed government in a secondary role: 'While it is primarily up to the private sector to provide the employment opportunities to sustain a vibrant labour market, the government has a clear responsibility to create the environment in which business can flourish to the greatest advantage of all Canadians' (Roberts 1983: 5).

8 From time to time, departmental spokespersons reiterated this theme. John Edwards, associate deputy minister, gave the standing committee this interpretation of the evolution of training policy in Canada: 'The [CJS] changes build on, but go far beyond the changes we introduced with the National Training Act of 1982 ... The National Training Act emphasized the relevance of the skills that were to be taught by introducing the concept of skills of national importance and by focusing the nation's training capacity in areas of greatest need using the Skills Growth Fund. In so doing, it redirected federal training policies away from the social goals that underlay the programmes under the previous legislation and focused instead on economic objectives ... There has, however, been a subsequent and much more profound shift in federal training policy with the introduction of the Canadian Jobs Strategy ... It has brought the emphasis of skills and training to all our labour market programmes, including programmes that were formerly concerned with short-term job creation alone' (House of Commons, Standing Committee on Labour, Employment and Immigration, 24 November 1986: 4, 8–10).

Chapter 6

1 Referring to social security, which in the United States covers both retirement pensions and unemployment benefits, O'Connor (1973: 138) comments: 'Although social security contributes to social and political stability by conservatizing unemployed and retired workers, the primary purpose of the system is to create a sense of economic security within the ranks of employed workers (especially workers in the monopoly sec-

tor) and thereby raise morale and reinforce discipline. This contributes to harmonious management-labour relations which are indispensable to capital accumulation and the growth of production. Thus the fundamental interest and effect of social security is to expand productivity, production and profits. Seen in this way, social insurance is not primarily insurance for workers, but a kind of insurance for capitalists and bureaucrats.'

2 A deliberate one in the opinion of opposition spokespersons. See G.W. Baldwin's criticisms in *Hansard*, 1973: 614–20.

3 For an excellent critical review of this literature see Paul Phillips (n.d.).

4 For other criticisms of the methodological characteristics of studies finding a positive relation between the 1971 act and unemployment, see Bodkin and Cournoyer (1978) and Osberg (1979).

Chapter 7

1 Crispo (1978: 282) notes other motives for employment standards legislation in the modern period. These include a desire to protect reasonable employers from unfair competition from unscrupulous operators and, in the case of minimum-wage legislation, a desire to maintain purchasing power. In terms of the analytical framework being used in this book, these motives clearly pertain to capital accumulation rather than to legitimation.

2 Craven (1980: 167–74) has an interesting discussion of whether this legislation is classified more appropriately under the legitimation or accumulation functions. The case for legitimation rests on interpretations that emphasize the desire of Macdonald's Conservative government to win working-class votes. Conversely, the legislation can be viewed as designed to attract and retain the skilled labour force necessary for economic development through providing a legislative environment for labour-capital relations which would be equivalent to that of Britain, whence much skilled labour was drawn, and produce wages and conditions sufficient to prevent out-migration to the United States.

3 These were the Conciliation Act (1900), the Railway Disputes Investigation Act (1903), and, most comprehensive, the Industrial Disputes Investigation Act (1907). At least one province also provided for conciliation and voluntary arbitration of disputes (Quebec in 1901).

4 On the Snider case, see Peter Russell (1973: 38–45).

5 Because of the war, and under the rubric of the War Measures Act, labour relations had once again become (albeit temporarily) an area of predominantly federal jurisdiction.

6 For some of the implications of this, see Haiven (1991).

7 Strikes over jurisdictional disputes, recognition issues, application and

interpretation of collective agreements, and during conciliation procedures were illegal. From time to time, extraordinary coercive measures were taken against unions exercising the right to strike. In 1959, Newfoundland, for instance, passed a special law declaring the International Woodworkers Association, a union long since purged of its communist leadership, a 'criminal organisation' and membership of it 'a criminal act' (see Lembke and Tattam 1984). Such incidents remind us that accounts of Keynesian-era toleration toward unions can be much exaggerated.

8 For a useful comparison of the details of these provisions see Gerald E. Phillips (1977: 172–80).

9 Newfoundland's cabinet possessed wide discretionary power to limit the exercise of this right by designating employees 'essential.' The Federal Public Service Staff Relations Board had a similar, but less extensive, capability.

10 The aptness of the 'permanent exceptionalism' characterization, especially where it is construed as implying a systematic restructuring of the industrial relations system, is a matter of dispute. For an interesting discussion see Bob Russell (1990: chapter 7, especially 255–7).

11 Only Saskatchewan and Quebec opted out of the program; they set up their own provincial boards to regulate wages.

12 For critiques of the view that this did represent a partial victory, see the articles by Annis, Chudnovsky, and Pollack in Argue, Gannage, and Livingstone (1987).

13 For an assessment of the legislation and a review of significant labour criticism of it, see Gonick (1987b).

14 Writing of an earlier era, Kwavnick (1972: chapter 9) documented the CLC's inability to influence government policy outside of a narrow range of directly labour-related policy areas on which the government chose to regard the CLC's representatives as legitimate.

15 For a less critical interpretation of government policy see Adams (1982).

16 See the earlier discussion of this issue in chapter 5.

References

Abella, I.M. (1973) *Nationalism, Communism and Canadian Labour: The CIO, the C.P. and the CCL. 1935–1950* (Toronto: University of Toronto Press)

ABT Associates (1984) *Evaluation – Developmental Use of UI Funds for Job Creation* vol. IV *A Final Report* (Ottawa: Employment and Immigration Canada)

– (1985a) *Evaluation – National Institutional Training Programme (NITP): Final Report* (Ottawa: Department of Employment and Immigration)

– (1985b) *Evaluation of the Critical Trade Skills Training Programme: Final Report* (Ottawa: Department of Employment and Immigration Canada)

Adams, Roy J. (1982) 'The Federal Government and Tripartism,' *Relations industrielles* 37, 606–16

Alberta Federation of Labour (1988) *Presentation to Alberta Minister of Labour, January* 11

Albo, Greg, and Jane Jenson (1989) 'A Contested Concept: The Relative Autonomy of the State,' in Clement and Williams, eds (1989) 180–211

Annis, Ruth (1987) 'The Impact of the BC Government "Restraint" Program on Provincial Employees, Social Services and Women,' in Argue, Gannage, and Livingstone, eds (1987) 137–42

Apple, Nixon (1980) 'The Rise and Fall of Full-Employment Capitalism,' *Studies in Political Economy* no. 4, 5–39

Argue, Robert, Charlene Gannage, and D.W. Livingstone, eds (1987) *Working People and Hard Times: Canadian Perspectives* (Toronto: Garamond)

Armstrong, Pat, and Hugh Armstrong (1990), 'Lessons from Pay Equity,' *Studies in Political Economy* no. 32, summer, 29–54

Armstrong, Philip, Andrew Glyn, and John Harrison (1984) *Capitalism since World War II* (London: Fontana)

Ashton, D.N. (1986) *Unemployment under Capitalism: The Sociology of British and American Labour Markets* (Brighton: Wheatsheaf)

Atkinson, Michael M., and William D. Coleman (1987) 'Is There a Crisis in Business-Government Relations?' *Canadian Journal of Administrative Science* 4 no. 4, 321–40

Aucoin, Peter (1979) 'Public Policy Theory and Analysis,' in Doern and Aucoin, eds (1979) 1–26

Baggaley, Carman D. (1981) *A Century of Labour Regulations in Canada* (Ottawa)

Bank of Canada (1970–87) *Annual Reports* (Ottawa)

Banting, Keith (1986a) 'Economic Consultation and the Macdonald Commission Research and Recommendations,' in Murray, ed (1986) 46–67

– research coordinator (1986) *The State and Economic Interests*, vol. 22 of research studies for the Royal Commission on the Economic Union and Development Prospects for Canada (Toronto: University of Toronto Press)

– (1987) *The Welfare State and Canadian Federalism* 2nd ed (Kingston and Montreal: McGill-Queen's University Press)

Barber, Clarence L., and John C.P. McCallum (1980) *Unemployment and Inflation: The Canadian Experience* (Toronto: James Lorimer)

Barratt Brown, Michael (1984) *Models in Political Economy* (Harmondsworth: Penguin)

Bellemare, Diane, and Lise Poulin Simon (1988) 'Full Employment: A Strategy and an Objective for Economic Policy,' in Cameron and Sharpe, eds (1988) 63–93

Berger, G.A. (1973) *Canadian Experience with Incomes Policy, 1969–70* (Ottawa: Prices and Incomes Commission)

Bhaduri, Amit, and Josef Steindl (1983) *The Rise of Monetarism as a Social Doctrine* (London: Thames Papers in Political Economy)

Blackman, Tim (1987) 'The Politics of Full Employment,' *Political Geography Quarterly* 6 no. 4 (October) 313–33

Blair, Cassandra (1984) *Forging Links of Cooperation: The Task Force Approach to Consultation* (Ottawa: Conference Board of Canada)

Blais, André, and François Vaillancourt (1986) 'The Federal Corporate Income Tax: Tax Expenditures and Tax Discrimination,' *Canadian Tax Journal* 34 no. 4, 1122–39

Blank, Stephen (1977) 'Britain: The Politics of Foreign Economic Policy, the Domestic Economy, and the Problem of Pluralistic Stagnation,' *International Organization* 31: 673–722

Block, Fred (1987) *Revising State Theory* (Philadelphia: Temple University Press)

Bocock, Robert (1986) *Hegemony* (London: Tavistock)

Bodkin, Ronald G., and André Cournoyer (1978) 'Legislation and the Labour Market: A Selective Review of Canadian Studies,' in Grubel and Walker, eds (1978) 62–89

Borgen, W., and N. Amundson (1984) *The Experience of Unemployment: Implications for Counselling & the Unemployed* (Scarborough: Nelson)

Bornstein, Stephen, David Held, and Joel Krieger, eds (1984) *The State in Capitalist Europe: A Casebook* (London: George Allen and Unwin)

Bossons, John, and D.P. Dungan (1983) 'The Government Deficit: Two High or Too Low?' *Canadian Tax Journal* 31 no. 1, 1–29

Boston, Jonathan (1987) 'Thatcherism and Rogernomics: Changing the Rules of the Game – Comparisons and Contrasts,' *Political Science* 39 no. 2 (December) 129–52

Brenner, Harvey (1976) *Estimating the Social Costs of National Economic Policy: Implications for Mental and Physical Health and Criminal Aggression* A Study Prepared for the Use of the Joint Economic Committee, Congress of the United States (Washington, DC)

Brown, Douglas, Julia Eastman, with Ian Robinson (1981) *The Limits of Consultation: A Debate among Ottawa, the Provinces and the Private Sector on Industrial Strategy* (Ottawa: Science Council of Canada)

Brown, Lorne, and Caroline Brown (1978) *An Unauthorized History of the RCMP* (Toronto: James Lorimer)

Bruno, Michael, and Jeffrey Sachs (1985) *The Economics of Worldwide Stagflation* (Cambridge, Mass.: Harvard University Press)

Bulpitt, Jim (1986) 'The Discipline of the New Democracy: Mrs. Thatcher's Domestic Statecraft,' *Political Studies* 34, March 19–39

Cameron, David R. (1984) 'Social Democracy, Labour Quiescence, and the Representation of Economic Interest in Advanced Capitalist Society,' in Goldthorpe, ed (1984) 143–78

Cameron, Duncan, and Andrew Sharpe, eds (1988) *Policies for Full Employment* (Ottawa and Montreal: Canadian Council on Social Development)

Campbell, Robert (1987) *Grand Illusions: The Politics of the Keynesian Experience in Canada, 1945–75* (Peterborough: Broadview Press)

Canada, Department of Industry, Trade and Commerce (1978), *A Report by the Second Tier Committee on Policies to Improve Canadian Competitiveness* (Ottawa)

Canada, Department of Manpower and Immigration (1968/9 to 1976/7) *Annual Reports* (Ottawa: Department of Manpower and Immigration)

Canada, Department of Reconstruction (1945) White Paper on Employment and Income (Ottawa)

Canada, Statistics Canada a, *The Labour Force*, Cat. 71–001, various months and years

– b, *Historical Labour Force Statistics* 1, Cat. 71–201, various years

– (1984) *The Distribution of Wealth in Canada* (Ottawa, Cat. 13–580)

Canada/Ontario Agreement on Training (1980) 10 March

Canadian Labour Congress (1976) *Discussion Paper for the Meeting with the Prime Minister and Members of the Cabinet on July 12, 1976* (Ottawa: CLC)

Carmichael, E.A., W. Dobson, and R.G. Lipsey (1986) 'The Macdonald Report: Signpost or Shopping Basket,' *Canadian Public Policy* 12, Supplement, 23–39

Carnoy, Martin (1984) *The State and Political Theory* (Princeton, NJ: Princeton University Press)

Castles, Francis G., ed (1982) *The Impact of Parties* (London: Sage)

Chernomas, Bob (1983) 'Keynesian, Monetarist and Post Keynesian Policy: A Marxist Analysis,' *Studies in Political Economy* no. 10, 123–42

Chorney, Harold (1984) *The Deficit: Hysteria and the Current Economic Crisis* (Ottawa: Canadian Centre for Policy Alternatives)

– (1989) *The Deficit and Debt Management: An Alternative to Monetarism* (Ottawa: Canadian Centre for Policy Alternatives)

Chorney, Harold, and Phillip Hansen (1980) 'The Falling Rate of Legitimation: The Problem of the Contemporary Capitalist State in Canada,' *Studies in Political Economy* no. 4, 65–98

Chrétien, Jean (1978) *The Budget* (Ottawa: Department of Finance)

Chudnovsky, David (1987) 'The Impact of the BC Government Restraint Program on Teachers,' in Argue, Gannage, and Livingstone, eds (1987) 143–8

Clement, Wallace, and Glen Williams, eds (1989) *The New Canadian Political Economy* (Montreal: McGill-Queen's University Press)

Close, Lawrence J., and Ronald M. Burns (1971) *The Municipal Winter Works Incentive Program: A Study of Government Expenditure Decision-Making* (Toronto: Canadian Tax Foundation)

Cloutier, J.E. (1978) *The Distribution of Benefits and Costs of Social Security in Canada, 1971–75* (Ottawa: Economic Council of Canada)

Coleman, William D., and Grace Skogstad, eds (1990) *Policy Communities and Public Policy in Canada* (Toronto: Copp Clark)

Commission of Inquiry on Unemployment Insurance (1986) *Report* (Forget Report) (Ottawa)

Crane, David, ed (1981) *Beyond the Monetarists* (Toronto: Canadian Institute for Public Policy)

Craven, Paul (1980) *'An Impartial Umpire': Industrial Relations and the Canadian State 1900–1911* (Toronto: University of Toronto Press)

Crispo, John (1978) *The Canadian Industrial Relations System* (Toronto: McGraw-Hill Ryerson)

Crosbie, John (1979) *Budget Speech* (Ottawa: Department of Finance)

Cross, M.S. (1974) *The Decline and Fall of a Good Idea: CCF-NDP Manifestos, 1932–69* (Toronto: New Hogtown Press)

Cross, Michael S., and Gregory S. Kealey, eds (1984) *Modern Canada, 1930–1980's* (Toronto: McClelland and Stewart)

Cuneo, Carl (1979) 'State, Class and Reserve Labour: The Case of the 1941

Canadian Unemployment Insurance Act,' *Canadian Review of Sociology and Anthropology* 16, 147–70
- (1980) 'State Mediations of Class Contradictions in Canadian Unemployment Insurance, 1930–35,' *Studies in Political Economy* no. 3, 37–65
- (1990) *Pay Equity: The Labour/Feminist Challenge* (Toronto: Oxford University Press)
Daenzer, Patricia M. (1987) 'Canadian Jobs Strategy: In Support of a Buyer's Market,' *Canadian Review of Social Policy* no. 18 (May) 58–64
Davies, James B. (1986) 'Training and Skill Development,' in Riddell, ed (1986c) 163–219
Deaton, Rick (1983) 'Unemployment: Canada's Malignant Social Pathology,' *Perception* 6 no. 5 (Summer) 14–19
Department of Finance (1985) *Account of the Cost of Selective Tax Measures* (Ottawa: Department of Finance)
Department of Labour (1970) *Unemployment Insurance in the 70's* (Ottawa)
DiGiacomo, Gordon (1977) 'Institutional Barriers to the Development of Tripartism in Canada,' unpublished master's research essay, Carleton University
Dingledine, Gary (1981) *A Chronology of Response: The Evolution of Unemployment Insurance from 1940 to 1980* (Ottawa: Department of Employment and Immigration)
Doern, G. Bruce, ed (1981a) *How Ottawa Spends Your Tax Dollars: Federal Priorities 1981* (Toronto: James Lorimer)
- (1981b) 'Spending Priorities: The Liberal View,' in Doern, ed (1981a) 1–55
- (1982a) *How Ottawa Spends Your Tax Dollars: National Policy and Economic Development* (Toronto: James Lorimer)
- (1982b) 'Liberal Priorities 1982: The Limits of Scheming Virtuously,' in Doern, ed (1982a) 1–36
- ed (1983a) *How Ottawa Spends: The Liberals, the Opposition and Federal Priorities* (Toronto: James Lorimer)
- (1983b) 'Priorities and Priority Setting in the Trudeau Era: The Political Problems of Doing First Things First,' in Doern, ed (1983a) 66–92
- (1985a) 'The Politics of Canadian Economic Policy: An Overview,' in Doern, ed (1985b) 1–110
- research coordinator (1985b) *The Politics of Economic Policy*, vol. 40, Royal Commission on the Economic Union and Development Prospects for Canada (Toronto: University of Toronto Press)
Doern, G. Bruce, and Peter Aucoin, eds (1979), *Public Policy in Canada: Organization, Process and Management* (Toronto: Macmillan)
Doern, G. Bruce, Allan M. Maslove, and Michael J. Prince (1988) *Public Budgeting in Canada: Politics, Economics and Management* (Ottawa: Carleton University Press)

Doern, G. Bruce, and Richard W. Phidd (1983) *Canadian Public Policy* (Toronto: Methuen)

Donner, Arthur W. (1988) 'Labour's Shrinking Share,' *The Facts* 35 no. 3, 17–18

Donner, Arthur W., and Douglas Peters (1979) *The Monetarist Counter Revolution: A Critique of Canadian Monetary Policy 1975–79* (Toronto: Canadian Institute for Public Policy)

Dupré, J. Stefan, David M. Cameron, Graeme H. McKechnie, and Theodore B. Rotenberg (1973), *Federalism and Policy Development: The Case of Adult Occupation Training in Ontario* (Toronto: University of Toronto Press)

Economic Council of Canada (1964) *First Annual Review: Economic Goals for Canada to 1970* (Ottawa: Economic Council of Canada)

– (1965) *Second Annual Review: Towards Sustained and Balanced Economic Growth* (Ottawa: Economic Council of Canada)

– (1971) *Eighth Annual Review: Design for Decision-Making – An Application to Human Resource Policies* (Ottawa: Economic Council of Canada)

– (1976) *People and Jobs: A Study of the Canadian Labour Market* (Ottawa: Economic Council of Canada)

– (1982) *In Short Supply: Jobs and Skills in the 1980's* (Ottawa: Economic Council of Canada)

Edelman, Murray (1964) *The Symbolic Uses of Politics* (Urbana, Ill.: University of Illinois Press)

– (1971) *Politics as Symbolic Action: Mass Arousal and Quiescence* (Chicago: Markham)

– (1975) 'Symbolism in Politics,' in Lindberg et al, eds (1975) 309–20

Eichner, A.S., ed. (1979) *A Guide to Post-Keynesian Economics* (London: Macmillan)

Elster, Jon (1982) 'Marxism, Functionalism and Game Theory,' *Theory and Society* 11, 453–82

Employment and Immigration Canada (EIC) (1977/8 to 1989/90) *Annual Report* (Ottawa: Employment and Immigration Canada)

– (1985) *Canadian Jobs Strategy* (Ottawa)

– (1987) *The Canadian Jobs Strategy: A Review of the First 18 Months* (Ottawa)

– (1988) *Report to the Minister of Employment and Immigration on CJS Delivery* (Ottawa)

Employment and Immigration Canada (EIC), Programme Evaluation Branch (1979), *1977–78 Job-Experience Training Programme Evaluation Report* (Ottawa: Department of Employment and Immigration)

– (1982) *Evaluation of the Employment Tax Credit Programme* (Ottawa: Department of Employment and Immigration)

- (1984a) *Evaluation Assessment: New Employment and Expansion Development Programmes* (Ottawa: Department of Employment and Immigration)
- (1984b) *A Pre-Evaluation Assessment Study of the Critical Trade Skills Training Programme* (Ottawa: EIC)
- (1984c) *Final Evaluation Report of the Canada Manpower Training Programme (Institutional)* (Ottawa: Department of Employment and Immigration)
- (n.d.) *Evaluation of the Canada Manpower Industrial Training Programme* (Ottawa: EIC)

Esping-Andersen, Gosta (1990) *The Three Worlds of Welfare Capitalism* (Oxford: Polity)

Fine, Ben, and Laurence Harris (1987) 'Ideology and Markets: Economic Theory and the New Right,' in Miliband, Panitch, and Saville, eds (1987) 365–92

Finn, Ed (1978) 'Tripartite Consultation at the National Level,' *Labour Gazette,* 78 65–70

Finn, Ed, and Michael McBane (1990) 'Index on Unemployment Insurance,' *Canadian Forum* 64 (May) 32

Fournier, Pierre (1986) 'Consensus Building in Canada: Case Studies and Prospects,' in Banting, ed (1986) 291–335

Fricker, Michael W. (1988) 'Private Sector Labour Legislation in Alberta, 1983–88,' MA thesis, University of Calgary

Gamble, Andrew (1988) *The Free Economy and the Strong State* (London: Macmillan)

Gauvin, Michel, Nicole Marchand, and Cal McKerral (1975) *Collective Bargaining Legislation for Special Groups in Canada* (Ottawa: Labour Canada)

Gera, Surendra (1987) 'An Evaluation of the Canadian Employment Tax Credit Program,' *Canadian Public Policy* 13 no. 2, 196–207

Gerlach, K., W. Peters, and W. Sengenberger, eds (1984) *Public Policies to Combat Unemployment in a Period of Economic Stagnation: An International Comparison* (Frankfurt: Campus/Verlag)

Gerlach, K., and W. Sengenberger (1984) 'Introduction: Active Employment and Labour Market Policies – Concepts, Approaches and Institutional Arrangements,' in Gerlach, Peters, and Sengenberger, eds (1984) 9–31

Giles, Anthony (1982) 'The Canadian Labour Congress and Tripartism,' *Relations industrielles* 37, 93–125

Gold, David A., Clarence Y.H. Lo, and Erik Olin Wright (1975) 'Recent Developments in Marxist Theories of the Capitalist State, Part 2,' *Monthly Review* 27 no. 6 (November), 36–51

Goldman, Barbara (1976) *New Directions for Manpower Policy* (Montreal: C.D. Howe Research Institute)

Goldthorpe, John H., ed (1984a) *Order and Conflict in Contemporary Capitalism* (Oxford: Clarendon)
- (1984b) 'The End of Convergence: Corporatist and Dualist Tendencies in Modern Western Societies,' in Goldthorpe, ed (1984a) 315–43
Gonick, Cy (1978) *Out of Work* (Toronto: James Lorimer)
- (1987a) 'Final Offer Selection: Splitting the Manitoba Movement,' *Canadian Dimension* 21 no. 6 (October) 20–3
- (1987b) *The Great Economic Debate: Failed Economics and a Future for Canada* (Toronto, James Lorimer and Co.)
Gough, Ian (1979) *The Political Economy of the Welfare State* (London: Macmillan)
Government of Canada (1981) *Economic Development for Canada in the 1980s* (Ottawa)
Graham, Katherine A., ed (1990) *How Ottawa Spends* (Ottawa: Carleton University Press)
Green, Christopher, and Jean-Michel Cousineau (1975) *Unemployment in Canada: The Impact of Unemployment Insurance* (Ottawa: Economic Council of Canada)
Green, Jim (1986) *Against the Tide: The Story of the Canadian Seamen's Union* (Toronto: Progress Books)
Grubel, Herbert G., Dennis Maki, and Shelley Sax (1975a) 'Real and Insurance-Induced Unemployment in Canada,' *Canadian Journal of Economics* 8, 174–91
- (1975b) 'Real and Insurance-Induced Unemployment in Canada: A Reply,' *Canadian Journal of Economics* 8 no. 4, 603–5
Grubel, Herbert G., and Michael A. Walker (1978a) 'Moral Hazard, Unemployment Insurance and the Rate of Unemployment,' in Grubel and Walker, eds (1978b) 1–35
- (1978b) *Unemployment Insurance: Global Evidence of Its Effects on Unemployment* (Vancouver: Fraser Institute)
Guest, Dennis (1980) *The Emergence of Social Security in Canada* (Vancouver: University of British Columbia Press)
Gunderson, Morley, M. Noah Meltz, and Sylvia Ostry, eds (1987) *Unemployment: International Perspectives* (Toronto: University of Toronto Press)
Haiven, Larry (1991) 'Hegemony and the Workplace: The Role of Arbitration,' in Haiven, McBride, and Shields, eds (1991) 79–117
Haiven, Larry, Stephen McBride, and John Shields, eds (1991) *Regulating Labour: The State, Neo-Conservatism and Industrial Relations* (Toronto: Garamond)
Hall, Peter A. (1984) 'Patterns of Economic Policy: An Organizational Approach,' in Bornstein, Held, and Krieger, eds (1984) 21–43
Hamilton, Malcolm B. (1987) 'The Elements of the Concept of Ideology,' *Political Studies* 35, 18–38

Hawthorne, George V. (1973) 'Prices and Incomes Policy: The Canadian Experience, 1969–72,' *International Labour Review* 108, 485–503
Heald, David A. (1983) *Public Expenditure* (Oxford: Martin Robertson)
Heidenheimer, Arnold J., Hugh Heclo, and Caroline Teich Adams (1983) *Comparative Public Policy: The Politics of Social Choice in Europe and America* (New York: St. Martin's Press)
Henning, Roger (1984) 'Industrial Policy or Employment Policy? Sweden's Responses to Unemployment,' in Richardson and Henning, eds (1984) 193–216
Hibbs, Douglas A. (1977) 'Macroeconomic Policy and Political Parties,' *American Political Science Review* 71 no. 4, 1467–87
Hicks, Michael (1983) 'Cutback Management in Canada,' *Australian Journal of Public Administration* 42 no. 2, 193–206
Hirosuke, Kawansishi (1986) 'The Reality of Enterprise Unionism,' in McCormack and Sugimoto, eds (1986) 138–56
Hoover, Kenneth, and Raymond Plant (1989) *Conservative Capitalism in Britain and the United States* (London: Routledge)
House of Commons, Special Committee on Employment Opportunities for the 80's (1980) *Work for Tomorrow: Employment Opportunities for the 80's* (Allmand Report) (Ottawa: House of Commons)
House of Commons, Standing Committee on Labour, Employment and Immigration (1986) *Proceedings*
– (1987) *Proceedings*
– (1988) *Proceedings*
Hueglin, Thomas O. (1987) 'The Politics of Fragmentation in an Age of Scarcity: A Synthetic View and Critical Analysis of Welfare State Crisis,' *Canadian Journal of Political Science* 22 no. 2, (June), 235–64
Hughes, James J., and Richard Perlman (1984) *The Economics of Unemployment: A Comparative Analysis of Britain and the United States* (Brighton: Wheatsheaf)
Hunt, E.K., and J.G. Schwartz, eds (1972) *A Critique of Economic Theory* (Harmondsworth: Penguin)
Hunter, Lawrence C. (1980) 'The End of Full Employment?' *British Journal of Industrial Relations* 18, 44–56
Huston, Lorne F. (1973) 'The State as Socializer: OFY and LIP Programmes,' in Roussopoulos, ed (1973) 99–108
Ichiyo, Muto (1986) 'Class Struggle in Post-War Japan,' in McCormack and Sugimoto (1986) 114–37
Impact Group (1987) *An Evaluation of Ontario's Training Services Experiment* (Toronto: Ministry of Skills Development)
Ismael, Jacqueline S., ed (1985) *Canadian Social Welfare Policy: Federal and Provincial Dimensions* (Kingston and Montreal: McGill-Queen's University Press)

– ed (1987) *The Canadian Welfare State: Evolution and Transition* (Edmonton: University of Alberta Press)

Jackson, Michael P., and Victor J.B. Hanby (1982) *British Work Creation Programmes* (Aldershot: Gower)

Jamieson, Stuart (1968) *Times of Trouble: Labour Unrest and Industrial Conflict in Canada, 1900–1966*, Study no. 22 for the Task Force on Labour Relations (Ottawa)

Jenson, Jane (1989) '"Different" But Not "Exceptional": Canada's Permeable Fordism,' *Canadian Review of Sociology and Anthropology* 26, 69–94

Jessop, Bob (1982) *The Capitalist State* (Oxford: Martin Robertson)

Jessop, Bob, Kevin Bonnett, Simon Bromley, and Tom Ling (1988) *Thatcherism* (Oxford: Polity)

Johnson, Andrew F. (1981) 'A Minister as an Agent of Policy Change: The Case of Unemployment Insurance in the Seventies,' *Canadian Public Administration* 24 no. 4, 612–33

Johnston, Richard (1986) *Public Opinion and Public Policy in Canada: Questions of Confidence*, vol. 35 of research studies for the Royal Commission on the Economic Union and Development Prospects for Canada (Toronto: University of Toronto Press)

Jordan, Grant (1984) 'Pluralistic Corporatisms and Corporate Pluralism,' *Scandinavian Political Studies* 7, 137–53

Kalecki, Michael (1943) 'Political Aspects of Full-Employment,' *Political Quarterly* 322–31

Kaliski, S.F. (1975) 'Real and Insurance-Induced Unemployment in Canada,' *Canadian Journal of Economics* 8 no. 4, 600–3

– (1984) 'Why Must Unemployment Remain So High?' *Canadian Public Policy* 10, 127–41

Katzenstein, Peter J. (1984) *Corporatism and Change: Austria, Switzerland, and the Politics of Industry* (Ithaca: Cornell University Press)

Kesselman, Jonathon R. (1983) *Financing Canadian Unemployment Insurance* (Toronto: Canadian Tax Foundation)

Keynes, J.M. (1926) *The End of Laissez-Faire* (London)

– (1936) *The General Theory of Employment, Interest and Money* (London: Macmillan)

Kirst, Sharon (1983) *Unemployment: Its Impact on Body and Soul* (Ottawa: Canadian Mental Health Association)

Kramar, Myron (1984) *The Impact of Plant Closures on Older Workers: Consolidated Bathurst: A Case Study* (Hamilton: Social Planning and Research Council of Hamilton and District)

Kurzer, Paulette (1988) 'The Politics of Central Banks: Austerity and Unemployment in Europe,' *Journal of Public Policy* 8, 21–47

Kwavnick, David (1972) *Organised Labour and Pressure Politics: The Cana-*

dian Labour Congress, 1956–68 (Montreal: McGill-Queen's University Press)

Lalonde, Marc (1983a) *Budget Speech* (Ottawa: Department of Finance)

– (1983b) *The Federal Deficit in Perspective* (Ottawa: Department of Finance)

– (1984) *The Budget Speech* (Ottawa: Department of Finance)

Lang, John (n.d.) 'A Lion in a Den of Daniels: A History of the International Union of Mine-Mill and Smelter Workers in Sudbury, Ontario 1942–62,' MA thesis, University of Guelph

Langille, David (1987) 'The Business Council on National Issues and the Canadian State,' *Studies in Political Economy*, no. 2 (autumn) 41–86

Lazar, Fred (1978) 'The Impact of the 1971 Unemployment Insurance Revisions on Unemployment Rates: Another Look,' *Canadian Journal of Economics* 11 no. 3, 559–70

Lehmbruch, Gerhard, and Philippe C. Schmitter, eds (1982) *Patterns of Corporatist Policy Making* (London: Sage)

Lembke, Jerry, and William M. Tattam (1984) *One Union in Wood: A Political History of the International Woodworkers of America* (New York: International Publishers)

Likierman, Andrew (1988) *Public Expenditure* (Harmondsworth: Penguin)

Lindberg, Leon N. (1985) 'Models of the Inflation-Disinflation Process,' in Lindberg and Maier, eds (1985) 25–50

Lindberg, Leon N., Robert Alford, Colin Crouch, and Claus Offe, eds (1975) *Stress and Contradiction in Modern Capitalism: Public Policy and the Theory of the State* (Lexington: D.C. Heath)

Lindberg, Leon N., Charles S. Maier, eds (1985) *The Politics of Inflation and Economic Stagnation* (Washington, DC: Brookings Institution)

Lipset, Seymour Martin (1955) 'The State of Democratic Politics,' *Canadian Forum* 35, 170–1

Lithwick, N. Harvey, and John Devlin (1984) 'Economic Development Policy: A Case Study in Underdeveloped Policy Making,' in Maslove, ed (1984a) 122–66

Logan, H.A. (1948) *Trade Unions in Canada* (Toronto: Macmillan)

Lynk, Michael (1988a) 'Labour Law Erosion,' *CUPE Facts* 10 no. 2: 72–7

– (1988b) 'The Labour Law Factor,' *Canadian Labour* 33 no. 2 18–20, 36

McBride, Stephen (1983) 'Public Policy as a Determinant of Interest Group Behaviour: The Canadian Labour Congress' Corporatist Initiative 1976–78,' *Canadian Journal of Political Science* 16 no. 3 (September) 501–17

– (1985) 'Corporatism, Public Policy and the Labour Movement,' *Political Studies* 33, 439–56

– (1986) 'Mrs. Thatcher and the Postwar Consensus: The Case of Trade Union Policy,' *Parliamentary Affairs* 39 no. 3 (July) 330–40

- (1987a) 'Hard Times and the "Rules of the Game." A Study of the Legislative Environment of Labour-Capital Conflict,' in Argue, Gannage, and Livingstone, eds (1987) 98–111
- (1987b) 'Trends and Priorities in Job Creation Programs: A Comparative Study of Federal and Selected Provincial Policies,' in Ismael, ed (1987) 151–70
- (1988) 'The Comparative Politics of Unemployment: British and Swedish Responses to Economic Crisis,' *Comparative Politics* 20 no. 3 (April) 303–23
McCallum, John (1981) 'Monetarism in Three Countries: Canada,' in Crane, ed (1981) 48–62
McCormack, Gavan, and Yoshio Sugimoto, eds (1986) *Democracy in Contemporary Japan* (Armonk, NY: M.E. Sharpe)
Macdonald, Donald S. (1976) *Budget Speech* (Ottawa: Department of Finance)
MacDowell, Laura Sefton (1978) 'The Formation of the Canadian Industrial Relations System during World War II,' *Labour: Journal of Canadian Labour Studies* 3, 175–96
MacEachen, Allan J. (1980) *The Budget* (Ottawa: Department of Finance)
- (1981) *Budget Speech* (Ottawa: Department of Finance)
- (1982) *Budget Speech* (Ottawa: Department of Finance)
McKeen, Wendy (1987) *The Canadian Jobs Strategy: Current Issues for Women* (Ottawa: Canadian Advisory Council on the Status of Women)
McKinney, John C. (1966) *Constructive Typology and Social Theory* (New York: Appleton-Century-Crofts)
Macmillan, Harold (1938) *The Middle Way* (London: Macmillan)
McQuaig, Linda (1987) *Behind Closed Doors: How the Rich Won Control of Canada's Tax System* (Markham, Ont.: Viking)
McVittie, James (1984) 'The Canada Labour Relations Council, 1975–76,' unpublished manuscript, University of Western Ontario
Mahon, Rianne (1983) 'Canadian Labour in the Battle of Eighties,' *Studies in Political Economy* no. 11, 149–75
- (1990) 'Adjusting to Win? The New Tory Training Initiative,' in Graham, ed (1990) 73–112
Malles, Paul (1976) 'The Road to Consensus Policies: Challenges and Realities,' Occasional Paper No. 4 (Ottawa: The Conference Board in Canada)
Manga, Pran, Robert Bruyles, and Gil Reschenthaler (1981) *Occupational Health and Safety: Issues and Alternatives* (Ottawa: Economic Council of Canada)
Marks, Gary (1986) 'Neocorporatism and Incomes Policy in Western Europe and North America,' *Comparative Politics* 18, 253–77
Martin, Andrew (1985), 'Wages, Profits and Investment in Sweden,' in Lindberg and Maier, eds (1985) 403–66

Martin, Ross M. (1983) 'Pluralism and the New Corporatism,' *Political Studies* 31, 86–102

Maslove, Allan M. (1981) 'Tax Expenditures, Tax Credits and Equity,' in Doern, ed (1981a) 232–54

– ed (1984a) *How Ottawa Spends 1984: The New Agenda* (Toronto: Methuen)

– (1984b) 'Ottawa's New Agenda: The Issues and the Constraints,' in Maslove, ed (1984a) 1–30

– ed (1985a) *How Ottawa Spends 1985: Sharing the Pie* (Toronto: Methuen)

– (1985b) 'The Public Pursuit of Private Interests,' in Maslove, ed (1985a) 1–29

Maslove, Allan M., Michael J. Prince, and G. Bruce Doern (1986) *Federal and Provincial Budgeting*, vol. 41 of research studies for Royal Commission on the Economic Union and Development Prospects for Canada (Toronto: University of Toronto Press)

Maslove, Allan M., and Gene Swimmer (1980) *Wage Controls in Canada, 1975–78: A Study of Public Decision Making* (Montreal: Institute for Research on Public Policy)

Masters, D.C. (1956) *The Winnipeg General Strike* (Toronto: University of Toronto Press)

Meidner, Rudolf (1984) 'Sweden: Approaching the Limits of Active Labour Market Policy,' in Gerlach, Peters, and Sengenberger, eds (1984) 247–65

Miliband, Ralph (1969) *The State in Capitalist Society* (London: Weidenfeld and Nicolson)

– (1987) 'Class Struggle from Above,' in Outhwaite and Mulkay, eds (1987) 175–84

Miliband, Ralph, Leo Panitch, and John Saville, eds (1987) *Socialist Register, 1987* (London: Merlin)

Montgomery, Lee Ann (1986) *Overview of the Canadian Jobs Strategy*, Background Report for the Royal Commission on Employment and Unemployment, Newfoundland and Labrador

Moon, Jeremy (1983) 'Policy Change in Direct Government Responses to UK Unemployment,' *Journal of Public Policy* 3, 301–29

Moon, Jeremy, and J.J. Richardson (1985) *Unemployment in the UK: Politics and Policies* (Aldershot: Gower)

Morris, Joe (1976) *Towards a Corporate State* (Ottawa: Canadian Labour Congress)

Munro, John (1977) 'Federal Proposals to Improve Labour-Management Relations,' *Labour Gazette* 77, 357–9

Murray, V.V., ed (1986) *The Consultative Process in Business-Government Relations*, Edited Proceedings of the Annual Conference on Business-Government Relations of the Max Bell Programme for Business-Government Studies, Faculty of Administrative Studies, York University, 24, 25 April 1986

Muszynski, Leon (1985) 'The Politics of Labour Market Policy,' in Doern, ed (1985b) 251–305
– (1988) 'The Tax Reform Hoax,' *The Facts* 10 no. 3, 6–10
Neilson, Erik (1985) *Job Creation, Training and Employment Services*, A Study Team Report to the Task Force on Program Review (Ottawa: Task Force on Program Review)
Nuti, D.M. (1972) 'On Incomes Policy,' in Hunt and Schwartz, eds (1972) 222–32
O'Connor, James (1973) *The Fiscal Crisis of the State* (New York: St. Martin's Press)
OECD (1977) *Economic Survey: Canada* (Paris)
– (1979) *Economic Survey: Canada* (Paris)
Olsen, Gregg (1991a) 'Labour Mobilisation and the Strength of Capital: The Rise and Stall of Economic Democracy in Sweden,' *Studies in Political Economy*, no. 34, 109–45
– (1991b) 'Swedish Social Democracy and Beyond: Internal Obstacles to Economic Democracy,' in Haiven, McBride, and Shields, eds (1991) 172–97
Ontario, Ministry of Skills Development (1987) *Discussion Paper on the Canadian Jobs Strategy: Policy and Implementation*, Prepared for Meeting of the Federal-Provincial/Territorial Ministers with Labour Market Responsibilities, 29–30 January 1987
Ontario Women's Directorate (1986) *Employment Equity for Women in the Ontario Public Service 1985/86* (Toronto)
Ornstein, Michael (1986) 'The Political Ideology of the Canadian Capitalist Class,' *Canadian Review of Sociology and Anthropology* 23, 182–209
Osberg, Lars (1979) 'Unemployment Insurance in Canada: A Review of Recent Amendments,' *Canadian Public Policy* 5 (spring) 223–35
Ouellet, André (1983) *Labour and Labour Issues in the 1980's* (Ottawa: Labour Canada)
Outhwaite, William, and Michael Mulkay, eds (1987) *Social Theory and Social Criticism* (Oxford: Basil Blackwell)
Pal, Leslie A. (1983) 'The Fall and Rise of Developmental Use of UI Funds,' *Canadian Public Policy* 9 no. 1, 81–93
– (1985) 'Revision and Retreat: Canadian Unemployment Insurance 1971–81,' in Ismael, ed (1985) 75–104
– (1987) 'Tools for the Job: Canada's Evolution from Public Works to Mandated Employment,' in Ismael, ed (1987) 33–62
– (1988a) 'Sense and Sensibility: Comments on Forget,' *Canadian Public Policy* 14 no. 1, 7–14
– (1988b) *State, Class and Bureaucracy: Canadian Unemployment Insurance and Public Policy* (Kingston and Montreal: McGill-Queen's University Press)

Panitch, Leo, ed (1977a) *The Canadian State: Political Economy and Political Power* (Toronto: University of Toronto Press)
- (1977b) 'The Role and Nature of the Canadian State,' in Panitch, ed (1977a) 3–27
- (1979) 'Corporatism in Canada,' *Studies in Political Economy* no. 1, 43–92
- (1980) 'Recent Theorizations of Corporatism: Reflections on a Growth Industry,' *British Journal of Sociology* 31, 159–87
Panitch, Leo, and Don Swartz (1985) *From Consent to Coercion: The Assault on Trade Union Freedoms* (Toronto: Garamond)
- (1988) *The Assault on Trade Union Freedoms: From Consent to Coercion Revisited* (Toronto: Garamond)
Paquet, Pierre (1976) 'The Development of Canadian Policy in Occupational Adult Education and Manpower,' in Canadian Association for Adult Education, *Manpower Training at the Crossroads* (Ottawa: National Library) 5–8
Payne, James L. (1979) 'Inflation Unemployment and Left-Wing Political Parties: A Reanalysis,' *American Political Science Review* 73 no. 1, 181–5
Pentland, H.C. (1968) 'A Study of the Changing Social, Economic and Political Background of the Canadian System of Industrial Relations,' mimeo, Task Force on Labour Relations, Ottawa
People's Commission on Unemployment, Newfoundland and Labrador (1978) *Now That We've Burned Our Boats ... (Report)* (St John's: Newfoundland and Labrador Federation of Labour)
Phillips, A.W. (1958) 'The Relation between Unemployment and the Rate of Change of Money Wage Rates in the United Kingdom, 1861–1957,' *Economica* 34, 283–99
Phillips, Gerald E. (1977) *The Practice of Labour Relations and Collective Bargaining in Canada* (Toronto: Butterworths)
Phillips, Paul (n.d.) *Unemployment Insurance: Battleground in the Debate on the Economic Crisis*, Publication No. 18 (Ottawa: Canadian Centre for Policy Alternatives)
Pichelmann, Karl, and Michael Wagner (1984) 'Austria: Full Employment at All Cost: Trends in Employment and Labour Market Policy in Austria, 1975–83,' in Gerlach, Peters, and Sengenberger, eds (1984) 207–45
Piva, Michael J. (1975) 'The Workmen's Compensation Movement in Ontario,' *Ontario History* 7, 39–56
Pollack, Marion (1987) 'The Politics of "Restraint" and the Response of the Trade Union Bureaucracy in BC,' in Argue, Gannage, and Livingstone, eds (1987) 149–58
Prince, Michael J., ed (1986) *How Ottawa Spends 1986–87: Tracking the Tories* (Toronto: Methuen)
- ed (1987) *How Ottawa Spends 1987–88: Restraining the State* (Toronto: Methuen)

Prince, Michael J., and James J. Rice (1981) 'Department of National Health and Welfare: The Attack on Social Policy,' in Doern, ed (1981a) 90–119

Purvis, Douglas D., and Constance Smith (1986) 'Fiscal Policy in Canada, 1963–84,' in Sargent, ed (1986) 1–42

Queen's University (1983) *Canadian Labour Markets in the 1980s*, Proceedings of a Conference Held at Queen's University at Kingston, 25–26 February

Rea, K.J., and J.T. McLeod, eds (1976) *Business and Government in Canada: Selected Readings*, 2nd ed (Toronto: Methuen)

Rea, S., and G. Jump (1975) *The Impact of the 1971 Unemployment Insurance Act on Work Incentives and the Aggregate Labour Market* (Ottawa: UIC)

Rea, S.A. (1977) 'Unemployment Insurance and Labour Supply: A Simulation of the 1971 Unemployment Insurance Act' *Canadian Journal of Economics* 10, 263–78

Reasons, Charles E., Lois L. Ross, and Craig A. Patterson (1981) *Assault on the Worker: Occupational Health and Safety in Canada* (Toronto: Butterworths)

Reeves, M.A., and W.A. Kerr (1986) 'Implications of the Increasing Emphasis on Monetary Policy for the Federal State: The Case of Canada,' *Journal of Commonwealth and Comparative Politics* 24 no. 3, 254–68

Rice, James J. (1987) 'Restitching the Safety Net: Altering the National Social Security System,' in Prince, ed (1987) 211–36

Richardson, Jeremy, and Roger Henning, eds (1984) *Unemployment Policy Responses of Western Democracies* (London: Sage)

Riddell, Craig, research coordinator (1986a) *Labour-Management Cooperation in Canada* vol. 15 of research studies for the Royal Commission on the Economic Union and Development Prospects for Canada (Toronto: University of Toronto Press)

– (1986b) *Dealing with Inflation and Unemployment in Canada* vol. 25 of research studies for the Royal Commission on the Economic Union and Development Prospects for Canada (Toronto: University of Toronto Press)

– research coordinator (1986c) *Adapting to Change: Labour Market Adjustment in Canada* vol. 18 of research studies for the Royal Commission on the Economic Union and Development Prospects for Canada (Toronto: University of Toronto Press)

Roberts, John (1983) *Government of Canada Job Creation Programs* (Ottawa: Department of Employment and Immigration)

Robinson, Derek (1986) *Monetarism and the Labour Market* (Oxford: Clarendon Press)

Rokuro, Hidaka (1986) 'The Crisis of Postwar Democracy,' in McCormack and Sugimoto, eds (1986) 228–46

Roussopoulos, Dimitrios I., ed (1973) *The Political Economy of the State* (Montreal: Black Rose Books)

Royal Commission on Equality in Employment (1983) *Report* (Abella Report) (Ottawa: Supply and Services)

Royal Commission on the Economic Union and Development Prospects for Canada (1985) *Report*, 3 vols. (Macdonald Report) (Ottawa: Supply and Services)

Russell, Bob (1986) 'The Crisis of the State and the State of the Crisis: The Canadian Welfare Experience,' in James Dickinson and Bob Russell, eds *Family, Economy and State: The Social Reproduction Process under Capitalism* (London: Croom Helm) 309–37

– (1987) 'State Constructed Industrial Relations and the Social Reproduction of Production: The Case of the Canadian IDIA,' *Canadian Review of Sociology and Anthropology* 24 no. 2 (May) 213–31

– (1990) *Back to Work? Labour, State and Industrial Relations in Canada* (Scarborough: Nelson Canada)

– (1991) 'Assault without Defeat: Contemporary Industrial Relations and the Canadian Labour Movement,' in Haiven, McBride, and Shields, eds (1991) 14–44

Russell, Peter (1973) *Leading Constitutional Decisions*, revised ed (Toronto: McClelland and Stewart)

Rymes, Thomas K. (1986) 'Does the Bank of Canada Matter?' in Prince, ed (1986) 179–207

Sargent, John, research coordinator (1986) *Fiscal and Monetary Policy*, vol. 21 of research studies for the Royal Commission on the Economic Union and Development Prospects for Canada (Toronto: University of Toronto Press)

Sawyer, Malcolm C. (1985) *The Economics of Michael Kalecki* (London: Macmillan)

Scharpf, Fritz W. (1984) 'Strategy Choice, Economic Feasibility and Institutional Constraints as Determinants of Full-Employment Policy during the Recession,' in Gerlach, Peters, and Sengenberger, eds (1984) 67–114

Schmidt, Manfred G. (1982a) 'Does Corporatism Matter? Economic Crisis, Politics and Rates of Unemployment in Capitalist Democracies in the 1970's,' in Lehmbruch and Schmitter, eds (1982) 237–58

– (1982b) 'The Role of the Parties in Shaping Macroeconomic Policy,' in Castles, ed (1982) 97–176

– (1984) 'Labour Market Performance and Inflation in OECD Nations: A Political-Institutional View,' in Gerlach, Peters, and Sengenberger, eds (1984) 34–66

– (1987) 'The Politics of Full-Employment in Western Democracies,' *Annals of the American Academy of Political and Social Science* 492, July, 171–81

Sharpe, Andrew, Jean-Pierre Voyer, and Duncan Cameron (1988) 'Unemployment: Its Nature, Costs and Causes,' in Cameron and Sharpe, eds (1988) 19–46

Sherman, Howard J. (1976) *Stagflation: A Radical Theory of Unemployment and Inflation* (New York: Harper and Row)

Shields, John (1991) 'Building a New Hegemony in British Columbia: Can Neo-Conservative Industrial Relations Succeed?' in Haiven, McBride, and Shields, eds (1991) 45–78

Showler, Brian (1981) 'Political Economy and Unemployment,' in Showler and Sinfield, eds (1981) 27–58

Showler, Brian, and Adrian Sinfield, eds (1981) *The Workless State: Studies in Unemployment* (Oxford: Martin Robertson)

Siedule, Tom, Nicholas Skoulas, and Keith Newton (1976) *The Impact of Economy-Wide Changes on the Labour Force: An Econometric Analysis* (Ottawa: Economic Council of Canada)

Simeon, Richard (1987) 'Inside the Macdonald Commission,' *Studies in Political Economy* no. 22, 167–79

Smith, Douglas A. (1986) 'The Development of Employment and Training Programs,' in Maslove, ed (1984a) 167–88

Smith, Patrick, and Laurent Dobuzinskis (1987) 'From the New Reality to the New Economy: Job Creation Policy in Vander Zalm's British Columbia,' Paper for the 3rd National Conference on Provincial Social Welfare Policy, Banff, April

Smucker, Joseph (1980) *Industrialization in Canada* (Scarborough: Prentice-Hall)

Social Planning Council of Metropolitan Toronto (1982) *A Job for Everyone: A Response to 'Un'Employment Policies in Canada* (Toronto: Council)

Stanbury, William T., and Jane Fulton (1984) 'Suasion as a Governing Instrument,' in Maslove, ed (1984a) 282–324

Stanbury, W.T., Gerald J. Gorn, and Charles B. Weinberg (1983) 'Federal Advertising Expenditures,' in Doern, ed (1983) 133–72

Struthers, James (1983) *No Fault of Their Own: Unemployment and the Canadian Welfare State, 1914–1941* (Toronto: University of Toronto Press)

Sugimoto, Yushio (1986) 'The Manipulation Bases of "Consensus" in Japan,' in McCormack and Sugimoto, eds (1986) 65–75

Swimmer, Gene (1981) 'Labour Canada: A Department "of" Labour or "for" Labour?' in Doern, ed (1981a) 148–83

– (1984), 'Six and Five,' in Maslove, ed (1984a) 240–81

– (1987) 'Changes to Public Service Labour Legislation: Revitalizing or Destroying Collective Bargaining,' in Prince, ed (1987) 293–316

Swimmer, Gene, and Darlene Gollesch (1986) 'Affirmative Action for Women in the Federal Public Service,' in Prince, ed (1986) 208–49

Tanguay, A. Brian (1986) 'Recasting Labour Relations in Quebec, 1976–1985: Towards the Disciplinary State?' Paper Presented to the Annual Meeting of the Canadian Political Science Association, Winnipeg, June

Tarantelli, Ezio (1987) 'Monetary Policy and the Regulation of Inflation and Unemployment,' in Gunderson, Meltz, and Ostry, eds (1987) 94–102

Task Force on Labour Market Development (1981) *Labour Market Development in the 1980's* (Dodge Report) (Ottawa: Employment and Immigration Canada)

Task Force on Unemployment Insurance (1981) *Unemployment Insurance in the 1980's* (Ottawa: Employment and Immigration Canada)

Therborn, Goran (1986) *Why Some Peoples Are More Unemployed than Others: The Strange Paradox of Growth and Unemployment* (London: Verso)

Thurow, Lester C. (1984) *Dangerous Currents: The State of Economics* (New York: Vintage)

Tobin, James (1987) 'Macroeconomic Diagnosis and Prescription,' in Gunderson, Meltz, and Ostry, eds (1987) 12–40

Trebilcock, Michael J., Douglas G. Hartle, Robert S. Prichard, and Donald N. Dewees (1982) *The Choice of Governing Instrument* (Ottawa: Economic Council of Canada)

Tufte, Edward R. (1978) *Political Control of the Economy* (Princeton, NJ: Princeton University Press)

Tuohy, Carolyn (1990) 'Institutions and Interests in the Occupational Health Area: The Case of Quebec,' in Coleman and Skogstad, eds (1990) 238–65

Unemployment Insurance Commission (UIC) (1977) *Comprehensive Review of the Unemployment Insurance Programme in Canada* (Ottawa)

United Electrical Workers (1979) *Which Path for Labour? ... Collaboration or a Militant Class Struggle Fightback* (Toronto: UEW)

Uusitalo, Paavo (1984) 'Monetarism, Keynesianism and the Institutional Status of Central Banks,' *Acta Sociologica* 27, 31–50

Waldie, K.G. (1986) 'The Evolution of Labour-Government Consultation on Economic Policy,' in Riddell, research coordinator (1986a) 151–201

Walsh, W.D. (1975) 'The Canadian Experiment with Voluntary Incomes Restraint, Degree of Labour Organization, and Cyclical Sensitivity of Employment,' *Relations industrielles* 30, 390–407

Warskett, Rosemary (1990) 'Wage Solidarity and Equal Value: Or Gender and Class in the Structuring of Workplace Hierarchies,' *Studies in Political Economy* no. 32, (summer) 55–83

Webber, Douglas (1983) 'Combatting and Acquiescing in Unemployment? Crisis Management in Sweden and West Germany,' *West European Politics* 6, 23–43

Whitaker, Reg (1977) 'Images of the State in Canada,' in Panitch, ed (1977a) 28–68

Whiteley, Paul F. (1985) 'Evaluating the Monetarist Experiment in Britain,' Paper Presented at the Political Studies Association Annual Meeting, University of Manchester

Williams, A. Paul (1989) 'Access and Accommodation in the Canadian Welfare State: The Political Significance of Contacts between State, Labour and Business Leaders,' *Canadian Review of Sociology and Anthropology* 26, 217–39

Wilson, Michael H. (1984) *Economic and Fiscal Statement* (Ottawa: Department of Finance)

– (1985) *Securing Economic Renewal: Budget Papers* (Ottawa: Department of Finance)

– (1987) *The Agenda for Economic Renewal: Principles and Progress* (Ottawa: Department of Finance)

– (1988) *The Fiscal Plan ...* (Ottawa: Department of Finance)

– (1990) *Canada's Economic and Fiscal Performance and Prospects* (Ottawa: Department of Finance)

Wolfe, David (1977) 'The State and Economic Policy in Canada, 1968–75,' in Panitch, ed (1977a) 251–88

– (1984) 'The Rise and Demise of the Keynesian Era in Canada 1930–82,' in Cross and Kealey, eds (1984) 46–78

– (1985) 'The Politics of the Deficit,' in Doern, ed (1985b) 111–62

Wolfson, Alan (1983) 'Discussion' in Queen's University (1983) 145–7

Woods, H.D. (1973) *Labour Policy in Canada*, 2nd ed (Toronto: Macmillan)

Woods, W.D., and Pradeep Kumar, eds (1976) *Canadian Perspectives on Wage-Price Guidelines: A Book of Readings* (Kingston: Industrial Relations Centre, Queen's University)

Woods Gordon (1988) *Study of College and CITC Experiences with the Canada/Ontario Agreement on Training* (Toronto: Ministry of Skills Development)

Woolley, John T. (1982) 'Monetarists and the Politics of Monetary Policy,' *Annals of the American Academy of Political and Social Sciences* no. 459, 148–60

Yates, Charlotte (1990) 'Labour and Lobbying: A Political Economy Approach,' in Coleman and Skogstad, eds (1990) 266–90

Zakuta, L. (1964) *A Protest Movement Becalmed: A Study of Social Change in the CCF* (Toronto: University of Toronto Press)

Zoeteweij, Bert (1983) 'Anti-inflation Policies in the Industrialized Market Economy Countries,' *International Labour Review* 122, 563–78 and 691–708

Zussman, David (1986) 'Walking the Tightrope: The Mulroney Government and the Public Service,' in Prince, ed (1986) 250–82

Index

Abella Royal Commission on Equality in Employment, 210

accumulation: business preferences, 94; Conservative strategy, 104–5; criteria, 19–20, 67, 92, 121–2, 165–6, 189; and income distribution, 95–102; and industrial relations, 189, 191, 193, 206, 207, 216; and interest rates, 97–100; and labour market, 124, 127, 129–33, 136, 145, 149, 154, 157, 158, 215; and legitimation, 18–19, 20, 24, 57, 60, 102–3, 193–4, 207, 208, 213; and monetarism, 67, 91–2; and post-Keynesianism, 91; and the state, 17, 57, 71, 91–106; and tax expenditures, 102; and unemployment insurance, 164, 165–6, 175, 177, 178–9, 184

Adult Occupation Training Act (1967), 125, 134, 135

Alberta Federation of Labour, 204

Alberta nurses, illegal strike, 204

Allmand Report (1980), 133–4

Andras, Robert, 173

anti-communism, 195

Anti-Inflation Board, 72, 80, 89

Anti-Inflation Programme, 82–3, 199

Armstrong, Hugh, 145

Armstrong, Pat, 145

Atkinson, Michael M., 92

automatic stabilizers, 71–2, 74, 84; and social programs, 85, 105–6; and unemployment insurance, 162, 164–5

Axworthy, Lloyd, 176

back-to-work legislation, 197–202; see also industrial relations legislation

balanced budget, ideology of, 84

Bank of Canada: criticisms of government policy, 81; critics of, 81; gradualism, 73, 86, 107–8; and ideological legitimation, 107–8; and inflation, 50–1, 81, 89–90; and monetarism, 16, 73, 79–80, 86, 89-90; and monetary policy, 72, 79–80, 82

Banting, Keith, 113

Barber, Clarence L., 107

Basic Training for Skill Development, 149

Bellemare, Diane, 46–7
Blair, Cassandra, 113
Blais, André, 101
Blank, Stephen, 45
Bossons, John, 77
Boston, Jonathon, 36
Bouey, Gerald, 79
British Columbia Federation of Labour, 203
British Columbia Teachers Federation, 203
budget speeches: and government priorities, 109–11; and monetarism, 86–8, 91
business: and corporatist structures, 54–5, 179; and the deficit, 93–5; and full employment, 27–8, 56; and Keynesianism, 14, 60–1; and labour legislation (BC), 203–4; and monetarism, 14, 27; and post-Keynesianism, 68, 91; and social policy, 57, 94; and the state, 27–8, 89, 92–3, 188, 189, 218–20; and tax expenditures, 104; and tax reform, 92; and unemployment insurance, 160–1, 178, 180, 188; see also capital
Business Council of British Columbia, 203
Business Council on National Issues (BCNI), 91; policy influence of, 28, 92, 93; and the state, 91, 103

Cameron, David, 38
Campbell, Robert M., 55, 84–5
Canada Assistance Plan, 152
Canada Employment and Immigration Commission (CEIC), 124–5, 174, 178

Canada Manpower Industrial Training Programme, 129
Canada Manpower Training-on-the-Job Programme, 128
Canada Manpower Training Programme (CMTP), 125–7, 129, 133
Canada-Ontario Agreement on Training (1986), 152–3
Canada–United States Free Trade Agreement, 206, 218, 220
Canada Works, 138
Canadian Federation of Independent Business (CFIB), 146
Canadian Jobs Strategy (CJS): and federal-provincial training agreements, 148; interpretations of, 137, 149–58, 219; origins, 133, 146–8; and private sector, 149, 154; programs, 148, 153–5; and training, 122, 136–7, 148–9, 156–7
Canadian Labour Congress (CLC), and corporatism, 53–5, 207–8
Carnoy, Martin, 20
central banks, autonomy of, 43–4
Charter of Rights and Freedoms, 201, 205
Chernomas, Bob, 67
Chorney, Harold, 20, 93
Chrétien, Jean, 88
Clark, Joe, 88
class power, balance of: and corporatism, 53–5; and full employment, 40–1; and ideology, 25; and industrial relations, 73, 194–5, 212; and state policy, 27–8, 72–3; and unemployment, 27–8, 47, 56; and unemployment insurance, 161, 219; and welfare state regimes, 42
coercion: and industrial relations,

20, 51, 189–95 passim, 206, 212, 216; state and, 216–17; and trade unions, 92; and unemployment insurance, 160, 164, 165, 172, 178, 179

Cold War, 194, 195

Coleman, William D., 92

collective bargaining, 53, 60, 66; see also industrial relations policy

Commission of Inquiry on Unemployment Insurance: see Forget Commission

communists, 195

Community Industrial Training Committees, 152

Comprehensive Review of Unemployment Insurance (1977), 162, 181, 182, 183

concrete legitimation: and accumulation, 102–3; criteria, 20–1, 121–2; and full employment, 213; and industrial relations, 216; and labour-market policy, 141–56, 158, 215; state priority to, 23–4, 71, 92, 102–3; and tax expenditures, 102; and unemployment insurance, 160, 164–8 passim, 178, 179, 188, 215–16; see also ideological legitimation; legitimation

Conference Board of Canada, 82–3

Conservative government (Clark), 1979 budget, 88

Conservative government (Diefenbaker), 163

Conservative government (Mulroney): accumulation strategy, 104–5; and deficit, 93–4; labour-market policy, 137, 147–8, 150–2; and trade unions, 202; and unemployment insurance, 177

Co-operative Commonwealth Federation (CCF), 52, 195, 212

corporatism: business and, 54–5, 112; in Canada, 52, 53–5; defined, 37; and full employment, 37–40; and incomes policy, 25, 37–9; in Japan, 40; and labour, 53–5, 112, 207–8; and post-Keynesianism, 25; state and, 206–8; in Sweden, 37, 39; in Switzerland, 40; and welfare state regimes, 42

Craven, Paul, 227 n 2

Crispo, John, 227 n 1

Critical Trade Skills Training, 135, 136

Cuneo, Carl, 145, 160

deficit: and accumulation, 94–5; in budget speeches, 109–11; cyclical, 76, 77–8; effects, 71; inflation-adjusted, 76–7, 79; and monetarism, 15; reduction of, 90–1, 93–5; and revenues, 88; size of, 74, 75–6; and the state, 91, 93–5, 102; structural, 76–8, 88

Devlin, John, 103

Dingledine, Gary, 163–75

Dodge Report, 133–4, 146

Doern, G. Bruce, 85, 104, 108, 124

Dungan, D.P., 77

Dupré, Stefan, 125, 128, 129

Economic Council of Canada, 124, 125, 133–4, 168

Edelman, Murray, 22–3

Edwards, John, 220 n 8

Employers Liability Act (Ontario, 1886), 190

employment: part-time, 6; public

service, 75; *see also* full employment; unemployment
Employment and Immigration, Department of, 133
Employment and Immigration Canada, 154
employment equity, 144–5, 209, 210–11
employment standards legislation, 190–1, 194, 208–9
Employment Tax Credit Programme, 138–9, 146
Esping-Anderson, Gösta, 41–3
European Community, 33
expenditures, government: Bank of Canada and, 81; public debt and, 74; restraint, 73–5, 78, 90–1, 102–6

Factory Act (Ontario, 1884), 190–1
federal-provincial relations: and incomes policy, 82, 83; and training, 122–3, 149–50, 152–4, 157, 219
Finance: Department of, 78, 100; minister of, responsibility for macroeconomic policy, 72
First Ministers' Conference on the Economy: (1978), 145; (1985), 147
fiscal policy: defined, 71; effects, 72–3; stance, 77–9; trends, after 1975, 73–9, 83; *see also* macroeconomic policy
Forget Commission, 184, 186–7; opposition to, 187–8
Fournier, Pierre, 112
full employment: in Austria, 34; and capital, 60; in Japan, 34, 36, 40–1; and Keynesianism, 13, 58–60; and labour, 60, 192; and legitimation, 214; in Norway, 40; policies,

47–50; redefinition of, 64; and right-wing parties, 36–7; roads to, 40–1; sacrifice of, 216; in Sweden, 34; in Switzerland, 36, 40–1
full-employment commitment, 40–1; in Austria, 46–7; in Britain, 45–6; in Canada, 55, 56; in Japan, 47; in Norway, 46–7; in Sweden, 45–7; in Switzerland, 47
Fulton, Jane, 108–9
functionalism, 17, 18, 19

Gainers strike, 204
Gamble, Andrew, 218
General Industrial Training, 135
Gera, Surendra, 146
Gerlach, K., 47
Gill Committee, 163
Goldthorpe, John H., 38
Gonick, Cy, 82, 173
Gough, Ian, 19
gradualism: of anti-inflation strategy, 82
Gramsci, Antonio, 21–2
Gray, Herb, 103
Gregg, Allan, 107
Grubel, Herbert G., 182, 183

Hansen, Phillip, 20
hegemonic project, 22, 220
hegemony, 20–1, 23, 220
Hibbs, Douglas, 35, 36
Hicks, Michael, 74
Hoover, Kenneth, 21
House of Commons Standing Committee on Labour, Employment and Immigration, 153
Hueglin, Thomas, 17–18
Huston, Lorne F., 144

ideological legitimation: and Bank of Canada, 108; and budget speeches, 109–11; consultation, 110, 112–13; criteria, 20–3, 121–2; and employment equity, 144–5, 146; failed attempts at, 113–14; and government advertising, 115–16; and gradualism, 107–8; and hegemony, 220; and industrial relations policy, 206–11; and labour-market policy, 141–6, 148, 152, 154, 215; and legitimacy crisis, 24, 67; and public-sector incomes policy, 114; state and, 71, 106–7, 216–17; and throne speeches, 109–11; and tokenism, 110–11; and unemployment insurance, 160, 179–88; see also concrete legitimation; legitimation
immigration, 123
income distribution: and accumulation, 95–102; and Anti-Inflation Programme, 82; and fiscal policy, 99–102; and incomes policy, 82–3, 96; and macroeconomic policy, 78; and monetary policy, 96–9; and unemployment insurance, 164–5
incomes policy: and corporatism, 38–9; effects, 72, 82–3; federal-provincial co-operation, 82, 83; and industrial relations, 83; and post-Keynesianism, 13; public sector, 83, 114–15; in Sweden, 39; voluntary, 82; see also Anti-Inflation Programme; industrial relations policy; wage and price controls
Industrial Disputes Investigation Act, 192, 212

industrial hygeine, division of (Ontario), 190
industrial relations legislation, 190, 191–2, 194–5; conciliation procedures, 192, 194, 195; constitutional jurisdiction, 192, 195; excluded groups, 196–7; provincial, 195–6, 199, 202–5; public sector, 196–7, 200–2; special provisions, 197; in United States, 206; see also back-to-work legislation; collective bargaining; employment equity; employment standards legislation; incomes policy; Industrial Disputes Investigation Act; industrial relations policy; PC 1003; wage and price controls; Wagner Act
industrial relations policy, 51, 189–90, 194–7, 216; see also back-to-work legislation; collective bargaining; employment equity; employment standards legislation; incomes policy; wage and price controls
inflation: Bank of Canada and, 50–1, 81, 89–90, 107–8; in budget speeches, 109–11; control of, 47, 119–20; declining rate of, 83; delegitimizing effects of, 108; and monetary policy, 80–2; and state priorities, 73, 83
Institute for Occupational Health and Safety, 209
interest rates, 74, 80–1, 96–100

Jenson, Jane, 19
Jessop, Bob, 22–3
job creation, 123–4, 134, 137–41; community benefit, 138; confused

goals, 138; expenditures, 141–2,
143; incrementality, 140; number
of participants, 141–2, 144; private-sector benefit, 138, 140; programs, 137; role of, 142–6; and
training, 134; *see also* Canadian
Jobs Strategy; labour-market policy
Job Experience Training Programme, 138
Johnson, Andrew F., 163–4
Johnston, Donald, 103
Johnston, Richard, 11
Jump, G., 181, 182

Kalecki, Michael, 61, 62
Kaliski, S.F., 182
Katzenstein, Peter, 40
Keynes, John Maynard, 58–60; *see
also* Keynesianism; post-Keynesianism
Keynesianism, 58–62; and accumulation, 25–6, 57, 68; in Britain,
45–6; in Canada, 55, 61–2; capital's reservations, 60–1; and collective bargaining, 211; decline of,
84–9; dominant paradigm, 15–16,
84–5; and full employment, 13;
and labour legislation, 192, 194;
and labour-market policy, 68, 118,
119, 122, 124; and legitimation,
25–6, 57, 68; and macroeconomic
policy, 68; origins, 13; and public
policy, 3; and stagflation, 14; and
state's role, 13; and trade unions,
211, 227–8 n 7; and unemployment, 13; and unemployment insurance, 161–3, 188; *see also*

Keynes, John Maynard; post-
Keynesianism
Kurzer, Paulette, 44

labour: and corporatist structures,
53–5, 112, 179, 206–8; dissent
from reports, 113, 187; divisions
on corporatism, 54; and full employment, 27–8, 60; opposition to
legislation, 178, 203, 204; and the
state, 93, 189, 219; and unemployment insurance, 161, 188; and
wage and price controls, 68, 82,
197, 207, 209; *see also* Canadian
Labour Congress; trade unions
Labour, Department of, and legitimation, 206–7, 209–11
Labour Force Development Board,
179
Labour Force Development Strategy, 179
Labour government, New Zealand,
36
labour-market policy, 51, 214–15;
active, 118, 119–20, 124, 127–33;
confusion over goals, 121, 127–33;
definition, 118–19; early, 122–4;
expenditures, decline of, 149–54;
federal-provincial agreement, 147;
and Keynesianism, 68, 118, 119,
122, 124; and macroeconomic
policy, 119; and monetarism,
65–6; periodization, 122; and
post-Keynesianism, 64, 118,
119–20, 124; and privatization,
152; role under Mulroney government, 150–2; in Sweden, 36–7; *see
also* Canadian Jobs Strategy; job
creation; training

Labour party (UK), 46
labour policy: *see* industrial relations policy
Lalonde, Marc, 76–7, 88–9
Langille, David, 28, 92–3
Lazar, Fred, 182
legitimation: and accumulation, 18–19, 20, 24, 57, 60, 102–3, 193–4, 207, 208, 213; criteria, 19–20, 20–1, 67, 165–6, 223 n 5, 223 n 7; and industrial relations policy, 189, 191, 198, 199, 200, 204, 207, 208–9, 210–11, 211–12; and job creation, 142, 144; and labour-market policy, 127–33, 139–40, 143–4; state activities, 17, 206–11; and unemployment, 59; and unemployment insurance, 160, 164; *see also* concrete legitimation; ideological legitimation
Liberal government: and accumulation, 105; and economic development, 103; and social policy, 105
Lindberg, Leon, 47
Lipset, S.M., 60
Lithwick, N. Harvey, 103
Local Employment Assistance Programme, 137
Local Initiatives Programme, 138, 144

McCallum, John, 107
Macdonald, Donald, 73, 86–8
MacDonald, Flora, 147–8
Macdonald Commission, 111–12, 184, 185–6
McDougall, Barbara, 177
MacEachen, Allan, 88
Mackasey, Bryce, 165

Macmillan, Harold, 59
McQuaig, Linda, 100
McVittie, James, 207
macroeconomic policy, 50–1, 71, 78, 83, 213–14; *see also* fiscal policy; incomes policy; monetary policy; wage and price controls
Mahon, Rianne, 208
Major Projects Task Force, 208
Manitoba, views on Canadian Jobs Strategy, 150, 153
Manitoba Federation of Labour, 205
Manpower and Immigration, Department of, 124, 125, 127–33
Martin, Andrew, 39
Marx, Karl, 220
Maslove, Allan, 78, 85, 102
Matkin, James, 203
Meech Lake Accord, 218, 220
Miliband, Ralph, 23
monetarism, 15, 65–7; and accumulation, 25–6, 67, 91–2; and Bank of Canada, 86; and capital, 14, 43, 96–7; and corporatism, 55; dominant paradigm, 14–16, 84–91; and inflation, 14–15, 45, 51, 65; and Keynesianism, 14–15, 68; and labour-market policy, 65–6, 118, 120–1; and Macdonald Commission, 111–12, 185; and neo-conservatism, 3, 14; and privatization, 15, 66; and the state, 3, 14, 15, 57, 65, 86–8, 184, 212; and trade unions, 15, 45, 66, 197, 211; and unemployment, 3, 14, 45, 55, 57, 65, 67; and unemployment insurance, 66, 161–2, 175, 177, 179–88 passim
monetary policy, 72–3, 74, 79–82,

83; and accumulation, 96; critics of, 81; and inflation, 80, 82, 184; *see also* macroeconomic policy
Morris, Joe, 53
Mulroney, Brian, 113; *see also* Conservative government (Mulroney)

National Action Committee on the Status of Women, 155–6
National Economic Conference, 113–14
National Energy Programme, 81, 89, 104
National Institutional Training Programme, 136
National Training Act, 133, 134–6, 146
National Training Programme, 105, 125, 134, 135, 146, 149, 150
nationalization, view of Keynes, 59–60
neo-conservatism: and capital, 45; dominant ideology, 3; and employment equity, 145, 226 n 6; and labour-market policy, 147, 149; and monetarism, 3, 14, 23; and social democratic parties, 36; and social policy, 105; and the state, 218; and trade unions, 45
New Democratic Party, 52, 172
New Employment Expansion and Development, 139–40, 225 n 4
Newfoundland: federal employment programs in, 141–2; views on Canadian Jobs Strategy, 153–4

O'Connor, James: criticisms of, 18–21, 160; and fiscal crisis, 17–18; and state functions, 17–18, 159–60, 226–7 n 1

Ontario, view of Canadian Jobs Strategy, 150, 153
Opportunities for Youth, 137, 144
Osberg, Lars, 168
Ouellet, André, 200

Pal, Leslie, 144, 160–1, 178, 187, 188
Panitch, Leo, 16–17, 20, 199, 200, 228 n 10
PC 1003, 192, 194, 195–6; *see also* industrial relations legislation
Pentland, H.C., 189
permanent exceptionalism, 199, 228 n 10
Phidd, Richard W., 108, 124
Phillips, A.W., 62–3
Plant, Raymond, 21
policy paradigms, 3–4, 11–16, 57–8; and central banks, 43–4; changes of, 13, 14, 15–16, 23–4, 26–7, 67, 71; and class interests, 16; competition between, 84–91, 104; definition, 11–12, 223 n 8; and industrial relations policy, 190, 197; and labour-market policy, 14–15, 119–21, 158; and macroeconomic policy, 71, 213–14; and unemployment, 4, 27; and wage controls, 198
post-Keynesianism, 62–4, 84–9; and accumulation, 25, 91; capital's reservations about, 91; and collective bargaining, 13; and full employment, 62, 64; and incomes policy, 13, 63, 64, 193; and inflation, 13, 25, 62, 68; and labour-market policy, 14, 68, 118, 119–20, 123, 124, 162, 172; and legitimation deficit, 25; and state's

role, 13–14; and trade unions,
197, 211; and unemployment
insurance, 162, 172; *see also*
Keynesianism
Poulin Simon, Lise, 46–7
power resource theory, 42, 224 n 1
Prices and Incomes Commission,
197
prices and incomes policy: *see* Anti-
Inflation Programme; incomes
policy; wage and price controls
Prince, Michael, J., 85, 105
public debt: holdings, 98–9; servic-
ing costs, 74, 99, 103
public opinion: and the state, 107;
and unemployment, 11, 12; and
the welfare state, 106

quality of working life, 205, 208,
209

Rea, S.A., 181, 182
Regina Manifesto, 195
regulation approach to political
economy, 18–19, 223 n 1
revenues, government: forgone, and
the budget deficit, 74, 78, 88,
100–2; relative decline, 100, 101;
sources, 100, 101; *see also* tax expenditures
Rice, James J., 105
right to strike, public servants',
201–2
Roberts, John, 226 n 7
Royal Canadian Mounted Police,
193
Royal Commission on the Economic Union and Development
Prospects for Canada: *see* Macdonald Commission

Russell, Bob, 191, 228 n 10

Sawyer, Malcolm, 61
Say's Law, 58
Scharpf, Fritz, 41
Schmidt, Manfred, 30, 32, 33, 34,
36, 38, 39, 40, 52
Second Tier Committee, 207–8
Sengenberger, W., 47
Skills Growth Funds, 135
social democracy: in Canada, 52–3;
in Sweden, 36–7; in West Germany, 37
social policy, 102, 104, 105–6; and
Canadian Jobs Strategy, 154–6
Special Employment Plan, 128
Special Job Finding and Placement
Drive, 172–3
Stanbury, William T., 108–9
state: activism of, 52, 84–5, 89, 103;
and business, 56, 89, 92–3,
218–19; Canadian, in comparative
perspective, 216–17; fiscal crisis
of, 17–18; public perceptions, 107;
and public policy, 11, 19–20,
50–5, 83, 189; role of, 58–60, 64,
65, 91, 94, 220; theories of, 3,
16–25, 28, 213, 217–21; and unemployment, 3–4, 29, 49–51, 56
state activities, 16, 23, 26; and accumulation, 17, 57, 62, 71, 91–106;
and coercion, 189–95 passim,
216–17; and concrete legitimation,
23–4, 71, 92, 102–3; and ideological legitimation, 71, 106–16,
216–17; and legitimation, 17, 200,
206–11; *see also* accumulation;
coercion; concrete legitimation;
ideological legitimation; legitimation

Struthers, James, 160–1
Summer Job Corps, 137
Supreme Court of Canada, 201, 202
surplus, budget: effects, 71
Swartz, Donald, 20, 199, 200, 228
n10
Swimmer, Gene, 114, 201
symbolic politics, 22–3

Tarantelli, Ezio, 37–8
tax expenditures: business attitudes
toward, 104; and the deficit, 78;
scope, 100–2; see also revenues,
government: forgone
tax system: regressivity of, 99–102
Technical and Vocational Training
Act (1962), 122–3, 125
Thatcher, Margaret, 36
Thatcherism, 220
Therborn, Göran, 30, 33, 39, 40,
47–9, 51
throne speeches, 109–11, 208, 210
Times, The, 60, 62
trade unions: in Canada, 53; and
Keynesianism, 60; monetarist
views about, 15, 66; in western
Europe, 53; see also Canadian Labour Congress; labour
training: and accumulation, 124,
134; constitutional jurisdiction,
122–3; effectiveness of, 133–4;
federal criticism of provinces,
134, 149; federal role, early,
122–3; incrementality, 133; institutional, protection of, 152–3; and
privatization, 134; quality under
Canadian Jobs Strategy, 155–7; rediscovery of, 146–7; types, 125;
see also Canadian Jobs Strategy;
labour-market policy

Transitional Adjustment Assistance
Programme: recommendation,
185–6
Treasury Board, 129, 202
Trebilcock, Michael J., 115
tripartism: state promotion of,
206–8; see also corporatism
Trudeau, Pierre, 89
Trudeau government: and 'Just So-
ciety,' 164
Tufte, Edward, 35

unemployment, 14, 29–30, 221; in
budget speeches, 109–11; in Canada, explanations of, 52–5, 62;
definitions, 4–6, 14, 55; duration,
6; economic costs, 9–11; and inflation, 11, 13–15; national variations, explanations of, 27, 30–51,
56; rates of, 4–7, 31, 32; psychological impact, 7–9; public opinion and, 11, 12; social costs, 6–8;
types of, 58, 62, 63–4; see also
employment; full employment
unemployment insurance, 50, 66,
159, 162–3, 168, 170, 171, 188,
215–16; constitutional jurisdiction, 159, 160; costs of, 168, 169,
170, 171, 172–3, 175–6, 178; financing, 166–9, 175; government
contributions to, 166–8, 175–6,
177, 178; integration with labour-
market policy, 172, 177–8, 184;
legislative amendments, 169,
172–8, 188; and legitimation, 160;
origins of, 159, 160–2; task force
on, 176, 184; in the United States,
160; and work-disincentive literature, 181–5
Unemployment Insurance Act

(1971), 159, 163–5, 183; section
38 amendments, 139
Unemployment Insurance Commission, administrative controls,
169–70, 172, 173
unemployment insurance funds, developmental uses of, 139, 152,
174–5, 177, 178–9, 180, 185–6,
187
Uusitalo, Paavo, 43

Vaillancourt, François, 101–2
Vocational Training Coordination
Act (1942), 127

wage and price controls, 193–4, 197,
198, 199; and accumulation, 193;
in Britain, 46; and the BCNI, 91;
and post-Keynesianism, 16; public
sector, 199; see also Anti-Inflation
Programme; incomes policy

Wagner Act, 194, 196
Waldie, K.G., 206
Walker, Michael A., 183
War Measures Act, 195, 227 n 5
Warskett, Rosemary, 145
Webber, Douglas, 37
Weber, Max, 21–3
welfare state regimes, 41–3
Whitaker, Reg, 23
White Paper on Employment and
Incomes (1945), 61
White Paper on Unemployment In-
surance (1970), 164–5
Williams, Paul, 28
Wilson, Michael, 50, 90–1, 114, 178
Winnipeg General Strike, 193
Winter Works Programme, 123–4
Wolfe, David A., 62, 78, 85, 105
work-disincentive literature, 181–5
Workman's Compensation Act (On-
tario, 1914), 190